Psyop Docs

448049

D1477867

1

PSYOP: An Anthology

Bart van der Heide
Stedelijk Museum Amsterdam

It is tempting to look upon digital and technological impact from a distance, as a matter of objective hardware influencing the lives of others. Whether technological developments are considered a source of enrichment, enabling platforms that offer radical democratization and curation of knowledge and voices; or whether they are considered a slippery slope toward the loss of meaningful interpersonal connections, authenticity, and all things natural: as the antithesis to the warmth of the flesh, to the erratic heart and soul of mankind, technology should be observed from afar.

The privilege of artists has long been to acutely sense societal shifts and to be able to share what they sense by materializing it in objects. By doing so, artists enable the questions of our time to become public, and consequently, political. Distilling essences from the haze, artists use aesthetics to strike us with recognition of the latent "truth" that they bring into the light. The relationship between technology and humanity is irrefutably one of the most important challenges of our time, and exceptional artists are needed to make its societal impact tangible, offering an affective understanding that transcends the crisp knowledge of distanced reflection.

Metahaven are exceptional sensors, masterfully using the visual in all its guises to tease out what they have uncovered. Deeply invested in how the impact of technology looks and feels, Metahaven's work in design, and more recently their moving-image work, invites us into the very personal depths of our changing world, minds, and bodies—knowledgably playing with the many textures and faces of power.

Visualizing the digital protocol of these power structures is the main focus of Metahaven's practice, with the inhabitant as its vantage point. While researchers debate how social media platforms may shorten the attention span of teenagers growing up today, Metahaven's work pervasively engulfs us with our own intimate shrinkage of life down to a grid, our subtle impatience with the slow and unfiltered tapestry of the offline world. Metahaven's shrewd sensitivity seems to pick up on that which creates the ripples we see, submerging us in their source. Grasping for breath we emerge replenished.

The Stedelijk Museum is thrilled to work with Metahaven, proudly culminating in this book, *PSYOP: An Anthology*, as part of the solo exhibition *Metahaven: Earth* at the Stedelijk (October 6, 2018–February 24, 2019), simultaneously functioning as an accompaniment to the concurrent exhibition *Version History* at the Institute of Contemporary Arts (ICA) in London.

Together the publication and exhibition showcase Metahaven's interdisciplinary practice, encompassing graphic design, video work, installation, editing, poetry, and essays. I would like to thank Mondriaan Fund for recognizing the importance of the publication and for supporting its fruition. I am also grateful to Auto Italia South East, London who worked with Metahaven on an early concept of this book.

More than anything though, the exhibition and publication compound to show that Metahaven *live* the proposal made by their work: that generosity, warmth, and the ability to connect is within us, and that we are within technology. Walking through the exhibition with the book in hand, you will see names reappearing, names that testify to relationships built through their work, amidst and betwixt technology, intertwined, tangled, and overlapping with the heart.

Bart van der Heide, Chief Curator

previous

Stefan Kalmár
Richard Birkett
Institute of Contemporary Arts London

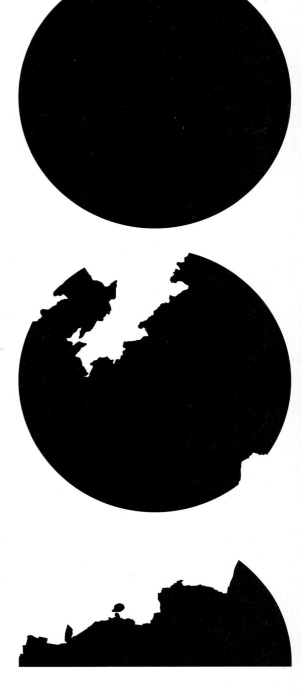

Magda Cordell and John McHale were central figures in the Independent Group of artists, designers, and critics who met at the Institute of Contemporary Arts (ICA) in London between 1952 and 1955, and are now synonymous with the address of mass culture "as found" and the coining of the term Pop art. Both were polymathic, with Cordell latterly described as an artist, futurist, sociologist, and educator, and McHale an "artist/graphic designer/information theorist/ architectural critic/sociologist/futurist."[1] In 1968, in the shadow of the Independent Group's entanglement with the promise of new technologies and mass communication, McHale and Cordell established the Center for Integrative Studies at the State University of New York (now Binghamton University), focused on long-range thinking about social, cultural, and ecological change, and the intersections between art and technology. In his 1969 book *The Future of the Future*, something of a manifesto for the center, McHale coined the beautifully paradoxical statement: "The future of the past is in the future; the future of the present is in the past; the future of the future is in the present."[2]

A compelling argument can be made for Metahaven as descendants of Cordell and McHale and their interdisciplinary and non-linear approach to future-thinking. Metahaven have also located their work at an agile intersection between the hypothetical and the texture of reality. Design as a mediating force within an economy of signs (or what McHale termed "an expendable series of ikons")[3]—and therefore design as a possible mode of critical thinking on the effects generated around this economy—is at the center of Metahaven's practice. The trajectory of their work articulates the importance of thinking beyond a diagnostic, problem-solving relationship to the complex conditions of the "now," instead looking to the speculative as a means to apprehend the ongoing collaborative fabrication of histories, presents, and futures.

Metahaven's mode of inquiry is acutely observant of cultural, technological, and geopolitical patterns, while seeking to render the felt dimensions of life in the thick of digital and physical layers. Such an integrated approach to the production and projection of ideas, affects, and aesthetic registers places Metahaven in a singular position within contemporary culture. They have defined a field of operation that runs parallel to the worlds of contemporary visual arts and film, while actively intervening within the political and affective dimensions of emerging processes and channels of information and media production.

The Independent Group stands as an important historical expression of the ICA's commitment to interdisciplinarity within forms of critical thought, and to addressing interwoven emerging cultural, technological, social, and political conditions—so too is Metahaven's exhibition at the ICA, *Version History* (October 3, 2018–January 13, 2019), a contemporary manifestation of such thinking. The ICA is proud to collaborate with the Stedelijk Museum Amsterdam for this monographic publication on Metahaven's work. In keeping with the editing and design of books as integral to Metahaven's practice, this volume moves beyond the monographic into the dialogical and hypothetical: it provides both a fitting accompaniment to simultaneous exhibitions at the ICA and Stedelijk, and a comprehensive entry point into Metahaven's recent moving-image work.

At a moment at which notions of veracity and falsity shape debates in politics and the media, Metahaven are vitally engaged with producing artworks, essays, and research that offer us pathways into the versioning of realities and histories, and the processes by which our coordinates are set to navigate within such "epistemic uncertainty."[4] The book is a reflection of Metahaven as a polyvocal entity, deeply engaged with the potential held within a network of collaborators and interlocutors. It also advances the principle expressed in their recent talk "Lyrical Design," that: "Especially amid all things post-truth, there are things that are beautiful, and there are things that are true, and there are things that need to be said."[5]

Stefan Kalmár, Director
Richard Birkett, Chief Curator

[1] Alex Kitnick, "Hip Artificer," in John McHale: *The Expendable Reader*, New York: GSAPP Books, 2011, 12.

[2] See John McHale, *The Future of the Future*, New York: George Braziller, 1969.

[3] John McHale, "The Expendable Ikon 1," *Architectural Design* 22 (February 1959): 82.

[4] See the conversation between Richard Birkett and Metahaven on page 99 of this publication.

[5] Metahaven, "Lyrical Design," lecture, Design Museum, London, July 20, 2018.

5

우주의 허위정보　　　Cosmic Disinformation

+

6

Information Skies (Crying Mother), 2016
mural, installation view, 11th Gwangju Biennale, 2016

Cloudy Weather
Karen Archey

7

Nation state? Black hole? An exceptional place, 2004
advertisement for the Principality of Sealand

Islands in the Net/Cryptonomicon/Guinness, 2013
Sealand Model, installation view, *Islands in the Cloud*,
MoMA PS1, New York, 2013

1
The research for this essay comes from the many conversations I had with Metahaven over the course of nearly two years (2017–2018) in locations ranging from the meeting rooms of the Stedelijk Museum Amsterdam to a mutual friend's wedding to dinners at their home. All of the quotes in this essay come from these conversations, unless otherwise indicated in footnotes.

2
See page 20 of this publication.

3
"US Hardliners Search for a Saddam Connection," *Gulf States Newsletter*, no. 9, September, 2001, http://www.gsn-online.com/us-hardliners-search-for-a-saddam-connection-911. Last accessed on August 29, 2018.

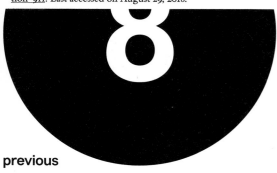

If knowledge and experience are the building blocks of reason, what is the role of the artist amid our current societal indifference toward truth? It could be argued that the artist today has a special role in conveying truth. As the currency of art is expression, perceived aesthetically, it evades our more defensive verbal faculties laden with buzzword traps and political mines. Aesthetic experience—whether at a museum or watching Netflix—is a vehicle for insurgent information. Historically tasked in the West with discerning how to navigate our present moment, the artist is faced with the erosion of basic values surrounding the acquisition of knowledge: patience, mutual understanding, empathy, literacy, and intellectualism are all cast as enemies of the common people. As metropoles grow larger and their constituents increasingly disconnected from their rural neighbors, how we may reach out of this paradox and into a universally agreed upon sense of reality may be up to the aesthetic ingenuity of artists.

Dutch collective Metahaven, comprising Vinca Kruk and Daniel van der Velden, have entered into this political moment as artists who aesthetically engender notions of reality and its embattlements. Metahaven has been active for fifteen years, with both Van der Velden and Kruk trained as graphic designers. They came together in 2003 to work on research inquiries relating to notions of political speculation within the field of design, bringing web vernacular into formal conversation with both decoration and knowing graphic design. Through many smooth transitions and some otherwise jarring left turns, as described in this essay, Metahaven has arrived in recent years at a fully mature filmmaking practice, embracing the duration and beauty of Andrei Tarkovsky with scripts reminiscent of riddles and poetry. While well-known in both the fields of design and contemporary art, their growth from the static to moving image is little known, perhaps owing to the idiosyncratically cross-disciplinary nature of their practice. Metahaven often transfers aspects from one field into another: for example, they envision their work conceptually as artists but execute it within the material practices of filmmaking and graphic design. So too are they writers, bookmakers, educators, mentors, and parents—their collaboration as life partners inevitably informing their collaboration in work. Considering the content of their work—with an early digital design project on extraterritoriality and most recently, films about Eurasian geopolitics and complex belonging—this all speaks to a deep investment in the world: its geography, landscape, and ultimately, its future.

Throughout their collaboration, Metahaven has developed aesthetic strategies that characterize their practice. Their graphic design work is recognizable for its use of web vernacular, layering, and experiments with surface and texture. Their designs are brassily exuberant, shamelessly interested in pop, and at times festooned with decoration. They play with notions of anachronistic bad design, such as drop shadows, novelty-sized text, and hazy auras of less attractive shades of CMYK such as puce and daffodil. Yet for all of Metahaven's joy and exuberance—their final designs sometimes planned and at times happened upon in the process—so too are their compositions visually complex and multitudinous in their interpretation. In their sketches for a recent carpet within the installation of their new film *Eurasia (Questions on Happiness)* (2018), a monochromatic political map of a cut-out state can merge into the contour of a star graphic found in a passport. Inspired by the visual language of anime, Metahaven's work often breaks down visual complexities into simple forms—take, for example, the immense simplification and enhanced emotional legibility within a manga character's face. Metahaven simplifies these forms, which are then often decontextualized and reformatted to create a new contextual mood board. While Metahaven's primary artistic output is film, the animation sequences often cut into their found and self-made footage and props such as scarves in their film *Possessed* (2018), represent this design aesthetic.

Work and Life

This essay treats the identities of Van der Velden and Kruk together as Metahaven, and at their behest quotes them collectively as such. Although Metahaven consists technically of only Kruk and Van der Velden, they identify most strongly as a collective, partially to distance their work from their prone-to-be-romanticized status as a couple, and to gesture toward

the incredibly collaborative nature of their work. Perhaps as a form of protection against simplistic inferences, Metahaven has developed a tight set of regulations when speaking about themselves (not as a "design duo" or "couple") and have a set of regular collaborators from diverse fields they often originally approached as fans, many of whom are contributors to this publication. Yet the only two people who direct all of Metahaven's activities are Van der Velden and Kruk, who come off as both constantly in synch and in negotiation.

As curator of their first survey exhibition, getting to know their idiosyncratic partnership over the last two years has been both a steep learning curve and engrossing. Following a brief feeling that I was peering into a hermetic world rife with its own histories and logics, I was rapidly brought into their work—and inevitably for them, also their lives.[1]

In a conversation with their frequent collaborators, musicians Mathew Dryhurst and Holly Herndon, Metahaven speak about the imperative to keep one's work in check with one's life:

> We operate in an economy where the actual making of work is the activity that's constantly under pressure […]. You need to find a unity between the production and distribution of work and the actual birthplace of ideas; both life and work need to be tied together and somehow be about the same things. So the caregiving and the love and so on need to be where the work is. Otherwise all the events of life will only be experienced as obstacles.[2]

While they stand by this, they emphasize that their work is not always based on the placid symbiosis of life and care: their simultaneous collectivity, autonomy, and individuality sometimes produces conflict, absence, and, well, the opposite of care. They are not always together, dispatching each other on errands, one teaching in Amsterdam or Arnhem while the other gives a talk in Moscow or visits a custom carpet manufacturer in Barcelona. Yet their remarkable productivity is marked by a constant connection, urgency, and self-reflective ambition, along with a tremendous sense of humor and iconoclastic spirit. For all of the sharing, caring, collaboration, and positivity found in Metahaven's practice, so too is it obsessive, monomaniacal, and borderline impenetrable due to its rooting in decades-long conversations between two incredibly close people. But above all, their extraordinary independence and idiosyncrasy is also necessary, particularly for artists who traverse such materially, conceptually, and practically diverse fields with such uncompromising ambition.

Transgressing Graphic Design

As teenagers, both Kruk and Van der Velden came to graphic design, like many of us in the arts, as a suitable environment for their social and intellectual needs—albeit in quite different ways. Van

der Velden's upbringing emphasized the role of visual art and a belief in being self-taught over formal training. "There is a part to graphic design that is about continuous learning. As soon as I entered graphic design, I found myself bouncing off the boundaries of what the field was," says Van der Velden. After a tepid year at university studying history, he transferred to the Academy of Visual Arts (now Willem de Kooning Academy) in Rotterdam. He then completed two years at the Jan van Eyck Academie in Maastricht.

Kruk, many of whose family members are academics, was brought up with the historical art canon. In high school, she was enticed by the visual and intellectual possibilities of conceptual art. After a relatively traditional design education, also at the Willem de Kooning Academy, she realized the economic implications and conceptual possibilities of design:

> Design had always been for me just a field of craft, and service; a possibility to express and produce visual work. I eventually came to the understanding that there was an economic aspect to design in which there's the connection between production of objects—for example, design being used to sell things, being a strategy to promote ways to consume, or to convey political ideas. And the introduction to that was both extremely exciting and terrifying. It was an important moment for me to then navigate how I wanted to either continue in that vein, or reject it.

Though their impetuses to study design are fairly disparate, Van der Velden and Kruk are still committed to identifying its peripheries and, ideally, redefining the field along the way. In 2003, while both doing research at the Jan van Eyck Academie before founding Metahaven, they began working together on a digital design project, the *Sealand Identity Project*—the framework of which would define their collaboration for the years to come. From their early speculative design work to their current film installations, Metahaven's projects always begin with a sense of fascination or challenge that is then turned into a research trajectory, followed and materialized until a project morphs into another set of concerns or media—or until the collective hits its deadline.

War on Terror

The year of Metahaven's first collaboration, 2003, also marks two years since the beginning of the War on Terror, which greatly influenced their practice. The Iraq War began in 2003 with an invasion of the country by a United States-led coalition that would overthrow the government of Iraqi President Saddam Hussein. Already having invaded Afghanistan, erstwhile US President George W. Bush contextualized the invasion of Iraq as an eye-for-an-eye response to the September 11, 2001 terrorist attacks—though of course no evidence then or now connects Iraq to Al Qaeda terrorists responsible for the attack.[3] While the US public was informed that the Al Qaeda plane hijackers originated from Afghanistan, the president's insistence that Iraq should somehow be culpable and potentially harbored "weapons of mass destruction," was enough to convince the nation to embark on what would become a fruitless nine-year war.

The confusion of the War on Terror—exacerbated by public trust in a government with ulterior motives—is emblematic of what Metahaven refers to as *the thickness of the now*[4]: the widespread inability of a populace to determine truth, exacerbated by a news cycle saturated with constant negativity, forestalling any optimistic or productive course of action. I recall my own reaction as a seventeen-year-old witnessing the collapse of the Twin Towers on TV. In the days preceding 9/11, I watched *Fight Club* (1999): in the final scene, the protagonist looks out over a fictional downtown scene as major bank buildings crumble to the ground due to a bombing campaign he orchestrates to destroy all record of consumer debt. As a teenager who had never been to New York, I could not help but meld this fiction fresh in my mind with reality. Did the punks bomb the World Trade Center? Was capitalism over? As the Pentagon was attacked and reality hit, out of concern my mind turned to my father, who was in the process of retiring as an FBI Special Agent in Akron, Ohio; I immediately felt confused and ashamed for this Hollywood-derived flight of fancy.

Of these coinciding—at times embarrassingly beguiling—fictions, Metahaven says: "During the War on Terror, strategies of speculation created a very disconnected, incomplete kind of fiction. The idea of speculation thinks through hypotheticals and the boundary between the real and the speculative." Their work applied this thinking to graphic design to both emulate and dismantle the speculative strategies they sought to address, using the digital medium of then-burgeoning online media.

Principality of Sealand

Metahaven's early work took the form of designed speculative visual identities. In 2003, they began researching the Principality of Sealand, an unrecognized state built upon a disused World War II sea fort in international waters, approximately seven nautical miles off the coast of Suffolk. Sealand was initially founded in 1967 by Paddy Roy Bates, a retired British major turned pirate radio show broadcaster, in an escalation of a territorial tiff with the British government. Sealand's existence flouts conventional notions of statehood, never mind formal requirements or constituents, with abundant humor. Bates naturally named himself prince and his wife princess, wrote a constitution, and developed national iconography including stamps, coins, and passports—the latter sadly classified by the Council of the European Union as a "fantasy passport."[5] Metahaven's design for this inscrutable "state" evinces their premise for it: "Through its existence as an image and a projection screen, Sealand has realized for itself the most radical, and most fictitious, condition of brand."[6] And further: "The appearance of objects in information

society consequently is no longer primarily visual, but informational. The informational imprint of a brand—or the lack thereof—provides a new paradigm for its management."[7]

Designed to exist on the internet alone, the actual material output of the *Sealand Identity Project* was entirely digital, comprising proposals for stamps, coins, posters, infographics, and images of many not-so-architectural models such as two Pringles cans holding up the Deleuze and Guattari book *A Thousand Plateaus* (1980), mimicking the sea fort's ⊓-like appearance. The very aesthetic of the *Sealand Identity Project* explores "the tension between the stable appearances of sovereign government (crests and coins), and the low resolution chaos of internet images when entering 'Sealand' as a query into the search engine, Sealand's identity becom[ing] entirely composed of the viewer's preconceptions—an inside formed by an outside."[8]

From (2000–2008), Sealand served as host to HavenCo, a data haven that attempted to woo customers by its extraterritoriality. When a data server physically lies outside the jurisdiction of a government—most of which have strict rules about the legality of content that it hosts—this means that all data is fair game. Though many data havens operate with their own code of ethics (including HavenCo),[9] theoretically, normally criminalized activity such as hosting child pornography, terrorist chat rings, and data leaks alike are not prosecutable. This sort of geopolitically emancipated data haven, attractive to activists evading government surveillance, whistleblowers, and data leakers, led to the nom de guerre "Metahaven."

The Sealand project brought Kruk and Van der Velden together, and Metahaven was founded thereafter in 2007, with a pi symbol acting as their logo. The actual physical carrier of identity design is not what most interests Metahaven—rather, they trace a constellation of aesthetic, theoretical, practical, and political interests through the material practice of graphic design:

> Design and especially identity design are always considered to be most successful when they are simple. We have often followed a reverse logic. If you start embracing those stories as part of the identity as it already exists, and start to design that or make work about it, visualizing it, you're actually enlarging and including some things rather than excluding and simplifying.

Their identity work reached out to political organizations, micro-nations, and other entities such as Independent Diplomat, the Icelandic Modern Media Initiative, and most notoriously, WikiLeaks—not-for-profits at the intersection of geography, information networks, and digital and human rights. While Metahaven's work wasn't always adopted by these organizations, their speculative identities were meant to make visible aspects of social and political struggle that would otherwise go unnoticed, and point to the pivotal potential of images as political tools in the service of propaganda and branding revolutions. Responding to the growing opaqueness of political power in the

4
Metahaven also note that the term implies that saturation of the now with "bads" and prompts makes it impossible to base one's actions on positive thoughts, viewing it as necessary, particularly for art. Technology greatly contributes to this condition in which nothing seems straightforward. See Metahaven's 2018 essay *Digital Tarkovsky*. Metahaven was influenced by Chris Dercon's statement "The extreme compression—the thickness—of the present" in "We Are Synchro Time," *032c*, no. 9 (2005), https://032c.com/2005/now-it's-synchro-time-chris-dercon. Last accessed on August 29, 2018.
5
See "Information Concerning the Non-Exhaustive List of Known Fantasy and Camouflage Passports, as Stipulated by Article 6 of the Decision No 1105/2011/EU," Migration and Home Affairs, European Commission, https://ec.europa.eu/home-affairs/sites/homeaffairs/files/what-we-do/policies/borders-and-visas/document-security/docs/list_of_known_fantasy_and_camouflage_passports_en.pdf. Last accessed on August 21, 2018.
6
Metahaven and Marina Vishmidt, eds., *Uncorporate Identity: Metahaven*, Baden: Lars Müller Publishers, 2010, 27–29.
7
Ibid., 52, 54.
8
See ibid., 40.
9
10
David Leigh, "How 250,000 US Embassy Cables Were Leaked," *The Guardian*, November 28, 2010, https://www.theguardian.com/world/2010/nov/28/how-us-embassy-cables-leaked. Last accessed on August 29, 2018.
11
See Esther Addley and Josh Halliday, "WikiLeaks Supporters Disrupt Visa and MasterCard Sites in 'Operation Payback'," *The Guardian*, December 9, 2010, https://www.theguardian.com/world/2010/dec/08/wikileaks-visa-mastercard-operation-payback. Last accessed on August 29, 2018.
12
Originally designed for the premiere of the Gwangju Design Biennale in September 2011, these scarves also appeared in a fundraiser for Artists Space, New York, during the 2013 group show *Frozen Lakes* and *Islands in the Cloud*, MoMA PS1, New York, 2013.
13
Metahaven, *Black Transparency: The Right to Know in the Age of Mass Surveillance*, Berlin: Sternberg Press, 2015, 5–6.
14
Melia Robinson, "Peter Thiel's Dream of a Floating Libertarian Utopia May Have Finally Been Killed," *Business Insider*, March 8, 2018, https://www.businessinsider.nl/libertarian-peter-thiel-utopia-seasteading-institute-2018-3/?international=true&r=US. Last accessed on August 29, 2018.

West, Metahaven began to think through and critically approach American political scientist Joseph Nye's notion of soft power—the power to attract, rather than rule by force—that informs the politics of branding and identity campaigns. This contextualizes Metahaven's investment in aesthetics and their function as a carrier and arbitrator of information: "I think that we very much did not want to belong with the type of design that is about form itself, but we also didn't want to belong with this idea where research means that you don't express yourself. We try to maintain both at the same time."

WikiLeaks

Among Metahaven's best-known campaign works is a partially realized study for WikiLeaks, which was founded in 2006 amid the Iraq War and on the brink of the Great Recession. Metahaven remarks on how the character of their work inevitably changed with WikiLeaks's shift from anarcho-libertarian freedom-of-information activists to their notoriety within liberal circles for dealing the final blow to Hillary Clinton's 2016 US presidential campaign:

Originally, WikiLeaks was set against the double commissions of the War on Terror and the financial crisis. When WikiLeaks became well-known in 2009, they focused on two things: the idea that there's a political and financial elite that actually runs the world, and that there is a secret war being run of which we don't see the human consequences and political cost.

Metahaven approached Julian Assange, offering to work on WikiLeaks's visual identity in June 2010, just weeks before the organization became a household name by leaking millions of classified documents. On April 5, 2010, Wikileaks released a series of videos entitled *Collateral Murder* involving three different, tactical shooter-view videos evidencing the purposeful killings of nonviolent Iraqi citizens and *Reuters* journalists. These evidentiary videos caused worldwide uproar about the United States's hawkish foreign policy and seemingly interminable, costly, and unfocused presence in Iraq. The surreal conditions that created the leak were striking: Private Chelsea Manning, then a military intelligence analyst known as Bradley Manning (quoted as "he" below), chose to capture confidential military information, exporting data via CD-RWs disguised as burned music CDs. David Leigh reports on Chelsea Manning's exfiltration tactics through her online chat conversations with friend Adrian Lamo, who turned her in, for *The Guardian* in November 2010[10]:

It was childishly easy, according to the published chatlog of a conversation Manning had with a fellow-hacker. "I would come in with music on a CD-RW labelled with something like 'Lady Gaga'... erase the music... then write a compressed split file. No one suspected a thing... [I] listened and lip-synched to Lady Gaga's 'Telephone' while exfiltrating possibly the largest data spillage in American history." He said that he "had unprecedented access to classified networks 14 hours a day 7 days a week for 8+ months"... He added: "Information should be free. It belongs in the public domain."

The fact that Chelsea Manning used a Lady Gaga CD-RW to disguise the largest intelligence breach in US history is both tantalizing and practically inconceivable. The fact that ISIS publishes a glossy lifestyle magazine, Putin commissions vanity shots of himself shirtless horseback riding, and North Korean dictator Kim Jong-un's brother Kim Jong-nam was assassinated with VX nerve agent by a young woman wearing dark lipstick and a shirt emblazoned with the acronym "LOL," are all part of a contemporary media landscape in which truth has genuinely become much stranger than fiction.

In 2010, major financial companies such as MasterCard, Visa, and PayPal blocked WikiLeaks,[11] leaving merchandising as the organization's main fundraising resource. To help, in January 2011 Metahaven met with Assange and switched gears from identity to merchandise design, including T-shirts, mugs, and perhaps most recognizably, scarves that aesthetically allude to transparency, opacity, glamour, and counterfeit. Graphically, a Louis Vuitton-like "WL" logo bleeds into camouflage, with the word WikiLeaks rimming the scarves' borders, following the design vernacular of luxury brand scarves.[12] To Metahaven, the knock-off Louis Vuitton scarf is a metaphorical "victory" over the power structure that pretends that there are still differences between original and copy. In exhibitions these scarves are usually shown pinned to fence-like frames, referencing the black market arcades in which such counterfeit luxury goods are often sold.

WikiLeaks, the "first intelligence service of the people," as they refer to themselves on a mousepad available for twelve euro in their official web shop, was a revelatory cause to champion in 2010 among leftists, government transparency activists, and hackers alike. Few took pause to consider that, above everything else, their defining principle was a lack of accountability to anyone, much less any political party, to the rankling of leftists throughout the world. The leaking of Democratic National Committee and Hillary Clinton campaign manager John Podesta's emails in 2016, and its aid in electing Donald Trump, seemed like a betrayal for an organization assumed to be progressive. This moment offered rather a clarification in WikiLeaks's allegiances, or a lack thereof—even if leaked information came from Russian agents and supported the Trump campaign, all leaks were created equal. In their 2015 publication *Black Transparency*, Metahaven states:

WikiLeaks' trajectory—from cyber-utopian political practice to major world power to post-empire downfall—says as much about the organization as about the rollercoaster of changes happening at that time. At the height of its fame, aligned with both the hacktivists from Anonymous and LulzSec and the activists from Occupy Wall Street, WikiLeaks seemed in control of global news cycles, and hoped that the managerial framework of sovereign technocracy would come tumbling down.

Given Metahaven's interest in the thickness of the now—the inability to determine truth and the fog of uncoordinated propaganda campaigns that precipitate such confusion—they inevitably became entangled in the trappings of the new world that they endeavored to give shape.[13]

Like the Principality of Sealand, WikiLeaks is similarly bound up with the desire to escape jurisdiction. "The design of an exclave, a space of exception, was the core of the Sealand study. WikiLeaks has taken this idea of its own role as an exception to levels of geopolitical chaos mongering that are just unprecedented," says Metahaven. Sealand's early HavenCo investors moved on to found the Seasteading Institute, a Silicon Valley group dedicated to the creation of extraterritorial floating cities, which never quite got off the ground.[14] Buttressed by a 1.7 million USD donation by billionaire PayPal co-founder and Trump transition team member Peter Thiel, Seasteading Institute and its commitment to extraterritoriality cozily finds its home in right-libertarianism. Thus the desire to escape jurisdiction—whether in order to hold the state ethically accountable via whistleblowing, or as a libertarian business venture, or simply as forum for lowbrow criminality—is perplexingly manifold, and not attributable to any one political affiliation or cause.

Transition to Moving Image

The unexpected and rapidly evolving allegiances among historically stable political positions contribute to the confounding nature of our current political moment that seems to serve those already in power. As such, Metahaven began to explore other forms of narration to tell urgent, complex political stories, ultimately taking up the moving image given their confidence in traversing media, information online becoming primarily video-based, and desire to work in longer durations both in terms of production processes and in material results:

Neither of us have felt hesitation about moving into a new question or territory when it comes to making things. We've always done that, whether it was to move into a sub-realm of graphic design, or to work from a hypothesis rather than an actual brief. The way we are working now with the moving image doesn't feel so different from the first projects that we did. Sealand, for instance, can be considered as a series of film stills, as a kind of storyboard, rather than a design proposal.

Karen Archey

next

Transparent Camouflage, 2011
WikiLeaks scarf
photo Meinke Klein

City Rising, 2014
video still with *New Babylon* model (Constant)

City Rising, 2014
video still with *New Babylon* model (Constant)

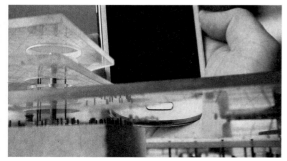

City Rising, 2014
video still with *New Babylon* model (Constant)

Their first moving-image work was a 14-minute film as part of the 2013 series *Black Transparency* that also includes prints, models, and video interviews examining the newfound cataclysmic power of the immediate worldwide transmission of Edward Snowden's and Chelsea Manning's leaks. These disclosures, and the widespread breadth and immediacy of their impact, were made possible by the communications networks that now circumscribe the Earth. Black transparency, then, is a renegade, newfound form of transparency—one that is wrongly classified in the US as unpatriotic or even espionage. The *Black Transparency* video interviews feature Anonymous expert and academic Gabriella Coleman, Icelandic information activist and International Modern Media Institute (IMMI) co-founder Smári McCarthy, as well as IMMI co-founder, poet, and politician Birgitta Jónsdóttir among others and mostly recorded via Skype. Like these interviews, the film features a graphic frame designed by Metahaven and a spinning "BT" logo. Departing from the interviews, *Black Transparency* combines found footage of riots, police violence, a data center under construction, and flowing magma with a voice-over narrating a poetic call to arms:

> There is no transparency without enlightenment.
> With the industrial revolution came the glass palaces.
> Life without secrets found its form in architecture.
> Under transparency the state loses the informational privilege that allows it to maintain itself.
> Black transparency is involuntary transparency.

Metahaven's next moving-image work, *City Rising* (2014), is set to narrated and edited selections from the essay "Is it Love?" (2014) by *e-flux journal* editor and frequent Metahaven collaborator Brian Kuan Wood, which examines how love is the substitute for the state's withdrawn social safety nets. *City Rising* is an homage to artist Constant Nieuwenhuys's utopian megastructure *New Babylon* (1959–1974) that envisions a utopian, fully automated society in which humans are freed from the obligation to work. Metahaven shot footage of a model of *New Babylon* found in the Gemeentemuseum Den Haag. Like *Black Transparency*, its editing is intuitive and characteristic of an early material experiment in a new medium. *City Rising*, as with much of Metahaven's graphic design work, was created to exist on and travel through the internet—specifically, it was made in the vein of a short Vimeo upload in order to reach a wide audience.

Yet *Black Transparency* and *City Rising* were also studio projects—anyone in the Metahaven studio could edit them, passing around files on a whim. After *City Rising*, Metahaven reconfigured this entirely open studio structure, keeping authorship of their artworks strictly between Van der Velden and Kruk. If a distinction can be made between artist and designer, the former holding conceptual authorship crucial and the latter delegation among a studio, this could be the moment at which Metahaven began transforming from a design into an artist collective.

Music Videos

In 2014, musician and composer Holly Herndon reached out to Metahaven to collaborate. This included album art for *Platform* (2015), T-shirts, and two music videos and GIF versions of them. Herndon's unique approach to electronic pop is at once emotive, experimental, and historically informed—later in this book she converses with Metahaven about taking inspiration from early music and its rooting in the power of the voice and self-expression. Her lyrics reflect on how mobile devices are simultaneously both impersonal and sources of ecstatic togetherness. Metahaven's music video *Home* (2014), for Herndon's song of the same name, combines shots of the musician with streaming patterns of National Security Agency icons, lifted from PowerPoint presentations leaked by Snowden in 2013. Metahaven refers to these colorful patterns as "data rain." Subsequent shots superimpose lyrics, bubblegum type, and shadowy silhouettes of checkerboards onto Herndon, imbuing the galvanizing catalyst of pop with a cryptic surveilled atmosphere. *Interference* (2015) juxtaposes lyrics with a waving white flag and pop-ups emblazoned with simple digital gradients in place of advertisements, as well as shots of Herndon reflected in water, decidedly more abstract than any of Metahaven's earlier moving-image works. The collective produced a copy of Situationist

International founder Guy Debord and writer Alice Becker-Ho's book that lays out a game, *A Game of War* (1987), which provides the backdrop for two arms coming together across the screen. Holding each other at the elbow, these arms suggest that the conflict of the game is overcome in solidarity.

The First Films

The quasi-natural phenomena in these music videos—plastic lily pads dotting bodies of water and data "rain"—as well as the videos' emotiveness and the creation of atmosphere continue in Metahaven's subsequent works, namely their film cycle (2016–2018). They note: "The music videos are very much a part of the development of the film cycle, because we start to work intensely with the notion of overlay and atmosphere." The cycle comprises four works (sometimes five depending on when and who you ask), beginning with the fiction-documentary *The Sprawl (Propaganda about Propaganda)* (2015) and followed by *Information Skies* (2016), *Hometown* (2018), and their latest film, *Eurasia (Questions on Happiness)* (2018). The fifth film is their 2018 cinematic debut *Possessed*, a collaboration with director Rob Schröder.

The cycle bears a preoccupation with Russia—its cultural history, particularly poetry and literature, as well as other filmmakers, most predominantly Andrei Tarkovsky. This interest arose partly in response to the cultural and political dominance of the US, and the nation's troubled relationship with global military aggression and capitalist expansion that, through some waxes and wanes, has boomed since the advent of the War on Terror. While a shared set of conceptual and visual concerns unite the cycle, whether or not *Possessed* fits into this remains an open question. Metahaven states: "The other films have specific questions about both the notions of digital media and epistemic uncertainty. While that's very strong in the four films it's less present in *Possessed* because it already assumes something about the way that digital media have impacted us. They have made us possessed."

● The Sprawl
(Propaganda about Propaganda)

The Sprawl is a fiction-documentary tracing several uncanny and seemingly disconnected events in 2014 between the more contiguous Ukrainian revolution, Russian annexing of Crimea, and widespread Western media coverage of Russian troll farms, and the more disparate downing of Malaysia Airlines Flight 17 (MH17) from Amsterdam to Kuala Lumpur and Ebola outbreak among other incidents. In addition to the many events it covers, so too does it shift rapidly in genre and atmosphere, its suspenseful, briskly changing electronic soundtrack composed by Berlin-based musician Kuedo. *The Sprawl* begins with footage of a dark forest with the voice-over of two men in eastern Ukraine discussing their involvement in a subversive, unstated

event that happened the night before, their associate receiving urgent phone calls, and their attempt to locate a car. It is July 18, 2014, the day after MH17 was shot down by a surface-to-air missile in eastern Ukraine. Amid the suspenseful electronic soundtrack the film cuts to a Google Earth walk-through, intersected with shots from the Russian forest overlaid with a graphic interface and play button. Shifting away from found footage is a scene filmed by Metahaven in which an actress stares at a black computer screen surrounded by billowing smoke. Narrated over this are selections from the poem *Requiem* (1935–1961), which Anna Akhmatova wrote over three decades in Stalin's Soviet Union. Early in the film is footage from the 1980s of former US President Ronald Reagan (who Metahaven jeeringly introduces as "Actor and former US President") telling a joke about the Soviet suppression of political dissidence, which he supposedly told Gorbachev directly. Not dissimilar to current US President Trump, Reagan delivers this joke with such outsized movie-star confidence that it feels as if we're sitting with him in his living room drinking a brandy—although, at the expense of many, his living room is our actual world.

The Sprawl embodies the conditions it seeks to document, taking on the jarring shifts in tone, content, and genre characteristic of the media today. The film could be located within a lineage of work by video artists such as Harun Farocki and Hito Steyerl, who maintain creative distance from the documentary format, or experimental documentary makers such as Adam Curtis. The societal conditions Metahaven seeks to address include the simultaneous democracy of authorship afforded by the internet and the supposed danger to truth that it poses, the subsequent proliferation of propaganda campaigns online, and the paralyzing nature of negativity that saturates our media landscape. The work reflects the wide-ranging nature of this content in its subsequent online version, sprawl.space (2016). This platform features the originally intended structure of *The Sprawl*, breaking down the film into "islands" or "shards" conceived as episodes and featuring this animated script that does not appear in the full-length version:

In 2014, a strange set of events unfolds.
Without apparent plan or structure, they seem connected.
Our views of the world are changing, as if we wake up from a dream.
We no longer see the internet as a means of communication,
but as a way to change the nature of reality itself.
Mind-warped, pixelated illusions replace our faith in information.
Ideologies collide in chasms of uncertainty and hope.
We are gazing at our screens, trapped in the sprawl.

This moment in *The Sprawl* marks Metahaven's interest in the aesthetic-

next

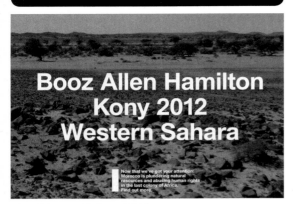

Free Western Sahara, 2014
campaign for Independent Diplomat

Free Western Sahara, 2014
campaign for Independent Diplomat

15
See Daniil Kharms, "Play" [1930], in *The Fire Horse: Children's Poems by Vladimir Mayakovsky, Osip Mandelstam and Daniil Kharms*, trans. Eugene Ostashevsky, New York: New York Review of Books, 2017.

16
See Ania Aizman, "The Secret Lessons of Soviet Children's Poems," *The New Yorker*, July 12, 2017, https://www.newyorker.com/books/page-turner/the-secret-lessons-of-soviet-childrens-poems. Last accessed on 29 August, 2018.

17
Samanth Subramanian, "Inside the Macedonian Fake News Complex," *WIRED*, February 15, 2017, https://www.wired.com/2017/02/veles-macedonia-fake-news/, and Emma Jane Kirby, "The City Getting Rich from Fake News," BBC News, December 5, 2016, https://www.bbc.com/news/magazine-38168281. Last accessed on August 29, 2018.

technical joinery known as the interface. To Metahaven, the interface represents reality's actual complexity, which has to be somehow reduced in order to become actionable:

> If we consider design to be a way of connecting one entity to another, and they are going to interact in one way or another, that is an interface. The interaction between these entities is going to be conditioned by the terms of the interface between them, which in turn affects their reality and behaviors.

The interface is a useful ideological tool in the advent of the thickness of the now as it introduces clarity within intolerable uncertainty—and if the same entities are doing the "thickening," or disorientation, and subsequently the clarifying, for them it is a double-win, an ideological repositioning and total reconditioning of public opinion. Metahaven explained their notion of the interface to me via the small, very basic LED monitor on my new e-bike that I rode to their studio. This monitor, which seems fairly banal and measures basic things such as my speed and the battery life, actually does simplify quite complex technological processes into layman ciphers, and comes with an IP, the ability to track me wherever I ride.

Theorist Benjamin H. Bratton speaks about the interface, and what he terms "interfacial regimes," within *The Sprawl*, slightly edited for clarity:

> At the level of the interface, this is where the capacity for a kind of real splintering in the way in which we perceive reality at a political level is possible. If you think of something like augmented reality, like Google Glass, Microsoft Hololens, Oculus Rift, or Facebook, what you have is a kind of an immediate lamination of a narration of the real that is directly into how it is that we perceive that reality. So it's not just that we see a person across the room, but I see their name and other information about them. Any interfacial regime, whether it's Google or Microsoft, or anything else, is a way in which this enormously complex system of the vast global super-computational network is made simple enough, and is narrated enough, that people can make use of it. In the course of this there's incredible reduction that takes place. And in that reduction of all the possibilities into just a set of buttons with words on them that you can click, there's inevitably a highly ideological distortion of all those possibilities into a framework.

The title *The Sprawl* refers to the seemingly unending divergent and disorienting information through which we must wade to determine truth. The film is visually inspired by the production vernacular of film and mass media: an actress wields a sword against a green screen, a "download" arrow button pops up alongside Bratton, a nighttime cityscape turned upside-down leads to a military compound viewed from a car, which is set against shots of a woman reading. Together, these moments suggest that our current sprawling information landscape is reduced through the interface of the

media, which is itself an immense simplification of ideologies.

The film is usually exhibited as a five-monitor installation: two screens run the first 35 minutes twice, two others run the second 35 minutes twice, and a central screen shows the film in full on loop with its soundtrack played in surround sound. The installation is configured as a forest: each monitor is installed on the stumps of faux birch trees. At the end of the room is a projection of a large red moon, which is also found within the film; it is subtitled with "REC," usually paired with a red dot, which together indicate that a video camera or similar device is recording. The red moon, to our eyes a small red sphere, stands in for the red recording dot, a widely recognized digital interface symbol. There's something humorously obvious and lo-fi about this gesture, but also poetic: it speaks to all of the unknown complexities and geographies of the moon, a rock so close as to be seen every day but also so far away, finding contrast in the false simplicity of the interface.

● Information Skies

Metahaven's subsequent, 24-minute film *Information Skies* is an entirely fictional sequel to *The Sprawl*. A couple, one of whom appears as a sabre-wielding actress in *The Sprawl*, follow a loose poetic narrative in a fantasy-driven but not-too-distant future. "Something happened this morning on our way to work," the film's female protagonist says at its outset. "It began raining facts from the ceiling." A voice-over narrates in Hungarian, with English and Korean subtitles, describing a condition of collapsed reality. Though the film references post-truth politics, here Metahaven illustrates rather than explains the effects of the characters' absorption in digital communication, which fundamentally limits their discernment of truth.

Wearing virtual reality headsets, the couple retreats into a forest where they withdraw into an unseen world in which they perceive that they're battling dragons. Anime scenes with landscapes doubling as faces rise and fall on the picture plane: the visual refinement echoes the simplicity the couple desire for their fantasy world. The presence of neo-feudal narratives in the entertainment industry, found both in role-playing games (such as *Skyrim*) and Hollywood-style programming (such as *Game of Thrones*), represents a vast consumer desire for the simplification of today's social complexities recapitulated as urgent needs for survival: food, water, a rampart, procreation. Within *Information Skies*, the soundtrack by Berlin-based musician M.E.S.H. suggests a dungeon theme from a 1980s video game, marked by digitized harpsichord strums and high piano notes played staccato. The combination of synthetic sound and extended takes of verdant, undulating landscape—for example, a worm's-eye view of a moss-covered tree and flowing brook—exemplifies the collective's in-depth study of Tarkovsky's similarly lush work.

From the early 1960s until his death in 1986 amid Soviet rule, Tarkovsky's films examined the conditions of Soviet life including industrialization, hopelessness, state censorship, blight, and spirituality.

Frequently in his films, the surface of water acts as a screen through which we examine its contents: in the opening scene of *Solaris* (1972), seaweed ripples under a glassine stream; throughout *Stalker* (1979), refuse such as rusting guns, religious memorabilia, and syringes appear covered in algae. The movement of water, and the abundant overgrowth in both Metahaven's and Tarkovsky's work, suggests the Earth's resilience, and its disconnection from our politics. Through infinite, perhaps brutal, adaptions, the Earth continues, though we might not recognize it as we knew it before.

Metahaven is likewise influenced by Tarkovsky's directorial style: unapologetically long, pensive shots; the striking casting of flora as both character and atmosphere; and particularly the absurdity of narrative, which responds to the absurdity of their historical moment. Both Tarkovsky's and Metahaven's sociopolitical approach to science fiction brings to mind that, like the War on Terror and speculative design, the genre itself is speculative, and thus invested in envisioning alternate realities. Science fiction dares to imagine life under fantastical conditions that, with a twist of the kaleidoscope, lay bare the truths of our own. Within Metahaven's practice, this embrace of Tarkovskyesque fiction represents a different way of dealing with documenting our historical moment: it is a departure from the attempt to give form to chimeric societal megastructures, and to instead discuss the circumstances created by those structures, particularly within the felt, lived experiences of the inhabitant.

Metahaven has deeply studied Tarkovsky, so too Russian poetry and literature, particularly children's poetry, described in their conversation with poet and translator Eugene Ostashevsky in this book. They reached out to Ostashevsky after reading his experimental work *The Pirate Who Does Not Know the Value of Pi* (2013) and *The Fire Horse* (2017), his volume of translations of children's poems by Russian futurist Vladimir Mayakovsky, modernist Osip Mandelstam, and absurdist Daniil Kharms. They are remarkably simple but devilishly sly in their subversion. Kharms's well-known poem "Play" (1930), the last featured in *The Fire Horse*, describes a cow clopping down the street, blocking attempts at progress:

A cow was walking down the road
Down the road,
Along the pavement
A cow was walking
Along the pavement
It was mooing
"Moo-moo-moo"
Just a real genuine cow
With some real genuine horns
Walked towards them on the road,
Taking up the whole wide way[15]

His use of metaphor—the cow standing in for an insurmountable barrier to progress, whether it be a potential revolution or society's industrialization—utilizes the rich imaginations of children to identify with the vehicles of, or perhaps obstacles to revolution.[16]

The characters in *Information Skies* are not children but young adults, and their game functions not as an imagined revolution but rather as its opposite: a societal withdrawal. This brings to mind the simultaneous connection afforded by digital communication technology and also its alienating effect, producing droves of young adults who would rather play role-playing games than go outside, much less show up for a protest.

● Hometown

Like Kharms's poems, Metahaven's scripts share this simultaneous simplicity of vocabulary that is paired with more complex, often paradoxical and subversive lyrics. Like *Information Skies*, *Hometown* is structured around a poem. Forcefully and playfully contradicting itself, the script doubles as a riddle or fable:

In a tiny village, as small as
four countries
Well-connected, without phone
or network
With no airlines flying to its busiest
airport
In this town, world-famous,
and known by nobody
Lives a retired woman, aged five or six
—who isn't me, unless you insist.

[...]

Before we continue,
let us agree on the time:
the station clock, always reliable,
wrongly says it's noon,
made out of one, and two.
So let us agree:
It's three

[...]

Here is where we disagree,
where one and one makes three.
Because I say so, because it's me.

But when one and one makes three
because the law says so
that's not me!—says who?

And is such a so-called law that
different from a law that says
that one and one makes two?

Displayed as a projection across two channels with a small gap in between, *Hometown* is about a fictional town compiled from footage shot in two real-life cities: Beirut and Kiev. As in *Information Skies*, it addresses the experiences and conditions created by the informational superstructures in *The Sprawl*. It focuses on "complex belonging"—another term coined by Metahaven, describing the dissonance between rational deduction of what is right, and what is felt as right—perhaps according to upbringing and psychological sensations such as experiencing déjà vu in a city you've never been to before. To Metahaven, the hometown does not exist as a single entity, but as a patchwork of real and imagined places. In the film, Ghina, a Lebanese woman and Lera, a Ukrainian woman, conflate their thoughts into one imagined shared space. Their biographies and other personal details are purposefully not made explicit. "The classical protagonist in a film is someone who you follow, and they undergo character development," Metahaven notes. "With our films you don't necessarily see this development, rather there's story development and you're prompted to consider how certain actions in the story implicate those figures." The film thus develops characters in a similar manner as would a poem, in which the experiences and reactions of a protagonist, rather than real-life verisimilitude, are central.

Throughout the 30-minute film Lera and Ghina traverse the unnamed fictional city, defined by its highway overpasses, concrete *Plattenbauten* dotted with satellite dishes, wild landscapes wrapped in barbed wire, and overgrown gardens. As the script quoted above suggests, the condition of this town is one in which truth is impossible to ascertain, yet life continues to flourish amid the contradictions laid out by the film. Interwoven are moments of what Metahaven calls "soft sci-fi," lemons cut into multi-sided prisms, as well as animated scenes that construe a sub-plot: a caterpillar, rife with its potential to become a butterfly, was murdered in cold blood, bleeding dark purple. This caterpillar, signified within the film as an augury of the "dawn of morality," and its killing, suggest two varying notions of unfolding morality: that of a society that has yet to fully realize itself, in a sort of ethically primitive chrysalis awaiting a metamorphosis of enlightenment; and, more simply, the overwhelming culpability one feels killing an insect as a child.

● Eurasia
(Questions on Happiness)

Eurasia (Questions on Happiness) is Metahaven's most recent work. As this book goes to print the film is being edited, its content and visual world are still developing and shifting into place. Part of the film is set in the Macedonian town of Veles, which in the last few years has been dubbed by the media as the "capital of fake news."[17] According to media outlets such as the BBC and *Wired*, in Velez a gaggle of teenagers create catchy headlines for stories plucked from right-wing news sites, then pay to "boost" them on Facebook, and watch them go viral while advertising revenue pours in from content monetization sources such as Google AdSense. Due to this sort of monetization, which rewards page views with a small payment, verity is exchanged for spectacle, catalyzing these stories to travel far and wide.

The film has several parallel and interwoven narratives, unrelated protagonists, and narrators. Sites are also characters, namely that particular landscape found between urban and agrarian environments

Karen Archey

next

Come to Iceland. Bring Data, 2012
campaign for IMMI, Iceland

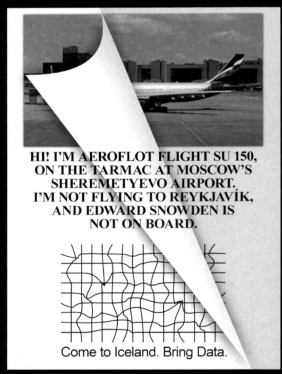

Come to Iceland. Bring Data, 2013
campaign for IMMI, Iceland

18
Laura Mulvey, "Visual Pleasure and Narrative Cinema,"
Screen 16, no. 3 (October 1975); 9.

—the kind of post-industrial zone that bears the touch of humans, but is eerily largely absent of human life. Its role in the film recalls Tarkovsky's work, in which the simultaneous presence and absence of humanity is portrayed by abandoned personal items and derelict industrial and domestic architecture. In *Eurasia*, looming infrastructure—highway underpasses, *Plattenbauten* strewn with cables, and pylons—contrast against majestic hills and towering trees. The landscape tells a story of connection between humans of the present and past, and also between nature, humanity, and technological and transport infrastructure. Metahaven's work attests to the scale at which humans are dwarfed by this infrastructure—so incalculably sublime, that we remain blind to it and its causes and effects. While this landscape is a generic one and exists in many cities and their surrounding areas throughout the world, *Eurasia* treats the contextual specificities of its shooting locations throughout Eurasia as actors, however imperceptible to the viewer: atmospheres become part of the film's plot, and landscape footage is cut against characters, placing them on an equal plane. Extended shots of steppes, an otherworldly crimson pool rimmed with black copper slag, and pylons dotting mountains, are enriched throughout by music composed by Kuedo. We hear:

It was not possible to still discern, with any degree of certainty, the way that the events had registered in, and made changes in the environment. But a peasant whom we met on the way, believed that this was a fully sentient territory. He believed that the grassroots and treetops were addressable, and that every such entity was acutely aware of the events as they had happened. He alleged, that even the vegetation had played a part in the disinformation campaign.

Can a landscape or site such as Veles bear witness? Complementing the "soft sci-fi" vernacular of the film, these landscapes are often tilted at a 45-degree angle in a somewhat nauseating shift in perspective that creates stark and stunning geometrical contrasts. Further, *Eurasia* combines cinematic footage shot by Metahaven with found footage, including several obscure YouTube clips that bring lightness and pun, as well as footage from the first-person-shooter survival horror video game *S.T.A.L.K.E.R.: Shadow of Chernobyl*—a real game created by a Ukrainian company. This use of sourced footage gestures back to *The Sprawl* and *Possessed*. *Eurasia* more seamlessly integrates found footage with Metahaven's own, folding in plots and layers of the film to situate fiction within reality, and reality within fiction. The film creates and plays with constructs of reality and believability, fictionalizing Eurasia itself in order to talk about "real politics." For example, Russia is referred to as DVD Zone 5—with its spoken languages of German, French, Italian, Macedonian, Russian, and Chinese reflecting the heterogeneity of the continental landmass.

A recurring theme in the film is that the drone that we see flying around and a camera that pries into its surroundings, catch sight of each other and of themselves. Amid the film's conclusion is a camera on a tripod in a bathroom, filming a mirror and thus capturing itself. This reference to the camera would suggest that *Eurasia* is a film about cinema itself—its history, its aesthetics, and even texture and logics. Due to their immersive and durational qualities, film and video are undoubtedly the most malleable media through which reality—and thus truth—are conveyed. And given the technological developments of the last ten years, no other medium is more changed in its accessibility.

At the same time these scenes of the drone and the camera also cast doubt on the very achievability of conveying truth through film and video. Much like their surroundings, the movements of the drone and camera are followed around like they're actors, their apparent gaze and unraveling self-awareness endowing them, and by extension perhaps also technology, with a power to witness that goes beyond factual registration. This adds another unnerving layer of non-objectivity to a vehicle entrusted to follow orders, it simultaneously being *Eurasia*'s medium of choice.

Creating Space

Part of Metahaven's work involves creating political, practical, and aesthetic spaces that suit their ideas and that previously did not exist—particularly in their treatment of film. Considering whether their work qualifies as film or video requires incredibly precise definitions of each. To Metahaven, the cinematic designates a complete temporal and visual unity, and subsequently, immersion. The Hollywood-dominated industry associated with cinema mediates professionalized production practices dictating how, where, and when such films are released, whether released in a theater or on platforms such as Netflix. Aware of this, Metahaven has concentrated their practice on emancipating the cinematic from this industry, rife also with conventions and limitations related to narrative strategies, the acceptability and complexity of content, duration, etc.:

> The cinematic as an experience, as a temporal and visual unity, represents something beyond the film industry. One of the things we're trying to do is reclaim elements of the cinematic from the situation where you can only be cinematic in a cinema, or on Netflix. But let's recognize the cinematic as things other than the usual story. In the confrontation between slowness and insipidity, there's an appropriate camera style. When combined with duration—how we would like times to run, if we had our way, if we could act as fast as the platforms make us think—that confrontation between slowness and insipidity, those sort of push-and-pull forces produces something that's cinematic on an everyday level.

Cinema and video operate psychologically in very different ways. Cinema is a psychological space well-defined by theorists ranging from eighteenth-century art critic Denis Diderot to contemporary feminist theorist Laura Mulvey. Theorizing theater rather than cinema, Diderot's concept of the "fourth wall" defines a performative convention that invisibly divides an audience from a realistic world portrayed by actors on stage. Mulvey's much later work considers the psychological effects of a viewer in the physically immersive, dark space of the cinema in which we are able to project ourselves onto the world playing out on screen. She writes:

> The mass of mainstream film... portray a hermetically sealed world which unwinds magically... producing [for the audience] a sense of separation and playing on their voyeuristic phantasy. Moreover, the extreme contrast between the darkness in the auditorium (which also isolates the spectators from one another) and the brilliance of the shifting patterns of light and shade on the screen helps to promote the illusion of voyeuristic separation... these conditions giving the spectator an illusion of looking in on a private world.[18]

Practically, the cinematic is further defined by the audience's intended attendance for the film's entire duration.

Metahaven's films are created within the industry, history, and material of cinema and are often shown within film festivals, as well as in art institutions. Artists' films and videos are shown in brighter, white-walled gallery spaces that are architecturally inhospitable to cinematic immersion, thus the nature of the viewing experience inevitably changes. These spaces are made to walk through, and thus there is a tacit assumption that a looped video will not be seen in entirety by every visitor. Works like Metahaven's 70-minute *The Sprawl* interestingly anticipate this, with its installation allowing for non-linear viewership and cinematic experience through a sequence of monitors screening different sections as described above.

The evolution from Metahaven's first project on Sealand to their current, immersive films charts their transformation from studying the vehicle of communication to identifying the ideological causes and effects of disinformation. In Metahaven's parlance, the interface itself describes the very human condition of wanting to understand, a basic desire for clarity. As citizens of the world, without moral or political clarity we find ourselves watching the wills and egos of giants play out in unsettlingly unpredictable ways as we're isolated in a defensive fog. No longer do we look for insurgence in the public square, but rather to Netflix in the quiet defeat of our bedrooms. Like cloudy weather, our current moment is defined by a situational lack of transparency, which, either by force or chance, will eventually lift.

Karen Archey
Karen Archey is Curator of Contemporary Art, Time-based Media at the Stedelijk Museum Amsterdam. She was previously based in Berlin and New York, where she worked as an independent curator, art critic, and editor of *e-flux conversations*. Her research analyzes contemporary art through social histories relating to technology, gender, and the economy. Her writing is regularly featured in magazines such as *frieze*, *LEAP*, and *ArtReview*. In 2014 Archey co-curated the survey exhibition *Art Post-Internet* at Ullens Center for Contemporary Art in Beijing and edited the associated publication *Art Post-Internet: INFORMATION/DATA*. At the Stedelijk, Archey has organized solo exhibitions of artists Stefan Tcherepnin (2018), Catherine Christer Hennix (2018), and Rineke Dijkstra (2017), as well as the group exhibition *Freedom of Movement* (2018). Archey organizes the Stedelijk's performance program, and leads the museum's research initiative on the collection, preservation, and presentation of time-based media artwork.

Cloudy Weather

next

What is
art?
What is
art.

QUESTION MORE

ЧТО ТАКОЕ ИСКУССТВО?

что

BB7

Bucharest
Biennale 7

Bucharest
International
Biennial for
Contemporary

May 26–
June 30
2016

18

Л.Н. ТОЛСТОЙ

Checkpoint Truth, 2016
billboard, Bucharest Biennale 7, 2016

INTERFERENCE—CHORUS—UNEQUAL
MORNING SUN—LOCKER LEAK
AN EXIT—LONELY AT THE TOP—DAO
HOME—NEW WAYS TO LOVE

PLATFORM
HOLLY HERNDON

Platform, 2015
album cover
courtesy of 4AD/RVNG Intl.

Pictogram

Maryam
Monalisa Gharavi

MH

next

Call, 2014
animated GIFs

20

Metahaven We're interested in your use of music to convey politics. In your songs "Home" and "Interference," that message is not immediately apparent or overt. This is perhaps because your politics are so personal, that they no longer correspond to what we think of as "political art" (and to the music's benefit, if we say so ourselves). Your work eludes literal reading, rarely offering direct statements. Its politics aren't hidden. In live performances and interviews, we see your political position combine aspects of queerness, cyber autonomy, and a third element, which is hard to pin down, but that we are tempted to call communion. Could you elaborate on how these politics are shaped by your music, how these ideas are reified as art?

Mathew Dryhurst and Holly Herndon Addressing the complexity of our contemporary political moment is a challenge, and we can only be certain of one thing: assuming an overt, kitsch political stance in the face of current issues is insufficient. We have some simple rules that we stick to in order to not explicitly make political artworks, but rather attempt to figure out a process for grappling with the complexity.

The first general rule is to be anti-nostalgic, which is liberating in the sense that it allows us to create freely and without being beholden to a predetermined goal. We couldn't make artworks tailored to a certain purpose, because that is not how we work. Despite the fact that our interests fall between the categories of art, technology, politics, and identity, it would feel disingenuous and limiting to let any one of these threads have too much influence on our decision-making.

The second rule is to attempt to incorporate new processes as close as possible to the subject matter. For example, with our songs "Home" and "Chorus," which explore the issue of surveillance, we made a point to surveil ourselves and see what arose from that. We often have to hack together our own tools to properly explore an idea. We've been doing something similar with artificial intelligence (AI), too: we're currently training our own AI child. If we want to really grasp something, we make an effort to directly engage with it, and spend a lot of our free time outside of the arts as a result. For example, we try to understand the art market as closely as possible, if only to most effectively ignore it. As a third rule, we try to be incredibly transparent about our practice with our listeners in order to engage them with our intellectual and practical processes.

This often chaotic combination of elements comes together to form a mutant practice in which even we have a hard time fully feeling at home. This feels true to our initial impulse, and often leads to richer and perhaps more complex results in our work.

As artists, how do you express a deep concern for politics without taking the bait and making kitsch and blunt political gestures?

MD&HH We are increasingly torn on the issue of vulnerability. On the one hand, we feel a responsibility to acknowledge through transparency that we are equally as vulnerable as everyone else. Yet on the other hand, we fear that expressing vulnerability online can become a kind of meta-vulnerability, as it is apparently an efficient way for those who scour networks to further understand their network subjects. Facebook's cataloging of depressed individuals is one of many examples of this. Mat recently tweeted: "The thing about ad driven platform capitalism is that the more detailed or aberrant your interests and beliefs are, the happier it is, as you are ostensibly expanding its model and pathways to sell ppl stuff." This sentiment could also apply to vulnerability and clearly legible gestures expressed online. One temptation is to conclude that if everything ultimately needs to be legible in order to be seen—and the criteria by which others even get to witness what you do is based upon a certain kind of network or machine legibility (for example, how one must in fact make *playlist music* to be featured on a Spotify playlist)—then the best one can do is attempt to make the most complex legible gestures and hope for the best. But this also feels like a compromise. I guess the contemporary equivalent of the glamorous, utopian futurity of CyberSyn is having the hubris—and necessary funds—to attempt to create one's own networks. This seems like an elusive goal. However, it is part of the reason we adhere to the "skin in the game" approach.

MH There is a paradox to making "political work" that challenges its own legibility. Working with you two has opened the floodgates of a more intuitive and emotive approach for us—an approach that perhaps has always been present, but was somehow packaged in other interests. By emotive we mean that we are working with motives that come from within. We now work from the belief that, in a sci-fi way, everything is nested inside everything else. In our age of technology a wooden table in a film is already perceived as a sentient object—you don't need to specify that it is either political or technological. The fantastical lies in the gaze and the frame, not in the subject matter.

Examples where sci-fi aesthetics and progressive politics were successfully merged are often on our mind. For instance, the Project CyberSyn operations room circa 1970, designed by Stafford Beer, Gui Bonsiepe, and others. It served as a kind of *Star Trek*-style command room that would coordinate supply and demand for the Salvador Allende government in Chile, a closed loop that in itself seems a bit quaint when looking back. But the idea that progressive politics could have its own kind of utopian cybernetics was firmly expressed in Project CyberSyn. The futuristic headquarters of the French Communist Party, designed by Oscar Niemeyer in Paris (1967–1981), is another example of a kind of glamorous futurism.

But right now we're in a very different situation. Technology and futurism are often not geared toward common goods, but toward spectacular space arks and Teslas on Mars, reflecting the interests of a technological Silicon Valley class that's become its own separate world. By necessity, the rest of us now think in terms of self-organization and small-scale (if any) initiatives. This brings to mind that asymmetry is still the root of many conflicts in the information age.

Vulnerability is a form of asymmetry, too.

21

MH For us it is revelatory that you use composition, vocals, performance, and media to feel or sense through complex political, technological, and social structures. This is distinctly different from the more common approach in which artists and musicians declare technology a formal subject matter to be critiqued in their work. We find it stimulating that you reverse this approach.

MD&HH Put simply, when you come to the conclusion that there are no formal boundaries between a technology and an individual or a collective, and see beauty in that, it feels like a missed opportunity not to approach that relationship in a discrete or analytical way. We also don't think that people experience technology in that way. So, if the goal is to make work that is resonant, or revealing, then we feel it's far better to immerse oneself and report back the complexity of that experience.

It helps to have at least one anchor, and for Holly that is almost always the voice. She has spent a decade now developing tools to be maximally communicative with that instrument. This provides a needed continuity. For example, we've been experimenting a lot with machine learning, and that has led us to ancient folk music, and feedback loops in the early development stages of languages, as well as early, "primitive" art, communion rituals, and social organizations. What would take a book to communicate in writing, could take ten seconds to express more powerfully and emotionally through the electronically processed voice.

We are assisted by the fact that music as a medium is largely unburdened by an expectation of legibility, or even tangible function. Your work seems to play with this tension.

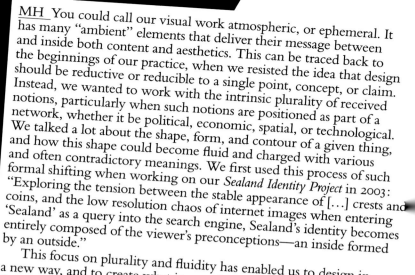

MH You could call our visual work atmospheric, or ephemeral. It has many "ambient" elements that deliver their message between and inside both content and aesthetics. This can be traced back to the beginnings of our practice, when we resisted the idea that design should be reductive or reducible to a single point, concept, or claim. Instead, we wanted to work with the intrinsic plurality of received notions, particularly when such notions are positioned as part of a network, whether it be political, economic, spatial, or technological. We talked a lot about the shape, form, and contour of a given thing, and how this shape could become fluid and charged with various and often contradictory meanings. We first used this process of such formal shifting when working on our *Sealand Identity Project* in 2003: "Exploring the tension between the stable appearance of [...] crests and coins, and the low resolution chaos of internet images when entering 'Sealand' as a query into the search engine, Sealand's identity becomes entirely composed of the viewer's preconceptions—an inside formed by an outside."

This focus on plurality and fluidity has enabled us to design in a new way, and to create what is now described as "research" and "speculative" design. However, if you keep questioning or digging, that process eventually undercuts the degree of certainty that design itself needs in order to "perform as" design. The process erodes the foundation of design itself and at some point there is either a moment when you can no longer call it design, or, the purpose of design becomes to feed itself. The notion of "feed" here intentionally touches on how contemporary design functions in the context of platforms like Instagram. Here, the functional requirements of providing a "legible" message are becoming overridden by the performative function of design as a system of organized and quantified visibility, not legibility.

However, the most important thing is what you build up while tearing down certainty. It's not a coincidence for us that our work has parallels with music. It's tempting to think of music, design, and cinema as, in a way, building together toward a new form of durational art.

We're curious to know who the important long-term predecessors to your way of working are. Is there, let's say, music from one hundred or more years ago that does similar things for you? And what has the twenty-first century added, do you think, to the way in which the position of the artist can be seen as being entangled with, or in opposition to, larger forces?

MD&HH We actually have to admit that we've learned a lot from you, in so much as there is little separation between your family unit and way of being and the work that you make, and that is a beautiful thing. Holly spends most of her time listening to early music from across the world, as it is jaw-dropping to follow the threads of expression back to their origins, and awe-inspiring to see how much complexity and diversity can arise from humble experiments in voice and harmony. Hildegard von Bingen is on constant rotation, as well as examples of Albanian iso-polyphony, Central-African homophonic parallelism, Baḥrī music of the Gulf, Christian music of the Deep South, and ancient Greek music. More recently, she feels gratitude toward artists like Meredith Monk, Trevor Wishart, John Chowning, Thomas Tallis, Charles Ives, Timbaland, Karlheinz Stockhausen, and Laurie Anderson. Ultimately the goal is to not attempt to do what they did, as the greatest lesson they can teach us is to respectfully deviate from precedent.

At the moment we are looking at traditional artist studio models, and pop music production studio models as a means to be able to react more quickly to events as they unfold. It feels that to somehow have skin in the game in the twenty-first century, one requires agility. This is perhaps not a new dynamic in music or art, but the rate of acceleration feels like new territory. We ask ourselves how we might mutate ourselves to compete with bots and content engines and are still unsure as to the preferred configuration.

We suspect that you are more agile as visual artists in the highly visual environment of the feed. How much emphasis do you place on this agility? For example, you were very early to warn people of the new role of propaganda online, specifically with regard to modern Russian information warfare. The augury of your work and the latent, now-topical public outrage on this topic was profound. Is there a temptation to double down and jump back into those conversations? There are commercial incentives to do so, and yet somehow we find your power to come from guiding the spotlight, rather than reveling in it. We struggle with this question, and often internally debate which approach is more impactful. On the one hand, operating in the background and attempting to navigate the discourse without being immediately visible is rewarding and feels intellectually honest. On the other hand, it can often feel like we are doing research and development for others to ultimately capitalize on, which threatens long-term sustainability.

MH With our slow shift to producing longer-running moving image projects, our relationship to the feed also got into a kind of crisis. When making a film, much more time passes by where you are not sharing online what you are working on in the studio, and you miss out on the gratification that comes from the sharing process. We operate in an economy in which the actual making of work is the activity that's constantly under pressure—due to precarity, communication and representation duties, social media, daily life, and caregiving, which are at the same time the essential components of one's existence—you need to find a unity between the production and distribution of work and the actual birthplace of ideas; both life and work need to be tied together and somehow be about the same things. So, the caregiving, and love, and so on need to be where the work is, otherwise all the events in life will only be experienced as obstacles.

Essentially, the platform continually demands the most algorithmically desirable version of a life, which users are willing to offer because this will deliver them the gratification that comes from sharing content online. In the long run, existence, when it's conditioned by platform visibility, also becomes curated by it. By tailoring itself to the exact mold of the platform, current design produces something that is infinitely desirable but entirely unsustainable on the same terms. The ephemerality and "stardust" of design is further detached from its material form, and becomes an object of pure techno-capitalist quantification. The migration from Tumblr to Instagram, for design, has meant the equivalent of a shift from "indie" to corporate-owned self-exploitation. Everyone who participates recognizes this on some level, but still engages in the same collaborative competition for attention. We don't consider ourselves an exception to this, and don't want our analysis to be seen as a judgment of other people's online practices. But the question remains: what are we accomplishing by pouring liquid post-cyber design into the phalanx-like square order of the Instagram grid?

The platform catch-all produces consolidation and centralization as a dominant standard. This goes hand in hand with the hyper-fragmentation of all entities on the platform, as they become measurable and quantifiable against all other entities: their identifications, economies, payments, and their experiences are fragmented to the extent that subjectivity itself becomes divisible to new degrees. Cohesion, then, becomes premised on actual or self-declared margins that all simultaneously claim their universality.

There exists a rightful use of the word "marginalized," of course. But let's not forget that there's also a massive amount of relatively privileged people in the West who have in recent years started behaving as if they are under some kind of existential threat, precipitating a massive political shift to the (far) right.

There is a hyper-fragmentation going on in terms of identities, but similarly in terms of territories. Unwittingly, in this increasingly divided patchwork of conflicting interests, actors that translate influence into real power and that do not care for fairness or rules, now have the winning hand. Alarmingly so.

MD&HH It's really fitting that you reference cohesion and coherence in relation to the feed, as in a sense we have come to the conflicted realization that despite the constant temptation to participate in the push and pull of online discourse, it is also a necessity—and perhaps

the greatest contemporary privilege—to make work that attempts to be discrete from those pressures and pleasures. While this runs the risk of taking the form of elitism, it also perhaps represents the only possibility to develop something with sufficient context, coherence, and community to challenge the elites. It is a hackneyed story, but Steve Jobs didn't let his kids have iPhones, and of course elites are generally insulated from the downsides of non-participation in platform capitalism, or basically anything. In a sense, through being less concerned with imitation, gamesmanship, and daily monetized battles on the feed, we begin to see that a cooperative platform perhaps already exists, but it has an architecture and interface problem. We are increasingly interested in offline cultures, not as a reactionary disavowal of the present, but instead as a model for how to bring the connections and threads spawned online into physical space. Online space is in some sense infinite, and so victories are often illusory.

Mathew Dryhurst
Mathew Dryhurst is a British art, music, and software producer. He writes and tours with creative partner Holly Herndon. He teaches technology and aesthetics at New York University's Clive Davis Institute. He also built the self-hosted publishing platform Saga, and serves on the board of the music streaming co-operative Resonate.

Holly Herndon
Holly Herndon is a musician and artist based in Berlin. Herndon received her MFA in Electronic Music and Recording Media from Mills College, Oakland, California and is currently doing a PhD at Stanford University in Music and Acoustics, studying composition. Her music can be described as primarily computer based and often uses visual programming languages Max/MSP, with which she creates custom instruments and vocal processes. She has released music on the labels RVNG Intl. and 4AD. *Platform* (2015) is Herndon's most recent full-length album. She will release her third studio album on 4AD in spring 2019.

23

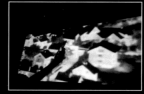

الجمهوريّة اللبنانيّة

وزارة الداخلية والبلديات

بلدية برج حمود

عدد: ١٥٢٧

تاريخ: ٢٠١٧/٣/٢٩

تصريح

إن رئيس بلدية برج حمود،

بناء على الطلب المقدم من المستدعية جنان شعيا، المتضمن طلب الموافقة على تصوير فيلم وثائقي قصير بعنوان Hometown في الفترة الممتدة بين ٢٠١٧/٠٥/٢٥ ولغاية ٢٠١٧/٠٥/٣٠ ضمن نطاق برج حمود،

يفيد ما يلي:

يصرح للمستدعية جنان شعيا بتصوير فيلم وثائقي قصير بعنوان Hometown في الفترة الممتدة بين ٢٠١٧/٠٥/٢٥ ولغاية ٢٠١٧/٠٥/٣٠ ضمن نطاق برج حمود أملاك .... على شرط عدم تكبير الطرقات والتنسيق مع رئاسة الشرطة السلامة العامة

الجمهورية اللبنانية

وزارة الداخلية والبلديات

محافظة مدينة بيروت

عدد:٥٠٨٩/م

دائرة المحافظة،

لإبلاغ الآنسة جنان شعيا موافقتنا على أخذ مشاهد من فيلم وثائقي بعنوان "Hometown" في مدينة بيروت وتحديداً:"الأشرفية — الرميل — مار مخايل البسطة — شارل حلو — السوديكو — الحمرا — القنطاري والروشة (ما عدا الاماكن العسكرية والادارية والخاصة) وذلك في الفترة الممتدة بين ٢٥ و ٣١ ايار ٢٠١٧، شرط التقيد بالآداب العامة والحشمة والقوانين المرعية الإجراء، وشرط عدم قطع الطرقات اثناء التصوير. يتطلب التصوير إيقاف شاحنة المعدات على جانب الطريق.

بيروت في ٢٣ ايار ٢٠١٧

القاضي زياد شبيب

محافظ مدينة بيروت

Republique Libanaise

Direction Generale de
la Sûreté Generale

Bureau des Medias

Service des Imprimées

الجمهورية اللبنانية

المديرية العامة

للأمن العام

مكتب شؤون الاعلام

دائرة المطبوعات

إجازة رقم ١٣٤ / م ط ص

بناءً على قرار المدير العام للأمن العام رقم ٤٣٧ / ش ر تاريخ ٢٠١٧/٠٥/٢٠

إن دائرة المطبوعات

تجيز لـ: جنان الدو شعيا

تصوير شريط وثائقي

المرعية

نص تحدد

٢٠١٧/٠٥/٢
دائرة المطبوعات

فؤاد قازان

22 MA

---

previous

+

24

Maryam Monalisa Gharavi The first image has certain hallmarks of beauty: the gauzy backdrop, the off-center hand entering the frame, the visual mimesis of the black rectangle. Because I've lately become concerned—the truth is, *obsessed*—with what digital device exposure is doing to organic bodies, the first thing this image prompts is bone loss: a combination of radiation, close proximity, and carpal bones silently chewing away. Fifty years from now, will we be holding mobile phones in our hands, or do-everything devices analogous to the things we currently call phones? Will today's devices look as kitschy and clunky as those box booths from the 1980s? If by then they have disappeared inside our skin, maybe no one will care.

That's why the second image is such a palliative. All those devices branching out from a tripod look safer, like the quiet eyes on the feathers of a peacock

Hometown

In a tiny village, as small as four countries
Well-connected,
without phone or network
With no airlines flying to its busiest airport.

In this town, world-famous, and known by nobody
Lives a retired woman, aged five or six
—who isn't me, unless you insist.

Here is our epic. Don't worry, it's short.
It's the secret that everybody has heard.
Before we continue, let us agree on the time
The station clock, always reliable
Wrongly says it's noon, made out of one and two
So let us agree: it's three.

We grew up with the seeming, probabilities, unlikelihood,
revolving doors and mirroring walls.
Favors. Bread, milk, sugar.
Self-made clothes. Self-rendered currency.

Grandfather is a scientist.
When he picks me up from school
and I'm wearing the yellow jumper—
he says it's red.
He holds both my hands, counts five fingers on each hand—
he holds in his hands my hands, counts the fingers on each.
How many?
He draws a caterpillar—
says it is a butterfly instead.

How so, granddad? You are only joking.
When it rains
the sun must shine.
Overcast again, daytime—
syntax error. A puzzle. Laughed—solved!
The sun is hiding in moonless blue.

Now under the gaze of the satellites
Between the nodes, connected underground.
Over ground
a crime happened:
a caterpillar got murdered in cold blood.
Dark purple, ink-like.

Here is where we disagree, where one and one makes three.
Because I say so, because it's me.
But when one and one makes three
Because the law says so
That's not me!—says who?
And is such so-called law that different
From a law that says that one and one makes two?

We grew up with the seeming, probabilities, unlikelihood,
revolving doors and mirroring walls, many-sided coins,
the coming and going of helicopters from there and to there,
the TV news.
A printing press was forced to "close its doors."

After school, in my hand the melting ice cream drips.
Once frozen, the glacier, now unleashed
Tastes of fruit, the orchard, of our ancient soil
And data center heat, you choose.

Родной город

В селе, как четыре страны небольшом,
отлично соединенном
без телефонов или сети,
ни один корабль не причаливает в аэродром

В этом городе, на весь мир знаменитом,
забытом давно,
Живет на пенсии женщина лет пяти-шести,
она — не я. Если, конечно, не все равно.

Здесь эпос наш. Не беспокойся, не долгий,
Это секрет, давно услышанный всеми.
Перед тем, как продолжить, давайте часы сверим:
надежные, те, что на станции,
неправильно показывают полдень,
собранный из одного и двух;
мы думаем — три.

Мы выросли с этим, кажущееся, вероятное,
маловероятное, вращающиеся двери
и зеркальные стены.
Одолжения. Хлеб, молоко, сахар.
Одежда своими руками. Деньги своими руками.

Дедушка был ученым.
Он забирает меня из школы,
на мне голубой свитер —
он говорит, бордовый.
Он держит в ладонях обе мои руки,
считает пальцы на каждой. Сколько?
Рисует гусеницу,
говорит — бабочка.

Как же, дед? Ты пошутил.
Когда дождь идет
солнце должно светить.
Опять облачно, днем —
ошибка в синтаксисе. Головоломка.
Рассмеялся — решил.
В безлунном небе солнце скрылось.

Под взглядом спутников,
меж узлов подземных сетей
над землей
преступление совершено:
гусеница хладнокровно убита.
Темно-пурпурно, в чернилах.

Итак, согласиться не можем мы,
здесь один плюс один дают три.
Так вам говорю я.
Но когда один и один дают три,
потому что таков закон,
говорю не я! — но кто говорит тогда?
И так уж ли разница велика между этим законом
так называемым,
и законом, что говорит,
что один плюс один равно два?

Там, где мы выросли, нас окружало кажущееся,
вероятное, маловероятное,
вращающиеся двери и зеркальные стены,
монеты многосторонние,
вертолеты туда и оттуда, выпуски новостей.
Печатный станок остановлен,
закрылся издательский дом.

После уроков, мороженое в моей руке капает.
Когда-то вечная мерзлота, ледник теперь тает
привкусом фруктов из сада, древней почвы
и теплом дата-центров. Сам подумай.

 Hometown

next

Suhail Malik I'd like to address some of the themes that seem to have preoccupied you for some time, and not just in the content of your work, but also in terms of how your work operates. I am particularly interested in how your collaborative practice—and your transdisciplinary practice, too, as artists, designers, writers, and editors—contributes to a renewal or a transformation of our understanding of propaganda. One of the most striking concerns evident over the course of your practice is how the status of propaganda has recently changed. Could you explain how and why propaganda became a theme for you?

Metahaven We initially viewed propaganda as something quaint, a dusty relic that, at least in the West, appeared to have "ended" after the Cold War, and was supplanted by equally deceptive soft power. In this period, military power is wielded multilaterally through an increasingly dysfunctional system of collaborative agreements, among which the "coalition of the willing" that okays the Iraq invasion in 2003. At or about the same time, cloud platforms begin to emerge, simultaneous to growing rifts and ruptures within the liberal West—mainly focused on immigration and religion—and between the West and other parts of the world. Our current work develops from an awareness of the ways in which the moving image is taking a critical role in the reemergence of propaganda, in particular between Russia and the West.

SM How is your more recent interest in propaganda connected to your pre-2010 work on state branding and the commodification of identity and status?

MH Nation-states in the post-1989 era were presumed to become market actors, having left behind a competition for political hegemony. Soft power is then simply the brand image of an actor in this marketplace—which is not just economical, but also one of ideas. The idea of soft power, like propaganda, is premised on telling stories. In convergence with a planetary "cloud," the means to tell stories proliferate and become more evenly distributed. Propaganda emerges as the former marketplace of ideas is transformed into an increasingly unregulated arena of free speech, where it is possible to achieve remarkable results even when holding comparatively little actual power, aided by the scaling and network effects of the platform itself. From pseudo-television to hacking, this proliferation of the means to tell stories and advance interests through the computational "megastructure" has been paired with a decreasing focus on democracy and rule of law as foundations for legitimacy. These principles are being taken for granted, or gradually replaced by more base-level ideas of "effectiveness." It's not an accident so much as a design feature of this new model of power that during the July 2016 so-called coup d'état, Turkish President Recep Erdoğan addresses the nation via FaceTime.

The assumption that digital platforms would somehow be naturally inscribed with liberal values and would thus inherently serve as instruments of soft power—for example, for the United States and its allies—led the US to enter the 2010 cycle of revolutionary events in North Africa and the Middle East. The idea was that Twitter and other platforms would provide the additional soft power that would give these events a certain political signature, while in fact, the era of soft power lay just behind us.

SM This became explicit when Egyptian authorities blocked the use of Twitter in Tahrir Square during the Arab Spring because the platform was said to be the main organizing medium there. It then became clear that the US state was heavily backing Twitter and putting pressure on the Egyptian authorities to keep it open; the Egyptian state ultimately complied.

MH Many media stories claim that this or that revolution or uprising started "with my Facebook post," a myth, a standard techno-determinist narrative, framed to benefit the role of the West. In *Uncorporate Identity* (2010), we addressed the unpairing of political outcomes from their standards of communication, as is exemplified by the hypothetical case in which the US has disappeared off the face of the Earth but everybody keeps on speaking English.

SM But cloud platforms have also become actors themselves.

MH YouTube was created in 2005 and bought by Google in 2006. Russia Today also started in 2005. There are a whole bunch of influential platforms that were founded in the mid-2000s and became more visible later on.

SM I want to come back to the "it all started with my Facebook post" meme. What's quite telling about that claim is the way in which an individual actor can have systemic effects. Before the internet you needed to go through mediating institutions to amplify your claims or criticisms. The "it all started with my Facebook post" myth speaks to how small actors can now have large effects, and to how large-scale actors don't necessarily have large effects. There's a kind of scrambling of scales between announcements and actions or effects going on.

The usual verification processes break down, so any transmission is at once the signal, the content, and also propaganda somehow. It's not clear what counts as content, what counts as affect, and what counts as persuasion. What seems to be at the core of *The Sprawl* (*Propaganda about Propaganda*) (2015) is the feeling that propaganda has become another name for communication itself.

If so, the modern and critical view of propaganda as distinct from truth, as a kind of deception that undercuts truth, or as a form of communication that's dictated only by power, doesn't hold for network-based communication anymore. Instead, you cannot tell whether communication conveys power or truth—whether it's subjective truth, or epistemological truth, and so on.

MH Maybe.

SM However, one faction of the critical left, and also of liberalism for that matter, certainly held on to this distinction. There was a clear sense from the Enlightenment onward that propaganda was to be treated with suspicion—that, at least in principle, it should be possible to demarcate a rational claim from propagandistic claims. That's the critical task. Rationalists argued for the elimination of propaganda as a basis for action. Politics, on the other hand, is

Sunrise, simulation
Nightfall, prepaid

I didn't kill the caterpillar
It was I who killed the caterpillar
Never not intentionally.

My hometown.
To a forgotten city, forever remembered,
on the very top of the deepest valley,
to this place, snowcovered,
in the blistering warmth,
I return, feeling fresh, after a long, hard journey.

The station clock came to a standstill:
It's always the same hour.
Let's agree on a place.
After thinking for long, I had the idea right away:
I'll see you at dawn,
where the road splits in two.

Crumbling like sand cake
Our new tomorrow
Is like the blackbird's song:
A solemn voice, a silent pulse of tomorrow.
As inheritance, seriously, I got: the future of the ruins.

Now in the sunken city, look around.
People dwell, lost, and entranced.
They forgot about,
how children taught them,
what cannot be taught:
a dawn of morality from within.
Their children bear names of,
what cannot be named:

Luka, of light,
Nadezhda, of waiting,
Alyosha, of help.

United we are, in chaos.
Once frozen, the solid mass, now a river,
becomes our life,
and washes away the memory banks,
of the town.

Pay cut, or power cut, there is no choice,
nightfall, a free-for-all,
magic, without wires,
unleashing vertical fire.

My hometown.

Рассвет — симуляция,
Закат — по предоплате.

Я не убивала гусеницу.
Это я убила гусеницу.
Никогда не нарочно.

Мой родной город.

В это забытое место, но сохраненное в памяти,
на самой верхушке глубокой долины,
укрытое снегом в палящей жаре —
сюда возвращаюсь я, чувствуя бодрость
после долгой, трудной дороги.

Часы на станции остановились:
время, всегда одно и то же.
Условимся же о месте.
Сразу решаю после долгих раздумий:
увидимся на рассвете,
на распутье.

Сыпучее, как песочное тесто,
наше новое завтра
как поет соловей:
пульсация нового дня.
Мне досталось в наследство — не шутка — будущее руин.

Мы в затонувшем городе. Вокруг
бродят те, кто затеряны в трансе;
забыли, как
дети учили их тому,
чему научить нельзя:
рассвету со чувственности изнутри.
Дети,
чьи имена говорят:

Лука, о свете,
Надежда, об ожидании,
Алеша, о помощи.

Едины мы в хаосе.
Раньше массив замороженный, теперь рекой
стала наша жизнь,
размывает памяти берега
в городе.

Срезать зарплату или электричество отключить
без выбора мы:
закат в открытом доступе,
падает вертикальный пожар.

Мой родной город.

Hometown

In Spring
Yulia Yefimtchuk ● MH

Metahaven In an interview with *032c* magazine you say: "Ukraine was always politically and economically unstable. People have got great patience and capability to survive within such conditions, which will be strange a bit for citizens of (western) Europe."[1] Do you mean to say that in the West people are used to having stable political systems? Because to us, it sometimes feels like today the West is slowly catching up with Ukraine. We perceive a feeling of uncertainty and coping that seems increasingly present in Western Europe.

Rather than merely recycling Soviet-era or Russian World aesthetics, your work evokes feelings of both innocence and militancy. In the abovementioned interview you say: "I tend to think that wearing this kind of clothes is the silent protest against the old system. I like [it] when my clothes are worn by simple people without special knowledge of trends and fashion, it is more important what is inside their head and what is in their eyes."[2] You do not appear to be seeing your work as fashion design when you talk about it—though, of course, it does operate within that system.

Can you tell us more about this idea of the silent protest? Why protest and what is the value of its silence?

Yulia Yefimtchuk I create utilitarian designs with a somehow rebellious spirit, driven by a mission to present clothes as art while also addressing actual social issues in modern society. The idea is not to reject reality, but to transform it. Every day, people select what they're going to wear. It is a form of self-expression.

MH What are the social issues in modern society that you address or work with?

YY My work deals with themes that relate to the past and the future, as well as the connections between the two. I often use slogans in the style of text on Soviet placards. I like this aesthetic; it is precise and legible. My fall/winter 2016 collection was about the "new world" as a new ruling system, politically and socially. I printed the slogan "we build the new world" on the clothes, with which I mean to say that you should not rely on your neighbor—you should create the new world yourself.

So, how do you interpret political themes in your own art? What subjects are relevant for you?

MH Our work is constantly moving. Over the past few years we have worked with, and for, unconventional partner organizations, in the belief that design is most effective when it inserts an unexpected point of influence into the world. For example, from 2011 to 2013 we designed scarves and T-shirts for WikiLeaks.[3] We were simultaneously interested in telling our own stories. We wondered whether or not our stories could be influential in the same way as design. The traditional role of (graphic) design has been to exert influence leveraged by a client's platform; your story is read through someone else's; your voice speaks through the actor for whom it was made. Alongside our graphic design practice, we have always written essays and books, and designed them ourselves. The step toward moving-image work was a really logical one. Our first video, *Black Transparency* (2013), is an animated poem or lecture of sorts, made with found footage, about a generation of internet nomads whose only weapon is (in)visibility. A trove of secrets.[4] We think that your orange "Spring" prisoner jumpsuit embodies the idea of silent protest perfectly. Would you agree?

YY Orange coveralls are strongly associated with the uniforms of (political) prisoners. The jumpsuit from my collection features a color, cut, and slogan that symbolically enact a silent protest against the global political system. The slogan "весна" (spring) suggests hope for a better future. It refers to Mikhail Kaufman's 1929 silent experimental documentary film *Весной* (*In Spring*), which depicts Kiev as it transforms from winter to spring. Scenes of urban renewal are juxtaposed with shots of nature's rebirth in springtime, symbolizing the political awakening of society. Kaufman experimented with hidden cameras in accordance with the avant-garde Kino-Eye theory, which argued that cinema's goal should be to document reality without any alterations or imaginary scenes.

On the topic of the absurdity of the modern world, I would like to share the lyrics from the song "Верой, смыслом, радостью"(With Hope, Sense, Joy) by the musical group Труд (Labor):

How not to go crazy with the latest news?
How to preserve yourself in all this absurdity?
When the whole world, seemingly, lost its mind,
And quiet horror filled my everyday life.[5]

MH The film *In Spring* is truly dream-like and amazing! These lyrics, somehow, speak to our shared reality. The notion of coping with a world that has lost its mind is something that relates to our films *The Sprawl (Propaganda about Propaganda)* (2015) and *Information Skies* (2016). What inspired us in the latter were events in our personal lives, and also an idea about propaganda that was already present in *The Sprawl*: that objective facts can sometimes come second to belief.

Yulia Yefimtchuk+ Fall/Winter 2016-17
stylist Yulia Yefimtchuk
photo Daniil Shumikhin

MMG Some months ago, I drew a diagram in my notebook:

SECURITY ⇄
UNKNOWABILITY ⇄ LOVE

It was a formula to help me remember that security can never lead to love (substitute here: life, vitality, or anima, the interior spirit of mortal beings). Security, the sum total of all knowledge within a given threat scenario, can only loop in paranoid circles back to unknowability. To be secure is deeply enmeshed with *knowing*. The hubris of security is the foundational Abrahamic myth of the Garden of Eden—no wonder the ground falls out from under them at the foot of that apple tree.

YY Your graphics for *The Sprawl* are fantastic; I like them a lot. In my spring/summer 2017 collection I also explore the question of propaganda. There is currently a propaganda program in Ukraine related to the process of "decommunization." Large amounts of money are wasted on the demolition of public art, such as monuments and symbols of the Soviet Union. Art of the Soviet period is very powerful; it transmits the spirit of the time and is highly emotive. It should not be destroyed. All this money could be spent on the development of new art. But everyone believes that "decommunization" will make life better. Thus, this collection is about good and bad propaganda—its ambiguity. Our thoughts intersect here; this is a silent protest.

MH We would like to ask you some questions based on the script of Andrei Tarkovsky's film *The Mirror* (1974).

YY I have not seen his films yet. I have a small list of artists that I want to discover when I am emotionally ready. I expect Tarkovsky's work to be very powerful. I am afraid of the impact that his films might have on me; it could change my approach. I first want to understand my own relationship with the world in a pure way.

MH That Tarkovsky scares you is easy to relate to and understand. His films—and their unceasing duration—are impressive, monumental, and quite incomprehensible. If one reads about the way he conceived his screenplays, one cannot but be touched by the process he went through to reach the final form in almost every one of his films.

He developed his initial script for *The Mirror* around one hundred questions addressed to mothers. In the original proposal he wrote: "It will be a film about a mother, any mother capable of arousing an interest in the authors. As all mothers, she must have had a full and fascinating life. This must be the ordinary story of a life, with its hopes, its faith, its grief, and its joys."[6] Tarkovsky and his co-writer, Aleksandr Misharin, continue further on in the same proposal: "We want to trace the principle of the spiritual organization of our society—which is the most important thing for us—through the rightful fate of one person; a person whom we know and love, who is called Mother."[7]

We would like to ask you five questions out of the hundred that Tarkovsky and Misharin asked the figure of the Mother:[8]

15. Do you think men or women the stronger?

YY If I judge from my own experience, I'd say that women are stronger psychologically. But today there is no dominant sex; I do not know whether that's good or bad.

MH 29. Your favorite composer?

YY All classical composers are engaging in their own way. My musical preferences tend to lean toward French impressionism and Russian avant-garde. Among contemporary musicians, I really like Carsten Nicolai.

MH 47. Tell me, when it was all too much, where did you find the strength to keep going?

YY An inner restart system always helps. It's hard to explain how it works, perhaps it is a belief in both yourself and a higher power. Being optimistic also helps a lot.

How do you deal with such moments? And do you consider yourselves optimists?

MH There is an inherent optimism in creating and finding fulfillment in producing things. We are optimists in the sense that we really believe, really care, and can never be angry for too long.

68. Which human qualities do you value most of all?

YY The Truth.

MH 89. Do you know how to forgive?

YY Yes, I do, even if I need to overstep myself. It is very important especially in relationships with loved ones. You need to learn how to let things go.

Yulia Yefimtchuk+ Spring/Summer 2016
stylist Erik Raynal
photo Michael Smits

1
Yulia Yefimtchuk, interview by Jeppe Ugelvig, "Ukranian Designer Yulia Yefimtchuk's Extremely Soviet Vision of Post-Soviet Youth," *032c*, March 30, 2016, http://www.yuliayefimtchuk.com/press. Last accessed on August 30, 2018.
2
Ibid.
3
See David Hellqvist, "The Dark Glamour of Transparency," *Dazed*, December 19, 2011, www.dazeddigital.com/fashion/article/12222/1/the-dark-glamour-of-transparency. Last accessed on August 29, 2018.
4
Metahaven, *Black Transparency: The Right to Know in the Age of Mass Surveillance*, Berlin: Sternberg Press, 2015, ix–x.
5
The English translation is by Yulia Yefimtchuk; the original Russian lyrics are: "Как не сойти с ума от свежих новостей? Как сохранить себя во всем этом абсурде? Когда весь мир, казалось бы, рассудок потерял, И тихим ужасом наполнены все мои будни." Труд, "Верой, смыслом, радостью," Moscow: город Москва, 2013, MP3, https://trud.bandcamp.com/track/--16. Last accessed on August 30, 2018.
6
Natasha Synessios, ed., *Andrei Tarkovsky: Collected Screenplays*, London: Faber and Faber, 1999, 257.
7
Ibid., 258.
8
All questions are quoted from ibid.

Yulia Yefimtchuk
Yulia Yefimtchuk is the founder of the independent Kiev-based fashion label Yulia Yefimtchuk+. Yefimtchuk studied at the Kyiv State Institute of Applied Arts and Design, researching, among others, socialist ideology and Soviet material history. The label is known for its conceptual womenswear and unisex clothes with strong cuts and minimalistic elements taken from uniform and workwear. Yulia Yefimtchuk+ presents "clothes as art, to transmit actual social issues of modern society, researching the past, predicting the future, finding connections."

considered the domain of propaganda—full of interests and distortions of the otherwise neutral informational operation of market pricing. But this perspective seems to assume that information *is* rationally communicative and *not* propaganda. Are you saying that this distinction was always untenable?

MH Let us explain. When you say that scientific knowledge has to some degree shattered our older belief systems, and that we now exist on a kind of ground zero where we understand truth scientifically...

SM That's the Enlightenment claim.

MH Then we've also been disenchanted on a cosmic scale. Peter Sloterdijk writes about the "celestial domes" that once seemed to hold our lives together, and asks: how do we keep on living now that these protective domes are shattered and now that we are naked under indifferent heavens? Sloterdijk claims that all human life has always only been possible within a bubble. In spite and precisely because of our cosmic disenchantment, we create bubbles for ourselves in which we temporarily, artificially restore the possibility of belief. And then our theory, which is not really a theory at all, is actually that propaganda bubbles, as pop-ups for alternative truths, say, "this may or may not be true, but let's act as if it is." It becomes a matter of version against version. The truth is decided on by the rendering speed of one bubble versus that of the other bubble. The most effectively, all-encompassingly rendered bubble thus produces a new fact. Both the averted

coup in Turkey and the Brexit campaign in the United Kingdom followed this logic.

The main point of this bubble theory of truth is that a fictional opponent is much stronger than a real opponent. Via platform-induced hypnosis, citizens got the idea that their Brexit vote made them into patriotic heroes saving the National Health Service, or that they would be casting a protest vote that wouldn't matter anyway, or doing this partially in virtual reality fantasyland. Because on the other side were the "all-powerful liberals"...

SM People like us.

MH Yeah, the people who also didn't see it coming.

SM Trump is another obvious example of this: there's a massive scaling from the individual contributions to Facebook, which is perhaps another version of the bubble that Sloterdijk is talking about. Internet activist Eli Pariser discusses how filter bubbles shatter social cohesion.

But why is this considered such a big problem? It's worth asking that question, not to throw the expectation of social cohesion under the bus but rather to better understand what it actually means. Its corrosion is only a problem if you hold on to an Enlightenment version of civil

society as a place of competing public interests that ultimately produce a perspective close to rational truth, through some kind of deliberative democracy. By contrast, the cloud-based bubbles you mention are specific, technically organized enactments of what in the late 1970s Jean-François Lyotard described as the breakdown of the metanarratives of modernity through information processes. For Lyotard, the grand narratives of the Enlightenment—notably, emancipation through knowledge, or rather emancipation *and knowledge* as producers of the "good" society—break down because they lose legitimacy through the horizontal distribution of information in network societies. This results in numerous different narratives—each coherent as a self-contained bubble—that spread subjective opinions that only reinforce themselves. This happens because the material condition of the network doesn't require any reference to a greater, socially organizing narrative as a basic normative constraint.

What's key in this transformation of the social bond is that subjectification becomes the condition for truth. The bubble refers to subjects who live within a certain interpretation of truth due to the information they're getting, but also how it feels to be inside that self-reinforcement. It's what Stephen Colbert in 2005 called "truthiness": you don't necessarily know what the truth is, but that it just *feels* right. It's truth

from the gut, not from the head, which is to say truth without or an epistemological foundation. What Colbert presented as satire at that time is what Trump now does in earnest. It's the basic condition for what's called a post-truth or post-fact politics, which has been reinforced by social bubbling.

To come back to your practice more directly: it seems to me that the key issue that your work deals with—made explicit in *The Sprawl*—is that this move toward a post-truth or post-fact condition *requires* propaganda as the only viable mode of political communication, if not of social composition altogether.

MH Yes. And at the same time, *The Sprawl* is about *being inside*. It's much more as if you're in flight mode *inside* propaganda. This also allows you to discern different qualities of truth-making in propaganda that can be more, or less, elegant. So, when you're talking about Trump's truth-making—Trump-making—it is the crudest form of truth-making (or lie-making) possible. It's the low-res of post-truth.

SM What's important about refinement though? Isn't that a way of maintaining a critical distance, which is more typical of a skeptical position that looks for truth behind the propaganda? Also, though I think I disagree with your version of what Trump is, why is he (or, as a propagandistic phenomenon, it) at low resolution?

MH The issue with propaganda and bubble-making is not just about *what* the bubble is, but also *how* it is. So, the *treatment*, let's say, of a certain proposition, is of vital importance.

SM Are you then like connoisseurs?

MH Hobbyists, rather! It's not that once there were facts and now there are only post-facts. The idea that we have entered a fundamentally new era is tempting to believe in, but it's a techno-determinist idea. If you look at newspapers in the 1950s that stood for a certain party line, you would not recognize the same bubbles. We also don't believe that the only alternatives to "post-facts" are "facts."

Information Skies

Something happened this morning on our way to work.
It began raining facts from the ceiling.
A happy world since time immemorial broke apart.
We stopped, searched for parts of that bursted bubble.
Remember: this story exists only if you want it to.
Find the pieces. Enter the missing dream.
Press play.

The fighter sits.
His long-nailed girlfriend is absentminded on her phone.
We adorn.
We are the silver.
We are dragons, newborn from the mouth of an unverified source.
Desperately seeking, we seem to have found
that source, the road through the forest, the clearance,
each other, another.

The supermarket opens to a queue of early risers.
The mundane is only the best excuse to talk.
Let's talk about the apartment,
or about the dishes, and who left them unwashed in the sink.
Our daily rituals are paintings,
our shopping lists, the poems.
Full circle, face the void.

The hole in the sky
left as a courtesy by the last person who used the bathroom.
The weight of the soul, measured in terabytes.
I'm looking at you, but I'm staring at the plains.
With my eyes closed, at least I can remember.

We have a plot
formerly known as dream.
Now we have a video to prove it.
Everyone can see myself from the emptiness within,
an eyeless face inside an idea.

Someone just disappeared into the station hall, the crowd.
He came to steal the future—his truth for all.

Suicide bombers are also people.
Think about it, we all have mothers.
When we were born, we were not allowed to die.

Death is virtual reality.
Catch up with this world, watch the mothers wave
their children goodbye, crying.

The fathers dig a grave, sweating, scorching heat,
in a steppe of pixels.

There is no one in the grave.
Their only relief is bottled water.

The fighter watches TV.
His long-nailed girlfriend is still on Snapchat.
We have an OK life.
We are gold-plated.
We are reflections.

That large screen ahead is beaming with stars.
Waiting, emblazoned with signs
of you being right, that's what they say.
All this time, they say—together, metallic, lit from behind,
shared a thousand times, and counting.

These faltering batteries, dim light of your echo
our kiss in a fur coat of darkness.
I'm holding you close, I can see through the mountains blinded by color.
Please help me. I'll pay you much later.

We have a plot
formerly known as dream.
Now we have a video to prove it.
Everyone can see myself from the emptiness within,
an eyeless face inside an idea.

Valóságos egek

Ma reggel valami történt velünk munkába menet.
Valóság csöpögött a mennyezetből.
Egy ősi boldog világ hullott darabokra.
Megtorpantunk, ripityára törött részei után matattunk.
Vésd észbe: ez a történet csak akkor létezik,
ha te is úgy akarod.
Találj darabkákat. Lépj be a hiányzó látomásba.
Indíts.

A harcos ül. Hosszú körmű barátnője
szórakozottan mobilozik.
Szépülünk.
Ezüstök vagyunk.
Sárkányok vagyunk, frissen, ismeretlen forrásból születettek.
Kétségbeesetten hajszolva jobbára rátaláltunk.
A forrásra, az erdőn átvezető útra, a tisztásra.
Egymásra. A másikra.

A csemegebolt a koránkelők sorának nyit.
A profán a legjobb apropó a beszélgetésre:
Fecsegjünk a lakásról. Vagy a tányérokról, és arról,
aki koszosan hagyta őket a mosogatóban.
Napi szokásaink festmények, bevásárló listánk költemény
A kör teljes, nézz szembe az ürességgel.

Az égből nyílt lyuk a fürdőt utoljára használó ember figyelmessége.
A lélek súlya, terrabájtokban mérve.
Rád nézek, de a pusztát kémlelem
Csukott szemmel, így legalább emlékezem.

Van egy tézisünk
Korábban belerévedtünk
De íme egy videó, nem tévedtünk.
Bárki láthatja a tükröződést
A belső megcsömörlést
S hogy vak arcból szól az ötletelés.

Valaki épp beleolvad az állomáscsarnok tömegébe
A jövőnket lopja – csak hogy igaza legyen.

Az öngyilkos merénylők is emberek
Gondolj csak bele, mindannyiunknak van anyja.
Amikor megszülettünk, tilos volt meghalnunk.

A halál virtuális valóság. Nyisd már ki a szemed,
lásd az anyák integetését,
Gyermekeiktől búcsúzva, sírón.

Az apák a sírt ássák, izzadva a perzselő melegben,
a pixeles sztyeppén.
Senki sincs a sírban.
Az egyetlen enyhülés a palackozott víz.

A harcos tévét néz – hosszú körmű barátnője továbbra is
Snapchat-ezik.
Elvagyunk.
Aranyozottak vagyunk.
Tükröződünk.

E nagy képernyő előttünk fényes a csillagoktól
Címeres jelképként várakoznak.
Igazad van – legalább is ezt üzenték.
Mindvégig igazad volt – mondták együtt,
fémes hátfénnyel
Ezer és egyszer sugallták.

(E) pislákoló izzók hordozzák félhomályos visszhangod
Csókunk a bundakabátod sötétjében
Ha közelre húzlak, átlátok a hegyeken
Elvakítanak a színek (kérlek segíts!), később
megfizetlek.

Van egy tézisünk
Korábban belerévedtünk
De íme egy videó—nem tévedtünk.
Bárki láthatja a tükröződést
A belső megcsömörlést
S hogy vak arcból szól az ötletelés.

Information Skies

next

SM No, but the key difference would be that you have diverse opinions represented in various media, which are supposed to lead to a kind of consensus through deliberative democracy. By contrast, the problem you're describing is one in which the whole field of discourse is now made up of divergent views without a consensual meeting point.

MH Pre-Trump, one Russian argument has been that no news platform can be objective. The claim was constructed as follows: every large mainstream broadcaster has ties with their national government's policy, the BBC and CNN as much as Russia Today (RT). The claim that you actually can exist in an objective space outside the influence of geopolitics is never really true. Based on this idea, RT has entitled itself to have their platform create not so much a single "national" story, but lots of possibilities, questions, and alternative theories around events reported in the news. By opening up a Pandora's box of possible, alternative hypotheses, RT catalyzes epistemic uncertainty; it does not offer a single counter-narrative, but different versions. The production of this kind of disinformation also often involves creating forms of analog, offline parallel constructions. The Russian manufacturer of the missile that took down Malaysia Airlines Flight 17 while flying over eastern Ukraine in 2014, created a Vladimir Tatlin-like experimental installation of one such missile, mounted on a wooden, constructivist structure. They then positioned a discarded missile to demonstrate that actually this plane fuselage next to it. They could not have been the weapon that downed the plane. They made a video of it that was subsequently released online. The degree of investment in creating this story is absurdly deep. It is an entire parallel reality, not just a few incoherent lines.

MH Right, and one of the problems with "post-facts" so far has been that in order to refute them, one first needs to repeat them. That reiteration of the untruth is part of the post-truth condition. Hillary Clinton tried to get around this by asking people to "go to hillaryclinton.com to check if what Donald just said is true."

SM Essentially, political discourse has become clickbait. I read something around the beginning of the Trump candidacy on this subject. Basically, Trump began his presidential bid as a promotional campaign for himself as a brand. His strategy was to "suck all the oxygen out of the room": he says things that will immediately become the talking points so that attention always goes to him and on his terms. Everything he says is simply meant to generate a reaction, which serves to propagate his brand.

It has been interesting to see this strategy become power, because what's key is that the content of what he says is entirely subordinated to his mediatized presence. Content becomes a mechanism of "likes" (however much one may dislike what he says). The question then concerns what the basis for communication becomes. If the common space of discourse—which in the modern period was called rationalism or community—is now weak or subordinated to these affective, rhetorical, persuasive power claims, which are the domain of propaganda, what is happening to communication in general?

SM For the sake of clarification, and because we're talking now about Russia, let's compare this propagandistic method to that of the Soviet Communist period. *Pravda*, which translates as "truth," was the newspaper for the Communist Party's propaganda. The paper and everything in it were clearly understood as Communist propaganda. So, there was a kind of enactment of clear political authority.

MH An official version.

SM Yeah, but it's clearly not the truth, and that was probably well understood by a good proportion of its readership. But it was one message, and you had to accept it even if you didn't believe it. But following what you've just said, propaganda today is completely different. It produces a multiplicity of narratives, each of which could be true, but the net effect of which is to discredit any official narrative from any side. Is the strategic aim just to get rid of the viability of a credible truth claim?

MH The Russian language has two words for truth. Not just *pravda*, but also *istina*, a higher spiritual truth that can't be grasped in the everyday. But the situation isn't particularly Russian. In general, in a fuzzy landscape where nobody knows what's real, and everyone gets to have their freedom of speech and their opinions without adhering to the meeting point of the real, power goes unchallenged and becomes medieval. Did you see the citation from Leo Tolstoy's "What Is Art?" in *The Sprawl*? Were you not, like us, thoroughly fulfilled by it?

SM Absolutely not.

MH Tolstoy is saying that in order to make us experience a wolf, there needn't be a wolf. It could have been invented. Isn't that a simple way to address an element

SM Could you say a little more about the high-definition version of this kind of disinformation? What do you find is more sophisticated about it?

MH The strategy is to disrupt, contradict, to make no sense, and produce information that spontaneously combusts.

MMG This image of yours is an analog, isn't it? There's "dysfunction" on two levels. First, the mask comes off: there's a kink in the visual surface on the user's end, revealing the system's activity monitor. (OK, maybe three dysfunctions, *since* that system shows an error code.) On another level, it's the threat of a world where design fails. I just read Daniel H. Pink's book on the power of right-brained or R-directed thinking, *A Whole New Mind: Why Right-Brainers Will Rule the Future* (2006). Design is one of six aptitudes he promises can beat the computer brain's logistical L-directed thinking. The breakdown of design that surfaces in these two images, is the embarrassing revelation of a hiccup in a normally functional L-directed system— like we've accidentally walked in on the world of what are usually indefatigable machines, failing at their one job.

Who knows what's true?
Who knows what's not?

Mother knows.
A parallel house. Mother knows where.
He's alive. She makes him breakfast.
The love of the morning, their laughter,
sounds of the kitchen, curtains waving, windows open,
sign in to watch the sequel.

Nothing happened of the sort, there still is a chance.
No proof, only rumors.

Defend us, please help her, she'll pay you for
the key to the door of that house.

Our laptops, our visors, globes turn dark,
short on imagination
movable titanium
switch off the haunted gaze.

A graceful landing on the soil.
The territory, the way things were,
is a trauma and a luxury

as readily a friendly older man sits down with us
and gives us tea.
He asks us to agree with him
that there was no house,
and there are no mountains.

An endless grassland with nothing there,
how could we disagree?
We grapple for words, gasp for air,
for the judge has not seen what we have seen.
Judge, we reply, we were just there, you weren't.

There are mountains all around us, we fought like dragons,
here's our flag, of digital satin,
and mother, of striped white cotton,
and her forlorn son back home,
our brother, hear his joyful laughter.

You must be dreaming—says the man—
or you spent too much time elsewhere.
Nowhere in this barren land are mountains.
I haven't met the woman you seem to know so well,
and hold so dear.
Her son: I know of him, he killed himself, and others.
There's nothing left but a name that's in the papers.

Hidden in the high grass lay the fighter
and his long-nailed girlfriend.
In their still encampment
they watch the stars again.

Thanking machines, mother, unknown movements
for their newfound harvest on the ridge.

Redcurrants.

Ki tudja mi igaz?
Ki tudja mi nem az?

Anya ismeri a párhuzamos házat.
Anya tudja, hol van.
A testvérem életben van.
Anya reggelit készít neki.
A reggel szeretete, a nevetésük
A konyha hangjai: függönyök húzódása,
ablakok nyitódása
Lépj be, hogy megtekintsd a folytatást.

Semmi olyasmi nem történt, még van esély.
Nincs semmi bizonyíték, csak pletyka—védj meg minket,
kérlek segítsd őt, meg fog fizetni a bejárat kulcsáért.

A laptopjaink, sisakjaink sötétbe hajló gömbök,
de képzelet híján
Csak cipelhető titánium.
No, csapd föl a rostélyt

Kecses érkezés a földre
A területre, ahol összetorlódik trauma és luxus.
Olyan könnyedséggel,
mellyel egy régi barát lehuppan hozzánk és teával kínál:
Úgy kéri, értsünk egyet vele
Abban hogy sem ház nem volt, sem hegyek nincsenek
És a végtelen füves pusztán nincs semmi sem.
Hogyan is ellenkezhetnénk?

Dulakodunk a szavakért, levegőért kapkodunk,
hiszen a bíró nem látta, amit mi láttunk
Bíró úr, válaszoljuk, mi voltunk ott, nem maga.
Hegyek magasodtak köröttünk, és sárkányokként
küzdöttünk.
Itt a zászlónk, digitális szatén, anya, fehér csíkos vászon,
Aki tékozló fiának, testvérbátyámnak,
végre otthon hallja vidám nevetését.

Biztosan csak álmodsz—mondja az ember—
vagy túl sok időt töltöttél távol
Mert sehol e kopár földön nincsenek hegyek
És nem találkoztam a nővel,
kit láthatóan oly jól ismersz és kedvesnek vélsz,
A fia: na felőle hallottam,
megölte magát, és másokat.
Semmi sem maradt
Csak a neve az újságokban.

A magas fűben rejtőzve fekszik a harcos
és a hosszúkörmű barátnője
Dermedt táborhelyükről nézik a csillagokat.

Hálásak gépnek, anyának, ismeretlen menetelésnek,
A friss aratásért a dombtetőn.

Ribizlik.

Information Skies

Propaganda is Now Another Name for Communication Itself
Suhail Malik ●MH

Suhail Malik

Suhail Malik is a writer based in London. He is co-director of the MFA program at Goldsmiths, University of London where he holds a readership in critical studies. Malik was previously a visiting faculty member at the Center for Curatorial Studies at Bard College, Annandale-on-Hudson, NY. He writes on the compromised formation of contemporary art and the speculative reorganization of time in complex global societies. Publications include *On the Necessity of Art's Exit From Contemporary Art* (2019) and an extended essay on finance in *Collapse 8: Casino Real* (2015). Malik is co-editor of *The Flood of Rights* (2017), *The Time-Complex. Postcontemporary* (2016), and *Realism Materialism Art* (2015).

of post-truth that goes missing in the discussion? Are we losing our ability to cope with fiction, and is this becoming exploited by political actors who use our fading fiction-literacy for their own gain? Besides, Tolstoy—who asserted that art should never be used in service of any power—returns to the emotional truth of a shared narration.

SM I guess. It makes sense to me on its own terms, but it's an expressionistic and representational notion of art. When Tolstoy says a successful work of art is an individual expressing something that the recipient understands and feels, then there is perhaps a kind of truth. But it's an affective truth, set into a subjective basis as a unique experience. However, in the conditions you have been describing, it's important that there are *many* bubbles, not just the extension of the artist's bubble to another person. And it's the aggregate effect of this production of multiple, unique subjective truths that I'm interested in. It seems to me that what you've identified in the idea of propaganda is the culmination of strategic and corporatized notions of art that have been prevalent as contemporary art for about half a century now. The consequences of this are very different from what Tolstoy is describing, as much as his account—if you are into it, which I am not—may be a good description of what art should do on the micro-level of subjective experience. You could say that such an aggregate-level effect is a consequence of postmodernity as Lyotard described and theorized it—there are only small narratives without any calibrating grand narrative—as it is the realization of now fairly ingrained posttructuralist claims that all so-called truths are power claims. And that feeds into the assumptions you'd expect for critical art practice: skepticism toward power and toward anything that claims to be the truth, because art is supposed to stand for something else.

So what interests me in your position regarding art is that somehow your work on propaganda addresses what certain state or state-corporate actors are now doing as large-scale network operators, as a kind of instrumentalized postmodern, posttructuralist avant-garde. What you're dealing with is how, in a sense, state-level organizations have caught up with the things that have been happening in art for some thirty to forty years now: the dismissal of the grand narrative, the primacy of the subjective position that this multiplicity of positions all have equal validity and so on. All you're left with here is a series of alternatives without a unifying horizon or a gathering narrative.

The problem then for contemporary art, or at least for art that makes critical claims, is that it sets itself up to be counter-statist, counter-hegemonic, anti-capitalist, and so on. But the dominant powers, perhaps most clearly exemplified by Russia, are now replicating or duplicating exactly what critical art practices have been doing for some time. If we still want to maintain a critical position via the received precepts of contemporary art, this is a crisis. We can no longer maintain any distance or separation from a powerful actor "over there."

But I wonder if your ambivalent position on our mini-narratives versus the untruths of big power takes a stance other than the paralyzing dilemma contemporary art now faces. Do you see some potential in the fact that there is a convergence between the way that art and the state operate, and that you're exactly at the intersection point between those two things? I'm wondering whether that feels like an opportunity or a curse, because it seems to me you nonetheless want to remain skeptical of the state.

MH We see many limits to rendering everything through a geopolitical lens, and in fact we also really need to expand the way that we tell stories, the way we work, and the way that we feel into things that people then can also feel.

Fact-Checker

Metahaven's earlier work's concern with state branding: Metahaven and Marina Vishmidt, eds., *Uncorporate Identity: Metahaven*, Baden: Lars Müller Publishers, 2010.

The US was heavily backing Twitter and putting pressure on the Egyptian authorities to keep it open through street protests: Sharon Gaudin, "Social networks Credited with Role in Toppling Egypt's Mubarak," *Computerworld*, February 11, 2011, www.computerworld.com/article/2513142/web-apps/social-networks-credited-with-role-in-toppling-egypt-s-mubarak.html. Last accessed on August 17, 2018.

During the so-called coup d'état in Turkey in July 2016, Turkish President Recep Tayyip Erdoğan addressed the nation via FaceTime: Reuters, "Erdogan addresses Turkey via FaceTime amid attempted coup–video," *The Guardian*, July 16, 2016, www.theguardian.com/world/video/2016/jul/15/erdogan-facetime-turkey-coup-attempt. Last accessed on August 17, 2018.

All so-called truths are only in fact power claims: Michel Foucault, *Power/Knowledge: Selected Interviews and Other Writings, 1972–1977*, ed. and trans. Colin Gordon et al., New York: Pantheon Books, 1980.

The Russian manufacturer of the missile that took down Malaysia Airlines Flight 17 created a Tatlin-like experimental installation of one such missile, mounted on a wooden, constructivist structure: "MH17 downed by outdated BUK missile fired from Kiev-controlled area – Defense system manufacturer," *Reuters*, October 13, 2015, https://www.rt.com/news/318531-mh17-experiment-almaz-antey/; the full press presentation held by manufacturer Almaz-Antey is available at Reuters, "Russian arms manufacturer Almaz-Antey delivers MH17 report," video, 2:35:21, October 13, 2015, https://www.youtube.com/watch?v=LKAXKwnUtg0; and more images of the installations can be found at https://www.metabunk.org/almaz-anteys-live-buk-explosion-tests.t6903/. Last accessed on August 30, 2018.

Leo Tolstoy, *What Is Art?* [1897], London: Penguin Classics, 1995.

Hillary Clinton asking people to "go to hillaryclinton.com to check if what Donald just said is true"; Jason Abbruzzese, "Hillary Clinton Turned Her Website into a Fact Checker for the Debate," *Mashable*, September 27, 2016, https://mashable.com/news/2016/09/26/clinton-website-fact-checker/. Last accessed on August 17, 2018.

Donald Trump began the Presidential bid as a promotion campaign for himself as a brand. His basic strategy was to "suck all of the oxygen out of the room": Eli Stokols and Ben Schreckinger, "How Trump Did It," *POLITICO*, February 1, 2016, www.politico.com/magazine/story/2016/02/how-donald-trump-did-it-213581. Last accessed on August 17, 2018.

An Enlightenment version of civil society—for which Jürgen Habermas has been the most notable advocate: Jürgen Habermas, *The Structural Transformation of the Public Sphere: An Inquiry into a Category of Bourgeois Society*, trans. Thomas Burger and Frederick Lawrence, Cambridge, MA: MIT Press, [1962] 1989.

Steven Colbert on truthiness: in the first episode of his series, *The Colbert Report*, "Truthiness," Comedy Central, October 17, 2005; Benajmin Zimmer, "Truthiness," or "Trustiness," *Language Log*, October 26, 2005, itre.cis.upenn.edu/~myl/languagelog/archives/002586.html; and "Stephen Colbert's 'Truthiness.' Word Describes 2016, www.washingtontimes.com/news/2016/aug/18/stephen-colberts-truthiness-word-describes-campaig/. Last accessed on August 17, 2018.

Eli Pariser on the filter bubble: Eli Pariser, *The Filter Bubble: What the Internet is Hiding From You*, New York: Penguin, 2012.

The breakdown of what Jean-François Lyotard called the grand narratives of modernity through information processes: Jean-François Lyotard, *The Postmodern Condition: A Report on Knowledge*, trans. Geoff Bennington and Brian Massumi, Minneapolis: University of Minnesota Press, [1979] 2010.

Peter Sloterdijk on celestial domes: Peter Sloterdijk, *Spheres Volume I: Bubbles*, trans. Wieland Hoban, Cambridge, MA: Semiotext(e)/MIT Press, 2011.

오늘 아침 일하러 가는 길에 무언가가 일어났다.
천장에서부터 '사실'이 쏟아 내리기 시작했고
태곳적부터의 행복한 세계는 산산이 부서졌다.
우리는 깨져버린 환상의 조각을 찾기 위해 멈춰 섰다.
기억하라, 이 이야기는 오직 당신이 원할 때만 찾아올 것이다.
조각을 찾아라. 잃어버린 꿈으로 들어가라.
재생 버튼을 누를 것.

전투사는 자리에 앉고, 손톱이 긴 그의 여자친구는 핸드폰에 정신이 팔려있다.
우리는 꾸민다.
우리는 은이다.
우리는 검증되지 않은 정보의 입에서 갓 태어난 용이다.
필사적으로 찾아 헤맨 끝에, 우리는 그 정보를 찾은 것 같다.
깨끗하게 정리가 돼버린 숲을 따라 난 길을 통해.
서로에게. 또 다른 누군가에게.

이른 시간부터 도착한 사람들을 위해 슈퍼마켓은 문을 열었다.
일상적인 것을 이야기하는 것이 가장 쉽다.
아파트에 관해서나 이야기할까
아니면 설거지, 누가 그릇을 씻지 않고 남겨뒀는지.
우리 일상의 습관은 페인팅이다. 쇼핑리스트는 우리의 시.
원점으로 되돌아가기, 공허함을 마주할 것.

하늘에 난 구멍이 마치 화장실을 마지막으로
쓴 사람이 깨끗이 치운 것 마냥 나 있다.
테라바이트 단위로 재어진 영혼의 무게.
너를 바라보고 있지만 사실 난 툰드라를 응시하고 있다.
나는 내 감은 눈으로 적어도 이것들을 기억할 수 있다:

우리는 이전에 '꿈'이라고 알려진 계획이 있고,
이것을 증명할 비디오도 가지고 있다.
모두 나를 볼 수 있다.
생각 안의 눈이 없는 얼굴, 그 공허함 안에서.

기차역의 사람들 무리에서 누군가가 방금 사라졌다.
그 사람은 미래-모두를 위한 그의 진실-를 훔치기 위해서 왔다.

자살 폭탄 테러범도 사람이다.
생각해봐라, 우리는 모두 엄마를 가지고 있다.
우리가 태어났을 때, 우리에게 죽음은 금지되어 있었다.
죽음은 가상현실이다.
이 세상을 따라잡기 위해서
그들의 자식에게 손을 흔들며 작별인사하고 우는 어미들을 봐라.
픽셀의 초원에서 아비들은 무덤을 파고, 땀을 흘리고, 더위에 그을린다.
무덤에는 아무도 없다.
병에 든 생수가 그들의 유일한 안식이다.

전투사는 텔레비전을 본다. 손톱이 긴 그의 여자친구는 아직도 스냅챗 중이다.
우리는 꽤 괜찮은 인생을 살고 있다.
우리는 도금된 존재이다.
우리는 반향이다.

우리 앞의 큰 스크린은 별을 비추고 있다.
별자리가 선명히 새겨진 기다림.
그들은 네가 옳다는 점에 대해 말한다.
금속성의 빛이 뒤에서 비치는 와중에,
그들은 지금껏 내내 이것은 수천 번 공유되었으며,
여전히 헤아려지고 있다고 말한다.

이 불안정한 배터리들은 너의 메아리를 흐릿하게 밝힌다.
어둠의 틸 코드 안, 우리의 키스
나는 너를 가까이 껴안는다. 나는 저 산 너머를 볼 수 있다-
색에 눈이 멀어버렸다- (제발 도와주세요) 나중에 갚을 테니.

우리는 이전에 '꿈'이라고 알려진 계획이 있고,
이것을 증명할 비디오도 가지고 있다.
모두 나를 볼 수 있다.
생각 안의 눈이 없는 얼굴, 그 공허함 안에서.

누가 무엇이 진실인지 알 수 있을까?
누가 무엇이 진실이 아닌지 알 수 있을까?

어머니는 안다.
평행의 집. 어머니는 어디에 있는지 안다.
그는 살아있어. 어머니는 그에게 아침을 만들어 준다.
아침의 사랑, 그들의 웃음.
부엌으로부터의 소리, 흔들리는 커튼, 열린 창문.
속편을 보려거든 서명하시오.

아무것도 일어나지 않는 것 같지만, 여전히 기회는 있다.
증거는 없고 오직 소문만 떠돈다.
우리를 변론해라, 그녀를 도와달라,
그녀가 그 집의 열쇠를 만들기 위한 돈을 줄 것이다.
우리의 컴퓨터, 우리의 헬멧, 천체는 어둡게 변하고,
상상력은 동이 난다.
움직일 수 있는 타이타늄
겁에 질린 시선을 거둘 것
우아한 착륙. 예전 상태로의 그 영토는, 트라우마이자 사치이다.

친근해 보이는 노인이 우리와 앉자마자 차를 건넨다.
그 노인은, 거기에는 집도 없고 산도 없으며,
끝없는 풀밭 말고는 아무것도 없는데
이것에 우리가 동의하는지 물었다.
우리가 어떻게 반대할 수 있겠나?

우리는 우리가 본 것을 보지 못한 판사 때문에 단어들과 씨름하고,
거칠게 숨을 내쉰다.
우리는 대담한다. 판사님, 우리는 거기에 있었지만,
당신은 아니었지요.

주위는 산에 둘러싸여 있었고, 우린 마치 용처럼 싸웠다.
여기 디지털 비단으로 된 우리 깃발이 있어.
그리고 흰색의 줄무늬를 입은 어머니도.
그리고 집에 돌아온 그녀의 불행한 아들도. 내 형제여,
그의 기쁨에 찬 웃음을 듣는다

'너는 지금 꿈을 꾸고 있는 거야. 아니면 너는 다른 곳에서
시간을 너무 많이 보내고 있던가' 라고 그는 말했다.
이 적막한 땅에서 '아무것도 아닌 곳'이란 산을 말한다.
난 네가 그리 잘 알고 아낀다는 그 여자를 아직 만나지 못했어.
그녀의 아들: 그에 관해 들어본 적이 있어. 자살했지. 다른 사람들도.
서류에 적혀진 이름을 제외하곤 아무것도 남아있는 게 없어.

전투사와 그의 손톱이 긴 여자친구는 키가 큰 풀숲에 누워있어 보이지 않는다.
고요한 그들의 야영지에서, 둘은 다시 별을 관찰한다.
기계, 어머니, 알 수 없는 움직임에 감사하면서.
산등성이에 있는 그들이 새로 발견한 수확물을 위해서.

레드 커런트 열매들.

next

Urgency
Laura Cugusi ● Jasmina Metwaly ● Philip Rizk ● MH

MH First thought: how is this storefront representing American soft-power based on twentieth-century credentials? Second thought: this is an interface, too. Third thought: we recently went to the Stedelijk Museum's Günther Förg exhibition with two young kids. Afterwards we went to the café upstairs for apple juice and macaroons. Then one of the kids said, macaroon in hand: "I know what this is called! An emoji!"

MMG I took this photo in the United Kingdom. I think that it's important to mention, because almost everywhere else I've been, which is mostly the global South, the junk food category isn't nearly as fetishized as it is in the UK. The reverence is more hallowed and encased in the UK—literally in the case of this storefront. There's not exactly an "invasion" of United States–based sugary and salty junk food that you see in South America or the Middle East. That stuff is often simply absorbed into industrial food production and you get some local version of Fanta. But there's a whole cabal of YouTube videos in which British people are filmed being introduced to North American candy. There's a soft power here, but not the same as when North Americans consume burritos. It's not *food* migrating back to the old empire as much as a consumer item, like a perfume or weird kitchen gadget.

36

previous

Metahaven What are artistic methods/politics and aesthetics in a (yet to be more tightly defined) crisis, or under circumstances of urgency? This slightly pompous tagline is to be taken apart/made more precise/thrown away/distorted or deformed in any way necessary/by the participants/all of us.

Philip Rizk There are a few words I avoid using because I find they have lost their meaning due to their being politicized or overused in a sense with which I cannot identify. Crisis and urgency, though, are not among them. I agree with what Jane M. Gaines writes in her text "Political Mimesis": radical aesthetics is most effective in moments of revolt, in moments of urgency.[1] There is a necessity for ranks, for a crowd on the ground. It is then that aesthetics can best play a part in revolt and become a tool to move the spectator. I do not believe in aesthetic work that moves people in periods of stasis, moments of complacency. Rather, I believe that in a time and place *of* movement, of revolt, in which radical aesthetics plays a role. It is a role just like that of those who tend to the injured, who are imprisoned, who are at the frontlines—all these positions must be filled. Aesthetics can play the role of upping the ante, countering the authorities that demand the status quo, pushing the discourse in order to get more bodies on the street. Because without bodies there is no revolt. Without bodies on the street, radical aesthetics act in a vacuum.

Radical aesthetics don't move a crowd, they may move with the crowd. I don't feel I can answer in a more direct way. I can't tell you *what* the aesthetics are, I can just tell you *about* their spirit.

Jasmina Metwaly If we consider that "behind every work of art is an uncommitted crime,"[2] then I think a more relevant question to pose would be about the perception of art within our collective consciousness. How we see things and cross the boundaries of what we know or take for granted is what constructs the very texture of the political. Art in such a sense is not about committing a crime per se, but about becoming an agent in mobilizing all parties involved, including the onlookers (audiences) and active participants (artists).

Laura Cugusi If radical aesthetics have the power to mobilize all parties involved in a crisis, including the onlookers, it is urgent to experiment with creative strategies and symbolic gestures that complement the necessary presence of the body in the street.

Artistic methods and aesthetics can't rely exclusively on the heroism of those who are left to protest with their bodies, and on the resilience of those who have been unjustly imprisoned. At the same time, we can't blame those who have migrated away from the fulcrum of attention or who are under real threat of retaliation from oppressive governments for not taking to the streets. Forms of protest and creative interventions that are not exclusively centered around the act of taking to the streets (in real life, or in its representation) cross the boundary of what we know and take for granted: that urgency will always manifest in the image of street protests.

Perhaps what it takes to move a crowd is for aesthetics to be radical, to have a radical power by evoking new imagery (that we struggle to find language for) rather than reproducing a familiar image such as that of the crowd of anonymous protesters, easily co-opted by pop culture and advertising.

For example, the protest against the murder of Khaled Saïd in Alexandria's corniche in 2010—where hundreds of people stood in silence reading books—operated a shift in the aesthetics of protests in Egypt at the time. Also, during another peaceful demonstration, in Cairo in October and November 2010, hundreds of workers from rural Egypt camped on the sidewalk, day and night, for at least three weeks. The urgency of that quiet protest manifested in their refusal to leave. It was a form of protest that cleverly managed to bypass the emergency law that prohibited public gatherings of more than six people. Although there were hundreds of protestors, they each sat two or three meters apart. You could only get a sense of the sheer scale of the protest by walking along its string of participants for a few minutes. Or from above.

During the eighteen days of occupation of Cairo's Tahrir Square in 2011, a friend of mine, who was conscripted into the army at the time, was asked to film the crowd on Tahrir Square from a helicopter. He told me he tried to hide his tears as he feared the consequences of higher ranking men noticing that he was

"with the people" in spirit. I anticipated seeing those images one day, but they still have not been released. The aerial footage of the June 30, 2013 protests instead has been made public: perfectly edited like a Hollywood movie.[3] The military junta had plenty of time to learn about the power of protest imagery and stage it in high quality so everybody would "feel" "something": the illusion of togetherness, the illusion of a "we, the people."

Writer and artist Johanna Hedva's Sick Woman Theory questions forms of political participation exclusively based on physical presence in public space. The author's chronic illness and vulnerability prevents her from going out and protesting with the crowd, but she refuses to surrender to invisibility.[4]

37

PR This statement is not so much about spreading guilt, it's rather about describing what I have seen. I am not saying that the only way to be "political" is to be a body on the street; I am saying that without bodies on the street there is no revolt. There is a big difference here. If there is a will, a desire, an intention to oppose police brutality but there are no people there to fight—whether those people are sick, imprisoned, or elsewhere—the brutality will go on. That is not to say that all those absent are guilty of doing nothing. That judgement is not for me to pass.

LC Those who are inclined to take to the streets perhaps do not even need a symbolic image to be moved to action. Rather, they need it to identify themselves as belonging to the collective narrative of the event after it has taken place, as being part of something bigger.

As writer Negar Azimi wrote: "a great deal of recent political art is affirmative; it affirms what we know (the wars of George W. Bush are bad; men are misogynists; gays are people too, etc.), it affirms that participation is necessary, and finally, it affirms that you—as the consumer of art—are, in fact, part of a community of like-minded peers."[5] In this sense, as Philip mentioned earlier, "radical aesthetics don't move a crowd, they move with the crowd" and they are vital. But an aestheticized struggle feels mediated, digested, not raw, less urgent.

PR I agree with you here. I don't know if I will be filming much next time.

LC I think filming was and is important. It is a need not always necessarily connected to the diffusion of the testimony. When filming a protest, your presence and movements are "legitimized" to an extent. But you can also become a target as your proximity to the action could seem threatening to governments that attempt to control the "official" narrative. Not only does documentation of protests serve a purpose, but also catching people in the act of filming validates the act—if what is happening is relevant, someone should document it.

I am talking about perception of involvement. I am not judging the level of involvement. The aestheticization of the footage can intensify the urgency that was already present for some, or dim it for others, depending on the level of their emotional investment and their proximity to the direct sources of information.

I think Philip's 2014 essay "2011 is not 1968: An Open Letter to an Onlooker on the Day of Rage," on activism and radical images, is still very relevant today.[6]

MH Here's a quote from that text:

The Internet helped create the aura that all this [protests on the streets in Egypt in 2010/2011] was familiar. By channeling the outrage on the streets through a medium that you recognized, the narrative presented on news channels diluted the mystery within the events and chained your imagination to what is familiar. The layers of interpretation painted over the images diminished your fear of the unknown. "This is only an act against dictatorship." "This is the individual cry for freedom." "This is a demonstration for democracy." "This revolution is nonviolent." The Internet replaced the Kalashnikov. These discourses silenced the structural dimensions of injustice and concealed the role of neoliberal policies promoted by the likes of the IMF, the EU, and the USA in deepening the stratification between poor and rich. They made you forget that it is out of these structures of injustice that the desire for social justice is born in the first place. These dominating narratives—the narratives of domination—localized the problematic, for instance, to that of a homegrown dictatorship. By isolating the crime, and highlighting the corruption of individuals, these accounts helped set the neo-colonial stage for the now empty shells of the old regime to be replaced by another that maintains the same logic of governance. [...] The images taken by the cameras of the BBC, CNN, or Al Jazeera become the private property of these institutions that then use them to tell their narratives, to celebrate what they desire to promote and silence what they want to suppress.

JM When thinking about people's movements I think about author Elias Canetti's open and closed crowds. He defines open crowds through their temporality and space, with entries and exits creating some kind of inclusion that lasts as long as there's agency, as long as there's growth. The capacity for crowds to move, expand, and disintegrate makes them politically unpredictable. Open crowds constitute themselves freely, outside the constraints of what one signifies as secure, outside the constraints of fear of the other, of touch. It starts small and grows only

MMG Humans kill 100 million sharks each year. It is one of those facts that is never too early to memorize.

What is actually newsworthy here? Almost nothing. There are sharks in the water, so the ones in its pathway are in danger. That might be worthy of explicit comment if it weren't so blandly obvious. But the ring of enthusiastic alarm here is of course implicit: the only thing that could make a hurricane worse is *a shark-filled hurricane*. This spuriousness based on fear and falsity is quite literally fake news.

A few months after this there are of course other headlines, including these from *The Guardian*: "Trump Is 'Obsessed' and 'Terrified' of Sharks—But His Fears Are Excessive" and "Reality Bites: Trump's Fear of Sharks Leads to a Surge in Charity Donations." It's wonderful that overnight people can be converted to show concern about animal welfare. But on what grounds? The president's galeophobia—an enemy-of-my-enemy-is-my-friend move—is boring.

when in flux, spontaneously swallowing more bodies. Its shape cannot be determined as it has no single entry point, as it grows indefinitely. I think that the aesthetics of a crowd in such a sense lies in its capacity to be "open every-where" and to move "in any direction." "The open crowd exists so long as it grows: it disinte-grates as soon as it stops growing."[7] It needs to fear that moment of disintegration at all times. That is its only constraint: the fear of disappear-ance of its political action.

I remember the first time I filmed a crowd of people. It was on a Friday, January 28, 2011, also known as the Friday of Anger. Nobody knew what exactly was going to happen as everyone was to a certain extent secretive about the plan for security reasons. Some people gathered in front of the mosque in Imbaba that day. I was there and had a small camcorder. It made me feel secure somehow, the fact that between me and the rest was a mediating device. There was a certain fear, anxiety that came with participa-tion in something that felt so much larger than any one of us. It was a relatively small group and it took a while for it to move. The march started eventually, and it was only a matter of time before it grew into a nonconforming geometry, with no beginning or end, with entry points, always in flux. There were few cameras that day and the internet was down.

LC_ I don't remember many particular clips of footage of protests in Egypt in 2011, but I remember a video by Jasmina very vividly. She presented it during the Alternative News Agency program at the Contemporary Image Collective in Cairo. It was a "left-over" image (a clip that was probably cut out of a more "relevant/newsworthy" one for the Mosireen archive).[8] In it were just dark silhouettes moving around in a back alley near the front lines. It did not show much "evidence" in the traditional sense, but it had the power to trigger my imagination and an urge to find out what happened before and after. It was then that I realized the gap of perception between those who experienced the uprising firsthand and those who didn't. I recognized the impossibility of representation and the incommunicability of mediated information.

JM_ In the legal realm, the "evidence of absence" suggests something that is missing, that doesn't exist. Lack of evidence becomes evi-dence, as it is the only thing left. In that sense, the left-over image is not only what is left and ignored, abandoned/found—it is what didn't serve its own premise. For about half a year, Essam, a worker from the Egyptian Starch and Glucose Company filmed around seven hours of footage of his factory as it was being illegally dismantled by the new owners. He did so to gather evidence to use against the new owners in court. This very personal diary and urgent evidentiary record was ignored by the courts of law, however. The footage turned into some-thing of an absent element in understanding what really happened in that factory.

Between 2011 and 2013 we filmed a lot of protests and testimonies. Many of these were happening in factory spaces. Philip and I recently discussed the particular urgency to film in these spaces, and the reasoning behind our choice of space and event; we had almost an obsession with covering every possible sit-in, protest, and chant. I think that for me, it was our way at the time to reconnect with the street that was slowly disappearing under the military rule of the SCAF (Supreme Council of Armed Forces, the transitional military body between the downfall of former Egyptian President Hosni Mubarak and the upcoming elections). In one of these videos, a worker from the Starch and Glucose Company shouts at the camera that he is with the people in Tahrir, that he is not less than the protesters gathered in Tahrir. With his body and voice, he chooses his Tahrir to be the factory. Back in 2011, everyone wanted to participate somehow, to discuss and debate, share political views, whether they were antagonistic toward the revolution or not. There was a sense of participation and construction of smaller, simultaneous narratives that were easily transformed into larger ones. Tahrir was a space of struggle, but also a space for street vendors, tea, and popcorn. I remember when we first discussed Mosireen and what role it could play, given that sooner or later the street would be taken from us again. We wondered how we could defend that space or create new ones and where. One way to do that was through video, countering the state's propaganda, opposing state-owned media. Through physical participation and interactions with people speaking directly to the lens, cameras became—sort of—extensions of our limbs: carefully, chaotically, urgently registering as much as possible, and when possible, moving with the crowd's flux. To capture without seeing sometimes, brutally engaging in the surrounding reality, editing while filming, and finally creating another reality. I think that this kind of relationship between fact and fiction is what lead me toward thinking about making a film in a tent, in a microcosmic Egypt, or elsewhere—where fiction is what's left of political agency.

LC_ This quote from your interview with scholar and art historian Angela Harutyunyan is also on point:

I am interested in the difference in reaction between when one looks at the reality itself and when one looks at its representation. I think that both documentary and art could create a similar response or feeling to image, but the line gets thicker when the image is taken to a different context. I can afford the work in the context of the gallery, but through my documentary practice, I want to produce a direct applied message without ambiguity, a message to reach as many people as possible.[9]

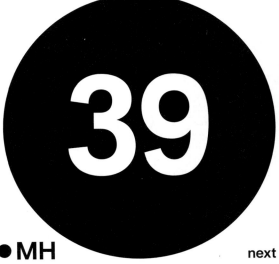

39

JM_ The fear of touching the image. I remember the Gaza War between 2008 and 2009. I was still living in London at the time. I came back in late 2009. The ceasefire was in January of that year. I remember watching the war in its different forms of representation, on a television screen mainly, but also in newspapers, printed material—material you could touch somehow. That was my only connection. I remember counting the casualties every day for six months. Operation Cast Lead. I still don't know what that means, but it sounds disgusting. The information coming from Gaza was very overwhelming, but it was also very terse. Fast-paced and effective shots creating information available for consumption by the general public: entertaining, overwhelming, entertaining. A lot of these images were shot from afar, over-looking the struggle without seeing the actual humans, just rocket strikes and explosions, like fireworks. Rafah, Gaza, and Khan Yunis are very densely populated areas, so you can imagine how difficult it is to actually see anything, to understand anything without actually being on the ground. It is always in splinters, formulated in bits and pieces of information, the representation of the very few.

I think this was the first time I thought about quitting painting. In that moment making pictures was irrelevant. Painting to me is very much about flattening the image to only its information is visible, flattening representation so only its surface is left, a bit like how bombs leave spaces emptied out of their histories. The process of flattening the image to only its surface can be painful because of our selective memory: our bodies protect themselves from overwhelming flashes of information. Our minds can only carry so much. These histories, these left-overs from an event, the second-hand experience of an event, the fear of touching information, leads to forgetting. As in painting, information gets flattened.

I forgot about Gaza and remembered it again with this image: a group of Israelis sitting with their backs to their settlement drinking Coca-Cola and watching the spectacle of bombs drop from the sky like fireworks. This is 2014. Israel launched Operation Protective Edge during which they did something called carpet bombing, which means that these bombs were unguided, random. Meaning they can kill more people at random but concentrated in a street, a house, a school. They killed 1,492 humans in seven weeks.

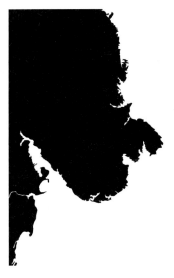

LC_ A *Reuters* article on the war in Syria noted:

War crimes investigators and activists have amassed an "overwhelming volume" of testimony, images and videos documenting atrocities committed by all sides during Syria's war, a U.N. quasi-prosecutorial body said in its first report.

[…]

"The volume of videos and other images— as well as the role played by social media—is unprecedented in any other accountability process with respect to international crimes to date," said the report…. "…It is not possible to prosecute all of the crimes committed, given their vast number," it added.[10]

On March 26, 2018, a UN spokesperson admitted that it's technically impossible to pursue all the war crimes and atrocities committed in Syria because the evidence is overwhelming. A few days later, the United States and the United Kingdom launched an attack on Syrian soil triggered by the diffusion of images of Syrian civilians gassed to death with "unauthorized chemical weapons." After seven years of horrific and unprecedentedly documented war in Syria— after there isn't much left to destroy—a series of clips (showing several men, women, and children with apparent signs of exposure to toxic chemical agents) half the world believes are staged, others consider long-awaited and unequivocal proof justifying foreign intervention. A threshold has been crossed. The red line is always the latest most outrageous, most shared and most commented upon video. Seven years of non-stop slaughter were not enough. A stronger image emerged and was skimmed like oil off the surface of an ocean of evidence.

Footage of crowds of migrants at Europe's borders triggers outrage and compassion in some and hysterical fear in others. The image is as thin as the border between adjacent filter bubbles.

Many claim that one image circulated widely years ago "shifted the perspective" on the migrant crisis and became a symbol: three-year-old Alan Kurdi. If anything, the image of his lifeless body washed up on a Turkish shore in 2015 made us even more numb to the death of refugee children. Now we need an even stronger, more cruel, more gruesome image to excite the same level of outrage. That image will drown in a sea of images.

40

I recently overheard a human-itarian worker talking about fundraising for 3D camera drones to report the migrant crisis more vividly. I have doubts about the impact of a generic "more" (more images, more pixels, more angles) as the human capacity to be moved is not infinite. It's like watching an ambulance with the siren on getting repeatedly stuck between cars in the traffic. It is an unbearable sight. At some point, unless you know how to clear the road, a defense mechanism kicks in and you turn away.

MH_ Alan Kurdi, a refugee who drowned in the Mediterranean Sea after his family had entered an inflatable boat that had capsized, lay on that beach, lifeless, himself and his clothes wet, but seemingly asleep. The power of the image was in its proximity to intimacy itself. Not only in the death of a child—a boundless tragedy—but also in its peacefulness, stillness, a slight but essential recall of a parent's experience of seeing their child asleep and caring for it endlessly; the exhibition of the sweetness and vulnerability of a Child, any Child, frozen in time and space. Therefore, as spectators we are drawn into a very difficult and perverse loop by remembering this child only for the image of his death. Would we have cared as much for him had he remained alive and been thrown against the fences of Hungary, endured the ordeals of Calais, or been captured by a lens in any other hellish place inside the EU? Our perverse privilege to declare him the Sacred Child as opposed to Vermin Scum is based on where and when images are taken, and whether they do or do not become flashes of proximity.

We lose track of the geopolitical trajectories that have made this Child's death a reality. With one hand we wipe away our tears at the sight of the pixels that represent Alan Kurdi, with the other we turn a blind eye to our government striking a deal with President Recep Tayyip Erdoğan's Turkey—both a covert ISIS

MH_ The Catalan independence referendum of 2017. Had we lived in times of less turmoil, this would, on its own, have dominated headlines for years to come. But how different does a national independence movement look in times of insurgent nationalism? An independent Catalonia, right now, would be just another little nation-state on an increasingly fragmented European map. That map is already starting to resemble a patchwork of rival fiefdoms, orchestrated by skillful populist demagoguery on social media. Somehow it is surprising that activists are looking at the nation-state as if it were the solution. There is a YouTube video from June 28, 2016 of then UKIP leader Nigel Farage addressing the European Parliament after the Brexit vote. He literally says, "the little people… want our borders back."

Maybe this belief in borders is more deeply connected to life with digital screens than to immigration issues: a user's desire for a reality that is as clearly addressable as an interface, where a border is a clear black line on a screen instead of a porous, clunky, textured negotiation.

collaborator and a NATO member.

Recently, the Rojava-based independence movement released files that feature identity documents, allegedly found in Syria, belonging to people allowed transit through Turkey to join ISIS; the files also include pictures retrieved from a smartphone in which a future ISIS fighter—with Kalashnikovs and flags—is initially clad in a Tommy Hilfiger sweatshirt. Our eyes are trained to judge Hilfiger wearers as unremarkable, middle of the road, *normal*, or normcore. Spike Jonze's 2005 TV commercial for the Gap plays on this perception. In it, a Gap store gets completely and violently destroyed by its clientele in a way that resembles a war zone. This tangent links us back to Hilfiger worn by an ISIS member; what was normal becomes normcore becomes actual violence.

The perception is about images—not about people. What Philip was talking about recurs throughout this conversation: it is about immediate and intrinsic actions, positions needing to be filled, and radical aesthetics as something moving with that.

MH › LC We met for the first time in 2010 in Spain, when you and Nida Ghouse were, together with Lina Attalah, working as the Take to the Sea collective, focusing on migration and memory in the Mediterranean space. As you recall, our American counterparts at the time seemed focused on unmasking the hypocrisy of the art world. Maybe at the heart of the confrontation, documented in an extensive, multi-camera video piece by Ergin Çavuşoğlu titled *Backbench* (2010) set in a cool gray stage design by Markus Miessen, was an uncommon idea about art—uncommon as in not shared, and therefore an unarticulated central problem.

LC At Manifesta 8, the fellow artists taking part in *Backbench* exposed their disillusionment at our seeming distance from the urgent matters they raised about the conditions of production, the corruption of biennials, and the pleas of the host communities. We recalled Luc Boltanski's *Distant Suffering* (1999), in which he argues that feeling guilty is not enough to move on to action and it won't make one change the world.[11]

Performing outrage and critiquing a space doesn't exempt one from the responsibility of being part of it and legitimizing its language

Artists and activists invest personally, financially, and emotionally in trying to make change—no matter how small—within and outside of institutions. But I think we cannot afford to romanticize this and keep reproducing the same practices without acknowledging the failures of political participation and socially engaged art.

MH "Crisis" has become a word thrown around by armchair critics. Is "urgency" going down the same path?

LC When did the crisis begin (to begin with)? And who does it belong to? Who are the agents of change if they have nothing to lose from the status quo? Where is the threshold when we no longer accept the flow of events, as we accept turbulent unexpected changes in the weather?

Once I imagined designing a "concern-meter" (or "urgencymeter") for events and phenomena that are perceived as a permanent crisis within this historical moment (such as forced migration or climate change or other long-term phenomena that the UN and various NGO leaders "urge" undefined audiences to take action upon, while expressing "concern" or "strong condemnation" and for which nobody can be held accountable). Once the threshold of collective outrage is crossed and all the angriest of the emojis have been used, the concernmeter would explode, splattering blood and emoji splinters all over the screen.

MH In response to that, what do you think about Ethan Zuckerman's Cute Cat Theory of political activism,[12] which posits that the mundane nature of most digital traffic through large platforms also guarantees political activists access to and use of these larger platforms for their ends?

LC The internet and social media are the platforms that can host the virtual "open crowds" that Jasmina mentions in reference to Canetti, where meaning can go in every direction and be shaped in a nonconforming geometry. I agree that, "If the government chooses to shut down such generic platforms, it will hurt people's ability to 'look at cute cats online', spreading dissent and encouraging the activists' cause."[13]

MH Emojis may represent the turn of everyday written communication to a single, pan-alphabetic, Unicode ideography, a kind of Esperanto-style universalism of the written image. Emojis are the ultimate form of trans-nationalist design—border-crossing communication standards and conventions. They appear exactly now, when the threshold that separates action from complacency becomes crucial—amplified by the idea of emojis exploding (reminiscent of yet another Jonze ad, for Sprite, in which a three-dimensional smiling sun jumps off a soft drink bottle and starts attacking people).

LC The compulsive diffusion of sensational images ceases to be a radical act when embedded in the cycle of consumption of information. The overload of visual content affects our emotional perception, making it almost impossible to decode it as relevant within the "noise" created by redundant and simplified

41

information, as we have a limited capacity for empathy in relation to time.

Images of conflicts are produced and disseminated by different actors conscious of the power dynamics of the attention economy. The ambivalent meaning and loss of symbolic power of images, allow the same images to simultaneously serve audiences with opposing belief systems; they will read opposite narratives in the same image.

Urgency is an armchair word because it is a permanent state right now. Without reaction it is hollow. All the energy is wasted in fear—waiting for the next imminent catastrophe. It dissipates when the catastrophe actually happens. There is no energy left to try to move those who do not care, and those who have the power to demand real change.

Urgency is a synonym for compulsivity: the urgency to react immediately to an event, to document and share the image as soon as possible. 4K sky-diving GoPro videos and shaky images of violent protests are consumed next to each other, putting our emotions through a spin cycle. As Doa Aly says: "on the Internet, as we rapidly process the stream of images, we are all witnesses to something that is impossible to testify to."[14]

MH This conversation *aspires to be* about "intimacy with an urgency"—about ways in which we *can't* be separated from what is urgent and immediate, ways in which urgency chooses us and forces us.

LC Urgency chooses us when we are directly or indirectly affected by an event.

Some events generate a sense of urgency in some people and leave others completely unaffected. For some groups of people an issue becomes urgent when it's already too late.

But the constant and accelerating exposure to aestheticized suffering makes it harder to be touched by images "deeply enough" to be moved to action. Everything is urgent in the news. So we live under the illusion that we'll only see war and melting icebergs in artsy documentaries. Urgency forces itself upon us when the consequences of information materialize in our lived experience.

MH It also aspires to be about "software and sovereignty," following design theorist Benjamin H. Bratton. In what ways is the artistic communication of urgency connected to the uses of certain technologies—regulated and controlled resources like software, technological stacks, YouTube, etc.—and even how we presuppose things like electrical grids as part of this apparatus? That is, hardware and sovereignty. The time that YouTube and Facebook were believably portrayed as harbingers of democratic revolution is behind us. How have our views on this technological stack developed?

PR In 2011, protesters in Egypt lost access to the net for some days. In a way it was crucial because—despite sounding rather obsessive, I will say it again—what really mattered were bodies on the street. There were phases of the uprising during which an obsession developed around the image, around being seen, around the television's eye. I wonder if we would have been better off for the entire period of 2011 and 2012 being offline. But that is hard to say because clearly it also served our communication. With the collective Mosireen that we were a part of, we always tried to push our information off the internet because for us, who it reached there was insufficient. We began screening footage and videos in Tahrir Cinema in the square. We distributed our videos on free CDs and via Bluetooth, the latter of which proved quite futile. We wanted our images to be free for everybody. It was around 2012–2013 that better phones became accessible. We wanted to bypass the centralization of the internet to share these videos. I was in touch with some researcher in the Netherlands who was doing work on large-scale Bluetooth dissemination, but he was still early on in his work. We didn't get very far, or maybe he didn't want to share his findings. Then another member of the group purchased some software that promised to disperse files via Bluetooth from a laptop to fifty recipients. It never worked and we had to give up on the idea.

In general, I think in the "urgency" of 2011, we didn't theorize too much about electricity or

even deeply about Facebook and YouTube. In the rush of things we just wanted "our" images, our narrative out there no matter the means, the more the better because we were up against a massive propaganda infrastructure on both the state and private levels. We were aware that YouTube might shut down our channel at some point, and always had physical backups. We also started to place our material elsewhere online. The tools we used were a crutch. We realized that, but we found no solutions to these issues.

When we had those screenings in the square, sometimes we would organize for an electrician to be there to help us access some power from a lamp post. Sometimes we couldn't, and someone would always just happen to show up and help us get power. I think at that point as middle-class types, we learned to connect with people on the margins who take what they don't get. And space on the street—and the electricity to go along with it—are two of those things. So we found a lot of solidarity and comradeship there.

The screenings at Tahrir Cinema eventually emerged into a much more powerful campaign called *Kazeboon* (Liars), where activists all over the country started setting up screenings to show images, particularly of military violence against civilians that were censored on TV and in mainstream media. Of course this required someone somewhere to have access to a laptop and a projector, so it was dependent on the software and the hardware and the know-how that went along with that—but it played a part. Months later the generals that ruled during that transitional period were removed by widespread popular consent.

LC In terms of technology, urgency happens when the infrastructure becomes evident in its violent interruption, or by an overload that makes it temporarily inaccessible—for instance, when underwater submarine internet cables are cut leaving entire regions in the dark. The limits of technology appear when Syrian children burn tires, making the sky turn grey, so drones cannot hit them.

Tahrir Cinema and Kazeboon were powerful artistic/activist actions (practices?) that could be imitated and reenacted elsewhere, in the future, or by different actors as a symbolic strategy.

MH › JM Your 2012 film *About the Donkey that Wanted to Become a Painting*, shows a dead donkey beside a dusty road, cars passing by. The handheld camera remains focused on the donkey as subtitles narrate the story of Nietzsche encountering a horse being beaten. Please tell us more about this piece. Does it reference Béla Tarr's *The Turin Horse* made that same year?

JM Nietzsche's eternal return. The inability to show, metaphorically speaking, is a condition when one's heart stops and there is a flat line on the cardiographic scan. The dead donkey is flattened to the surface of the ground. As in painting the process of the making, the gesture, slowly disappears under every new surface of meanings. The process of the making, the attempt to represent, will eventually die with the making. The last sentence is a quote from Nietzsche, "Mother I am dumb," which he spoke soon after throwing himself around a horse's neck to protect it from the blows of its owner. We don't know what happened to the donkey. The animal remains in a frozen image, looped in time. The body of the decomposing donkey and the narrative (the subtitled story) alternate without providing any further explanation. The image of the decomposed donkey, seemingly frozen, appears to be flattened to the surface of the ground. The last words, "Mother I am dumb," are flattened so only their meaning remains, and then everything starts again, collecting dust. I like Tarr. I like the fact that he said, "this is my last film," more than once.

MH › LC Describe the pathways that have led you from there to here, from then to now. Please—having always pursued such profound ways in engaging with people, reality, and art—describe your innermost urgency.

LC There used to be a phase for questions. Now those questions have been exhausted, saturated, after reshuffling the archive over and over. The need to justify motives for making art in times or geographies of crisis is problematic as much as it is problematic that to deserve freedom of movement you should pursue a noble cause.

According to this rhetoric, a migrant deserves freedom only when escaping war, but is not as deserving to compete in the labor market as a citizen with equal rights and a work permit.

An artist belonging to X group makes important work and is acknowledged internationally when the work is about issues perceived as urgent in a specific context.

The blackmail of gratitude: answers are predetermined and curiosities exterminated.

There is no path from there to here. I've been floating adrift. There is no romanticism in this. I had privileges, choices, and alternatives. I haven't been able to choose a medium or a language with enough conviction. There has been weather. Dead calm. High waves. A tsunami. Multiple shipwrecks. One thing I know now about where I am now is that "art is what you can do about not being able to do anything."[15]

I am too slow at reacting while the pace of everything else is accelerating—including people's ability to forget. My innermost urgency is to be able to escape the pressure to produce and consume information. To find the freedom and the energy to react, in case it's really urgent. In the imminent future we will use VR headsets just to see reality in slow motion, to slow down the present.

How the cinephile Kim Jong-il kidnapped a director to improve local films

MMG There's a North Korean movie from 2003 called *Our Fragrance* that's about a fashion show in Pyongyang, whose subtext is about the marital prospects of a young couple. Why would a spring fashion show—essentially a design competition—be the basis of a major film in North Korea? Because it is a perfect premise for a superimposition of nationalism and love—the inherent superiority of the former with the externalized radiance of the latter. The national spring dress is Yohji Yamamoto meets maternity wear with brightly colored bows. The film contains an extraordinary montage of a "before and after" transformation. Nations, like people, can aspire to getting facelifts. There's singing, synchronized dance, and people carrying flowers, more indexes of a wedding than a fashion show. The movie's subtext is to show off the skillfulness of a young couple who work diligently alongside each other, as much platonic co-workers as future newlyweds. The allusion to wedded bliss is summed up in one line: "The most beautiful fragrance of the young people comes from valuing things of the nation's own." National prospects rest on good—no, superior—design.

1
Jane M. Gaines, "Political Mimesis," in *Collecting Visible Evidence*, ed. Jane M. Gaines and Michael Renov, Minneapolis: University of Minnesota Press, 1999, 92–98, http://www.columbia.edu/itc/film/gaines/documentary_tradition/Gaines_PoliticalMimesis.pdf. Last accessed on August 13, 2018.
2
See Theodor Adorno, *Minima Moralia* [1951], trans. E. F. N. Jephcott, London: Verso, 1974.
3
Mido Tiger, "33 Million Protesters in Egypt—30 June 2013," video, 5:17, July 2, 2013, https://www.youtube.com/watch?v=dLnD_8nbM1c. Last accessed on August 30, 2018.
4
"Sick Woman Theory" by Johanna Hedva is adapted from her lecture "My Body Is a Prison of Pain so I Want to Leave It Like a Mystic But I Also Love It & Want It to Matter Politically," sponsored by the Women's Center for Creative Work, Human Resources, Los Angeles, October 7, 2015, https://vimeo.com/144782433. Last accessed on August 13, 2018.
5
Negar Azimi, "Good Intentions," *frieze*, March 1, 2011, https://frieze.com/article/good-intentions. Last accessed on August 13, 2018.
6
See Philip Rizk, "2011 is not 1968: An Open Letter to an Onlooker on the Day of Rage," *Mada*, January 28, 2014, https://www.madamasr.com/en/2014/01/28/opinion/u/2011-is-not-1968-an-open-letter-to-an-onlooker-on-the-day-of-rage/. Last accessed on August 14, 2018.
7
See Elias Canetti, *Crowds and Power*, New York: The Viking Press, 1962.
8
Mosireen is a non-profit media collective born out of the explosion of citizen journalism and cultural activism in Egypt during the revolution. From 2011 to 2014 it held a space in downtown Cairo that was a revolutionary activist hub dedicated to supporting and producing citizen media of all kinds—including publishing videos, providing training, technical support, campaign support, equipment, screenings, and events, alongside hosting an extensive archive of footage from the revolution. At its height, Mosireen's YouTube channel was the most watched nonprofit channel in the world. It remains the most watched nonprofit channel in Egypt. Campaigns and initiatives Mosireen supported include No To Military Trials for Civilians, Kazeboon, Operation Anti-Sexual Harassment, Freedom for the Brave, and Tahrir Cinema among others. Alongside their personal work, the preparation of 858.ma, a major video archive of material from the revolution, for public use is the current focus of the collective's work together. It was launched in January 2018, https://858.ma/. Last accessed on August 30, 2018.
9
See Angela Harutyunyan, "Active Interventions/Intervening Actions: Jasmina Metwaly in Conversation with Angela Harutyunyan," *Ibraaz*, April 5, 2012, https://www.ibraaz.org/interviews/17. Last accessed on August 13, 2018.
10
Stephanie Nebehay, "War Crimes Evidence in Syria 'overwhelming', Not All Can Be Pursued—U.N," *Reuters*, March 26, 2018, https://uk.reuters.com/article/uk-mideast-crisis-syria-warcrimes/war-crimes-evidence-in-syria-overwhelming-not-all-can-be-pursued-u-n-idUKKBN1H22GL. Last accessed on August 14, 2018.
11
See Luc Boltanski, *Distant Suffering: Morality, Media, and Politics*, Cambridge: Cambridge University Press, 1999.
12
Ethan Zuckerman, "Cute Cats to the Rescue? Participatory Media and Political Expression," draft essay for *Youth, New Media and Political Participation*, ed. Danielle Allen, Jennifer Light, and Ellen Middaugh, Oakland, CA: Youth and Participatory Politics Research Network, 2014. http://ethanzuckerman.com/papers/cutecats2013.pdf. Last accessed on August 13, 2018.
13
"Cute Cat Theory of Digital Activism," *Wikipedia*, last modified August 27, 2018, https://en.wikipedia.org/wiki/Cute_cat_theory_of_digital_activism. Last accessed on August 30, 2018.
14
Doa Aly, "The Image(s) Between Us," *Ibraaz*, November 30, 2015, https://www.ibraaz.org/essays/138 Last accessed on August 13, 2018.
15
Metahaven, Twitter post, June 29, 2016, 7:26am, https://twitter.com/mthvn/ status/748160830978527232. Last accessed on August 30, 2018.

Laura Cugusi
Laura Cugusi is an artist, researcher, photographer, filmmaker, and writer based in London. Cugusi studied media, sociology, and political science at the University of Bologna and in Santiago de Compostela. Her research focuses on migration and human rights narratives, artistic practices involving incomplete archives and collective memory, and informal urban practices in Egypt. Her work was included in the Tunisia pavilion, 57th Venice Biennale, 2017 and she is a member of artist collective Take to the Sea, with whom she has exhibited in the contexts of: Nile Sunset Annex, Cairo, 2013; Biennale Jogja XII, Yogjakarta, 2013; *Hydrarchy*, Contemporary Image Collective, Cairo, 2012; and Manifesta 8, Murcia, 2010–2011.

Jasmina Metwaly
Jasmina Metwaly is an artist and filmmaker based in Berlin and Cairo. Metwaly studied painting in Poznan where she focused on time-based works with strong correlations to painting. Rooted in performance and theater, her film and video work is focused on process-based practices that have a social function generating tension between participants and audiences. Metwaly's work has been exhibited at international art venues and festivals. Recent works include *We Are Not Worried in the Least* (2018); *Out on the Street* (2015), and *From Behind of the Monument* (2013). Just like Rizk, Metwaly is a member of non-profit media collective Mosireen.

Philip Rizk
Philip Rizk is a filmmaker and writer based in Cairo. With Jasmina Metwaly he directed the feature film *Out on the Street*, which premiered at the Berlinale in 2015 and was featured in the German pavilion of the 56th Venice Biennale later that year. He is a member of the non-profit media collective Mosireen. Rizk is currently working on an essay-travel film.

43

next

THE
NEW
EASTHETIC

+

44

Metahaven › Anastasiia Fedorova Recently, you suggested that the stunning music video for Jamie XX's song "Gosh" that Romain Gavras directed in 2016, and which was shot in Tianducheng, a disused tower block estate at the edge of the Chinese city of Hangzhou, was inspired by, or reminiscent of, the "New East" aesthetic of Eastern Europe. Here are a selection of fragments:

Eastern European skies are always colourless and bleak.

Dystopian cities are a staple of post-Soviet ruin porn. From disused military bases and abandoned industrial towns to locations of eco-logical disaster, dystopian urban environments are never far away in New East imagery. Ghost towns are not unique to Eastern Europe but they are certainly a key part of the largely region-specific genre of ruin porn.

Nothing screams Eastern Europe like a few rows of identical tower blocks. The vast and overwhelming cityscape has become, in recent years, stereotypic [sic] symbol of the emerging youth culture of the New East. Contemporary Chinese housing projects have borrowed a lot from their Soviet predecessors which creates an uncannily similar atmosphere of failed utopia: the idea of efficient life turned into a ghost town.[1]

Apparently there is a really tight set of visual codes, aesthetics, and cinematic patterns that invoke a specific geographical, social, and political imaginary corresponding to the "New East." But what does the New East stand for? Why is it so mysterious, yet so recognizable and even mappable—with the capacity to be reduced to such visual codes and patterns? Why does it inspire an "affect of the image": a particular feeling that the image immediately invokes? You also hinted at this when you wrote: "At the same time, post-Soviet youth culture has become a style obsession, with images of suburban skinheads, crumbled infrastructure, and Brutalist housing blocks becoming fodder for fashion blogs and mood boards."[2]

AF It's about one in the morning in St. Petersburg and I just got home from a cheap Soviet-style bar where I had 100 ml of Armenian cognac for 280 rubles, which was the most lush offering on the menu. The bar is not really Soviet, more like a 1990s imitation. There are a lot of nice contemporary bars nearby, and still young people go there a lot. For fun I guess, and I suppose because it's cheap.

I was born in St. Petersburg and lived here till the age of twenty-two. The truth is, I now feel very weird here. Walking past certain places that trigger memories, I feel nauseous and disconnected; the more trivial the memory, the worse the feeling is. Russian identity abroad is like wearing a Gosha Rubchinskiy T-shirt. It might seem like a great idea to wear "Russian" fashion designs in a different country, but it is awkward and embarrassing here.

The New East is not a place. It is a set of ideas and images, a myth, the great otherness, the strange edgeland. Why has French Hollywood actor Vincent Cassel spent half of his career playing Russians? Why does the French film La Haine (1995) look sort of Russian to us? It's not about Russia, or Eastern Europe, or the New East. It's about the notion of the cultural periphery. Without the periphery, there is no center, and without a dominant cultural identity, there is no need for an exotic other. Russia, Eastern Europe, and the broader territory of the former Communist sphere of influence has been imagined as an estranged, desolate borderland for a long time now. The Cold War shaped it as the cultural opposition to the West, so it's not surprising that this region remains a source of fear and wonder, and also a newfound aesthetic obsession.

I both love and hate those New East visual narratives. They really grab me, but sometimes I think the world around us is generally reduced to just a handful of archetypal images: a rainforest, Eastern European city, Asian city, etc. Our world is built from stock photos: we repeatedly consume and reproduce the same dozen images.

Have you ever thought about how reduced our vision has become?

MH We are currently sitting on a high-speed train in between the cities of Rotterdam and Amsterdam in the Netherlands. To save the little stamp-sized bits of nature that lie between these two cities, a large part of the journey is underground, in a long, internet-less tunnel in which the air pressure makes you feel like you're on a plane. At Schiphol airport, long queues of slow tourists board the train.

The route represents a lot of what Western Europe is currently about: a certain blandness and flatness, a particular level of convenience. Against the backdrop of this carefully designed productive boredom, other things stand in sharp contrast: bungee jumping from sky-high Soviet flats, dashcam videos. The "New Easthetic" started low-res, pixelated, and has only relatively recently become elevated to the level of full HD and 4K; it is tied in with the evolution of the technology stack. In general, we think people have trouble understanding the stack's reach; the moment that so many people have Premiere Pro or Final Cut Pro on their computers, and HD recording equipment on their phones—the moment that everybody makes music, that everyone is broadcasting.

The West's obsession with Russia as a villain who breaks all the rules, is an enduring fantasy about what the West (unconsciously) thinks it lacks: orientalist tropes such as risk, fate, wastelands, ruins, rawness, residual and unkept extra space, an unprocessed past, visceral experience, delirium, repositories of the imagination. It seems that the idea of a New Easthetic as an apolitical product of styling, monetized in fields such as fashion and music, could be a proto-political paradigm of space- and time-based distanciation or alienation that is forever prone to being captured and politicized anew, should the circumstances arise. Maybe we are talking about proxies for otherness, a difference that we project onto a political map that is no longer relevant—indeed, as you say: "the New East is not a place."

AF "Risk, fate, wastelands, ruins, rawness, residual and unkept extra space, an unprocessed past, visceral experience, delirium, repositories of the imagination" paints a very evocative picture. The New East image we're talking about—the brutal romanticism of tower blocks and wastelands—consists of a relatively recent set of stereotypes. The common cultural imaginary for most people in the West is still bears, ballet, the USSR, and caviar. On the one hand, I suppose every country has its images for export. The UK, for example, has Cool Britannia and the royal family. But on the other, I wonder whether it's more political than it seems. Did you know, for example, that The Guardian has a New East network? When I worked at The Calvert Journal, previously one of the network's content partners, I noticed that the articles The Guardian was most interested in republishing were those related to something Soviet.

Last week I got almost identical feedback from two different editors of two separate publications; they both commented: "your text is great, but could you mention Gosha Rubchinskiy and talk about your Soviet background?" Sometimes I fear that by being part of the creative industry, I am constantly allowing others to reshape my history and determine my narrative. Other times I think that today identity is fluid anyway and that mainstream media simply struggles to keep up. I am interested in what young Russians born in the 1990s would have to say; they grew up surrounded by relics of the Soviet past as well as by an avalanche of foreign cultures and goods, all bundled together into a new freedom to define oneself.

I am also interested in how young people in Russia perceive themselves while simultaneously seeing how they are presented in the international media. It must have quite an alienating effect. I can imagine them losing all hope of being understood. Talked about instead of with, the utopia of a globally shared common ground must

The New Easthetic

next

feel out of reach for them. I love what I see and hear in Russian music, fashion, and art in recent years, precisely because of the sharp, sarcastic self-reflective quality of this emerging generation.

MH › AF Can you tell us more about this feedback loop between young people's self-perception and how they are presented in the international media?

AF In Russia, I think a lot of people have come to believe in the existence of anti-Russian propaganda in the West. In fact, many Russians believe that their international image results from Western propaganda rather than from Russian politics. When it comes to young people, particularly in the creative industry, this perception seems to create a weird sardonic and cynical yet ironic posturing that they adopt when talking about their Russianness.

Today I was at my nephew's christening in a small, freshly built Orthodox church surrounded by crisp, freshly built tower blocks. I had to wear a cross and a headscarf and everything. The whole scene—the cityscape, the ritual, the social context—looked quite remarkable. I could almost visualize it from an outsider's perspective. But it wasn't staged—it was my hometown.

MH › AF In a piece you wrote for *032c*, you recall:

before 1991, there were no raves in Moscow. Come 9pm, the skyline was pitch black. That changed with the legendary Gagarin raves. Located at the space pavilion of the All-Russia Exhibition Center, the party pirated its name from the Soviet space hero. Three thousand ravers surrounded derelict satellites and rocket engines mounted on plinths, dancing to dark, pulsing acid house. In one night, Soviet heritage was rendered defunct by a wild, undefined energy.[3]

How do these and other remnants of twentieth-century utopian futurism relate to the utopias of the twenty-first century—artificial intelligence, the Human Genome Project, self-driving cars, cleaning up the plastic soup, TED Talks—that are in many ways super sanitary and often geographically connected to Silicon Valley?

AF It's interesting you brought up this particular passage. The editors and I were looking for a metaphor for how the specific heritage of Russian (and Soviet) culture clashes with modernity; something that would approximate the excitement about the first Rubchinskiy fashion shows. The 1990s mentioned in the quote above is a very recent chapter in history that still has a direct impact today.

Reflecting upon historical imaginaries of the future is a good way to evaluate our understanding of modernity. For me, it's also an emotional subject: it makes me think of my parents when they were young, when everyone was supposed to build a better future, a proletarian heaven. We are now a generation of writers, graphic designers, and marketing managers—and in Russia we're all children of rocket scientists, builders, and factory workers.

MH "Europa" was once a futuristic abstraction, too. The name was awarded fast cars and large buildings. Institutions worked in its name, redistributing resources such as coal and steel away from national monopolies to prevent another war. The end of the dream was arguably the common currency, the euro. This highlights a curious 1990s undercurrent. In a transition that took about two decades from the idealistic 1970s, the euro as prefix had come to stand for all things cheap: Eurolines, Euroshopper, etc.

The noble idea of Europe permeating the everyday should ideally have been its victory. But perhaps there is still hidden potential for that.

AF The most famous word with the euro prefix in Russian is Евроремонт. It translates into Euro-refurbishment, and stands for a certain interior design style popular in the early 2000s. It's a look that is supposed to be contemporary and Western, but often ends up as rather tacky. The circular building in which the Salute Hotel in Kyiv is housed is a masterpiece in Soviet modernism, yet the interior is a blend of an institutional idea of luxury (a lot of potted plants and ruched curtains) and this seemingly European new idea of comfort. Евроремонт has become a joke.

My reaction to Soviet utopia might be rather skeptical, but as someone who constantly needs to apply for visas, I had really wanted to believe in a united Europe. The fewer the borders, the fewer the papers, and the more human we are allowed to be.

I had an interesting conversation with an English friend the other day. We went to an exhibition on Russian cosmism at the Multimedia Art Museum in Moscow, a great show that combined real artifacts from Yuri Gagarin's travels through space, excerpts taken from Russian philosophy books, and contemporary art connected to space. My friend was very impressed by an artwork made from video footage of a rocket launch in Baikonur. "This is greater than anything the British have ever achieved," he said. I replied that synthesizing sustainable fuel from algae might not look as grand, but for me it's much more impressive and crucial for our future as a species. I think this is a very symptomatic divide: grand vision versus practicality and sustainability. As a child of engineers of the great failed utopia, I am immune to the traction of such grand visions.

MH › AF Rubchinskiy has talked about Russia's geopolitics and its "internal branding," so to speak, which he deems positive. He finds it is not so much about nationalism but about patriotism, emphasizing that all countries produce propaganda and that it's simply a matter of business. He also talks about there being great solidarity between youth cultures across the world who don't care about politics.[4] Do you agree with him?

46

AF Patriotism is an incredibly outdated bit of nonsense, and it should be laid to rest. Choosing to emigrate has been great for me, personally, because as an immigrant you end up in between: you're an outsider in every culture and you see everything from a distance. I love it, perhaps more so because I am a writer. All patriotism does is divide. I want to believe in a united future generation. Tomorrow this may come, but not today.

On another note, Ukrainian singer Luna creates an "Eastern" aesthetic that is totally different from the stereotypical brutalist tower blocks. Her work sounds and looks so nineties and yet is so contemporary, naive, and ironic at the same time.[5] I think her work reflects a certain "new Ukrainian romanticism."

MH › AF When we interviewed design theorist Benjamin H. Bratton for *The Sprawl (Propaganda about Propaganda)* (2015) a couple of years ago, we wanted to include parts of a Ukrainian dating video in the film from an agency called Anastasia Date, with headquarters in the Seychelles. It portrays Ukraine as a colony of the West, where characters who take on roles such as pensioners can go to purchase Extreme Femininity. The advertisement reminded us that the role given to Eastern Europe after the fall of Communism is bound to resource exploitation and biopolitical production. Bratton spoke about the ways in which planetary-scale computation has brought about a crisis of the nation-state, which in turn, he argues, can be seen as a crisis in male sexuality.

The "new Ukrainian romanticism" you mention as expressed by Luna appears very distinct from this. The video you refer to seems to rejoice in the soft-focus glitch. There is a sort of Snapchat tongue-in-cheek feel to the distortion of the women's faces in using a nineties video layer.

AF There is certainly a lot to be said about the myth of Eastern European femininity shaped by the Western male gaze: a blend of a ballerina, a honey trap spy, and a high-class prostitute. Eastern Europe is a sex tourism destination for the West—and that's where patriarchy shows its true face. In almost any culture, if you're an attractive woman, you're treated as exceptional, which is why it's great to see Kristina Bardash, aka Luna, taking control of her songs, her performance, and her aesthetics.

Do you agree that with the arrival of the Rubchinskiy fragrance the commodification of the New East trend has reached new heights?

MH We were on the verge of purchasing a Trump-Putin 2016 T-shirt online after seeing a newspaper photo of a Trump supporter wearing one with a certain cheeky pride. But we didn't end up buying it. We realized that this is some historically and politically absurd moment that we are living through right now, and that the boundaries between self-parody, art, life, and PSYOP have vanished. Merchandising is so interesting because that's where everything ultimately lands.

AF In the last few weeks I realized that I spend most of my time writing features for popular magazines such as *Dazed* and *i-D Magazine*, almost all of which are about the emerging trends in youth culture in Russia and Ukraine. I couldn't have imagined this five years ago. The New East movement seems so much bigger now, and it may be more geopolitically triggered than it seems. We recently hit twenty-five years since the fall of the Soviet Union, and in a way this has made everything feel very new.

Designer Anton Belinskiy and I have recently been joking about the latest image of post-Soviet youth culture: a second-hand market, skaters, and a rave next to a broken statue of Lenin. I would really like to get rid of that broken Lenin statue, at least. However, this new image that Belinskiy creates is very different from Rubchinskiy's: it's more forward-thinking, romantic, visually rich in terms of colors and references, and more playful, too—it has a different cultural foundation.[6]

MH › AF After viewing an exhibition by Danish artist Jesper Just at the EYE Filmmuseum in Amsterdam a few months ago, we're now finally starting to connect the dots about Tianducheng, the suburb of Hangzhou where Jamie XX's video is set. As you mention in the article we reference, the estate's architecture is in fact France-inspired, with a downscaled Eiffel Tower replica at its center. Nevertheless, we discussed its visuals as a New East phenomenon—a fiction of the Soviet past, whereas Tianducheng is simultaneously a Parisian fiction. In Just's video *Intercourses* (2013), a man aimlessly journeys along the edges of the ghost town, where the Versailles-style replicas quite abruptly

fade into wasteland. We're slightly overwhelmed by the layers of repetition and mirroring, by the overload of larger-than-life simulacra. Since the above conversation took place in 2016, Rubchinskiy has announced quitting seasonal collections. *GQ* published an article noting he "is a bit tired of doing season to season collections," and that he expressed a desire to switch to one-off projects. "Maybe that means a womenswear line sometime," the article continues, "or possibly more in the same vein as his high-profile collaboration with Burberry. In the short term though, Rubchinskiy wants to spend more time working on PACCBET, a line focused on skate wear that he runs with his friend (and pro skater) Tolia Titaev.[7] *Рассвет* = dawn, sunrise. In the logotype of Thrasher among others. These are all fictions.

MH › M.E.S.H. When we started working together on *Information Skies* (2016), we exchanged quite a few messages about Natalia Poklonskaya, the prosecutor of Crimea who was appointed by Putin as the interface for its annexation by Russia and who became an internet sensation. You seem very up-to-date about events in Russia and Ukraine. Why is that?

M.E.S.H. I was following a lot of the memes involving Natalia Poklonskaya and the Crimean/Donbas crises through a few European image boards. The visual language of these websites lends itself to the cartoonish revivification of anachronistic historical categories: dueling nationalist clades, rumored tsarists, cold warriors. I found it intriguing that a conflict can be two things at once—crude geopolitics with a surface dialectic that works itself out through images. It reminds me of Bratton in *The Sprawl*, talking about "subtitling the Real." I find it really unnerving to watch current events on this meta level of competing interfacial regimes—the narrowing of the gap between event and interpretation to the point where each new news tragedy is processed in real time, by everyone, often in hugely contradicting ways.

MH › M.E.S.H. While working together, we discussed composer Eduard Artemyev, who composed the music for Andrei Tarkovsky's film *Stalker* (1979). The key track for that score was "Meditation," which invokes an eerie, mountain-like, "Eastern" sense of cosmic spatiality, fitting with the film's originally planned shooting locations in Central Asia. Is Artemyev's music an influence for you, and if so, in what way?

47

M.E.S.H. I was only really aware of Artemyev's work through the Tarkovsky soundtracks, which I really love. I am drawn to the dissonant, spiritual side of music. I am also curious about the apocalyptic mysticism of composer and pianist Alexander Scriabin, and the interior, ascetic realms in composer and mystic G.I. Gurdjieff's music—just thinking of two other composers who represent some kind of Eastern "mystery" to Western ears, probably through diffusion of the New Age movement.

What prompted you to take a turn toward inner space with *Information Skies*? Does it come from a fatigue with the caustic nature of networked life?

MH › M.E.S.H. *Information Skies* developed into a film in which the image and the network have a different relationship than in, for example, *The Sprawl*, where everything feels quite manic while still being roughly structured around (the pretense of) documentary. There was a need for us to tell a story in a different way, creating a fictional "filter bubble" in which characters fight off an inner trauma by maintaining their own version of the truth. The term "filter bubble" was coined by internet activist Eli Pariser to denote how Facebook decides for you what you do and do not get to see. The direct inspirations for *Information Skies* came from working on *The Sprawl* and watching YouTube videos of pro-Russian fighters in the Donbas—an already pre-filtered experience of a filter bubble. The original title of the script was *Neo-Medievalism Explained*, and it explores how willingly and by design we can throw ourselves into conditions of not knowing or pretending not to know. Of course, *The Sprawl*—with its pursuit of fantasy narrative—left many questions unanswered. One of the strongest ones pertained to "belief": what if you really want to, or need to believe in something? We think of virtual reality as an extended phenomenon. By this we mean something that exists beyond the Oculus Rift and other technological/consumer units, and functions as a broader concept in society, as something that is going to challenge the idea of truth as we understand it, particularly in terms of legality. It's increasingly hard for adjudicating institutions to determine what reality is.

The situation with YouTube propaganda wars in Ukraine is ahead of the curve, not behind. This is not an ethnic conflict between warring peoples as a result of a state breakup, like in Yugoslavia in the 1990s. This is a fight over filter bubbles: both the idea of a "natural" Russian ownership of Ukraine, as well as the "original" mythologies of Ukraine as a ur-homeland, suppressed under Soviet rule, can be seen as fictions. This of course doesn't preclude them from also being realities.

You did this insanely beautiful score for Aleksandra Domanović's film *From yu to me* (2013–2014)—a documentary about Yugoslavian internet phenomena at the time of the war in the 1990s. The soundtrack accomplishes a similar type of futurism-with-archaic-elements that you have cited elsewhere as a mindset of yours. Is this the sonic equivalent of radical science-fiction films that do not show technology—like *Stalker*?

M.E.S.H. *From yu to me* was meant as a parallel history of the internet: it considers the development of networks against a backdrop of political disintegration. It relates to another project of Domanović's, *19:30* (2011), which grappled with the connections between the spread of rave music in former Yugoslavia, the evolution of computer graphics intersecting with nationalism via nightly news intros, etc. I think it's really fascinating when archaic symbols re-manifest themselves in high-tech form—when technology shapes itself to accommodate ancient drives.

"Radical science fiction that doesn't show technology" is a very interesting idea. I guess there is a similar tendency in electronic music to associate older synthesizer music and faithful recordings of vintage synthesizers with authenticity. I'm more interested in a form of extreme collage possible within digital audio software—the way spaces, moods, and instruments can be conjured and layered and remain convincing and "realistic" as sound objects. Maybe this type of "surface finish" relates somewhat to your work?

MH › M.E.S.H. We are more into "surface unfinished." Subtitles and interfacial ruins are working with and against the cinema layer. It's cinema for the interface.

1
Anastasiia Fedorova, "Watch: Is Jamie XX's Stunning New Video a Homage to Eastern European Bleakness?," *The Calvert Journal*, July 12, 2016, https://www.calvertjournal.com/features/show/6392/jamie-xx-gosh-easteurope. Last accessed on August 30, 2018.

2
Gosha Rubchinskiy, interview by Fedorova, "Gosha Rubchinskiy: Inside His Vertically Integrated Youth Universe," *032c*, June 14, 2016, https://032c.com/gosha-rubchinskiy-interview/. Last accessed on August 30, 2018.

3
Ibid.

4
"Being in Russia at the moment, I wouldn't call it nationalism. I'd call it the rise of patriotism and community. It feels positive." Ibid.

5
See, for example, Луна, "Он с тобою не…," video, 3:02, June 16, 2016, https://www.youtube.com/watch?v=jH3IWuAWau4. Last accessed on August 30, 2018.

6
Stas Galaktionov, "Anton Belinskiy S/S 17 Backstage," video, 2:58, October 5, 2016, https://www.youtube.com/watch?v=c5XY0-Q1gRw&feature=youtu.be. Last accessed on August 30, 2018.

7
Cam Wolf, "Gosha Runchinskiy Is Done Unless It's Not," *GQ*, April 4, 2018, https://www.gq.com/story/gosha-rubchinskiy-over-or-nah. Last accessed on August 30, 2018.

Anastasiia Fedorova
Anastasiia Fedorova is a writer and curator based in London. Fedorova finished her MA in journalism at the University of Westminster, London. She has written articles for, among others *Dazed*, *i-D Magazine*, *032c*, *Vice*, *Amuse*, *GARAGE*, *Wallpaper**, *Broadly*, *The Guardian*, *Highsnobiety*, *Vogue*, and *The Calvert Journal*. In her work Fedorova examines youth culture, the politics of contemporary fashion, identities in the global cultural space, immigrant consciousness, contemporary photography, and the new wave of creativity from Eastern Europe. In 2018, Fedorova curated an exhibition with "photography from the New East" called *Post-Soviet Visions: Image and Identity in the New Eastern Europe*, together with Ekow Eshun at Calvert 22 Foundation, London.

James Whipple/M.E.S.H.
James Whipple is an artist from California who lives in Germany. As M.E.S.H. he is a resident DJ at Berlin's Janus club night and has an ongoing series of releases on the record label PAN, including the albums *Hesaitix* (2017) and *Piteous Gate* (2015). He is known for a sound that can shift from the meditative to states of manic unease in its elaboration of the interior spaces of digital audio.

48

Home, 2014
music video for Holly Herndon
Courtesy of RVNG Intl.

Home

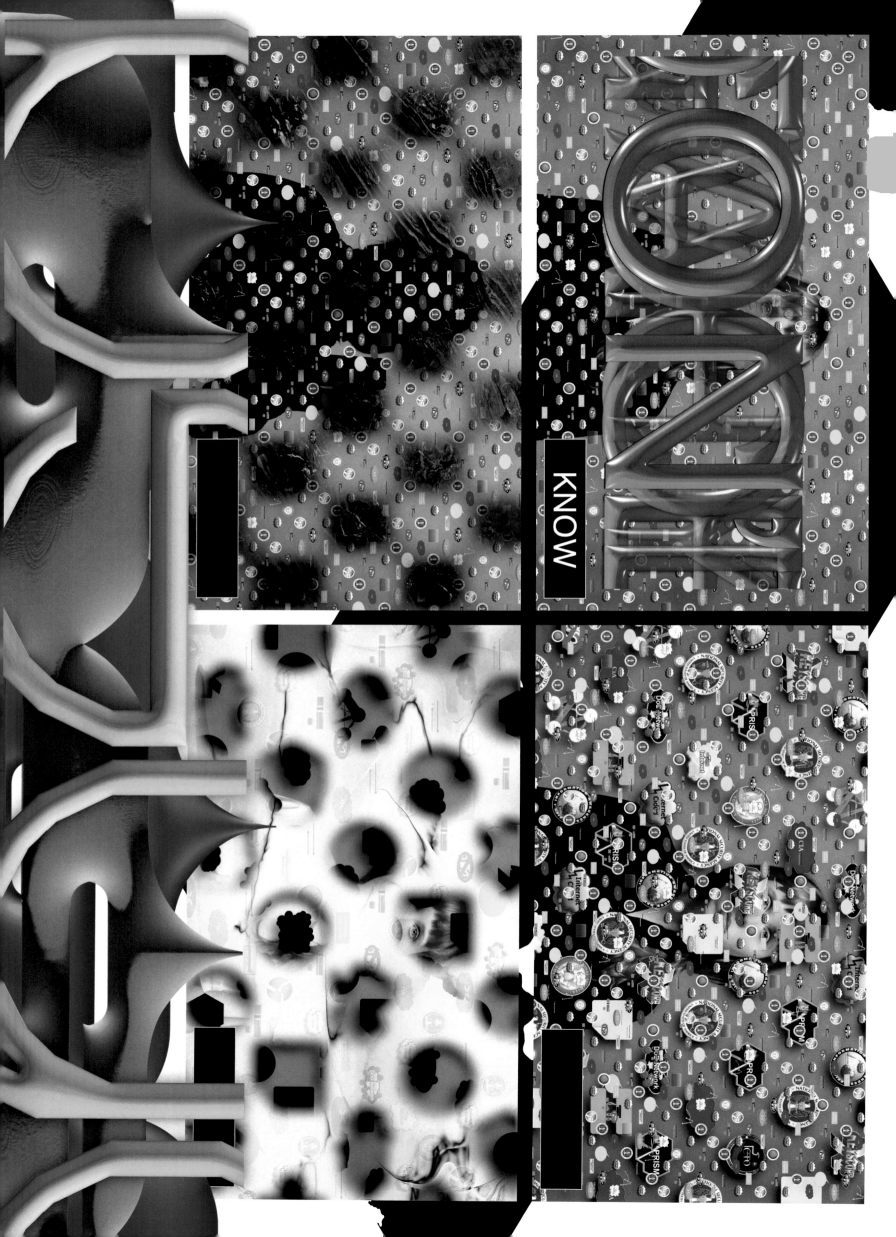

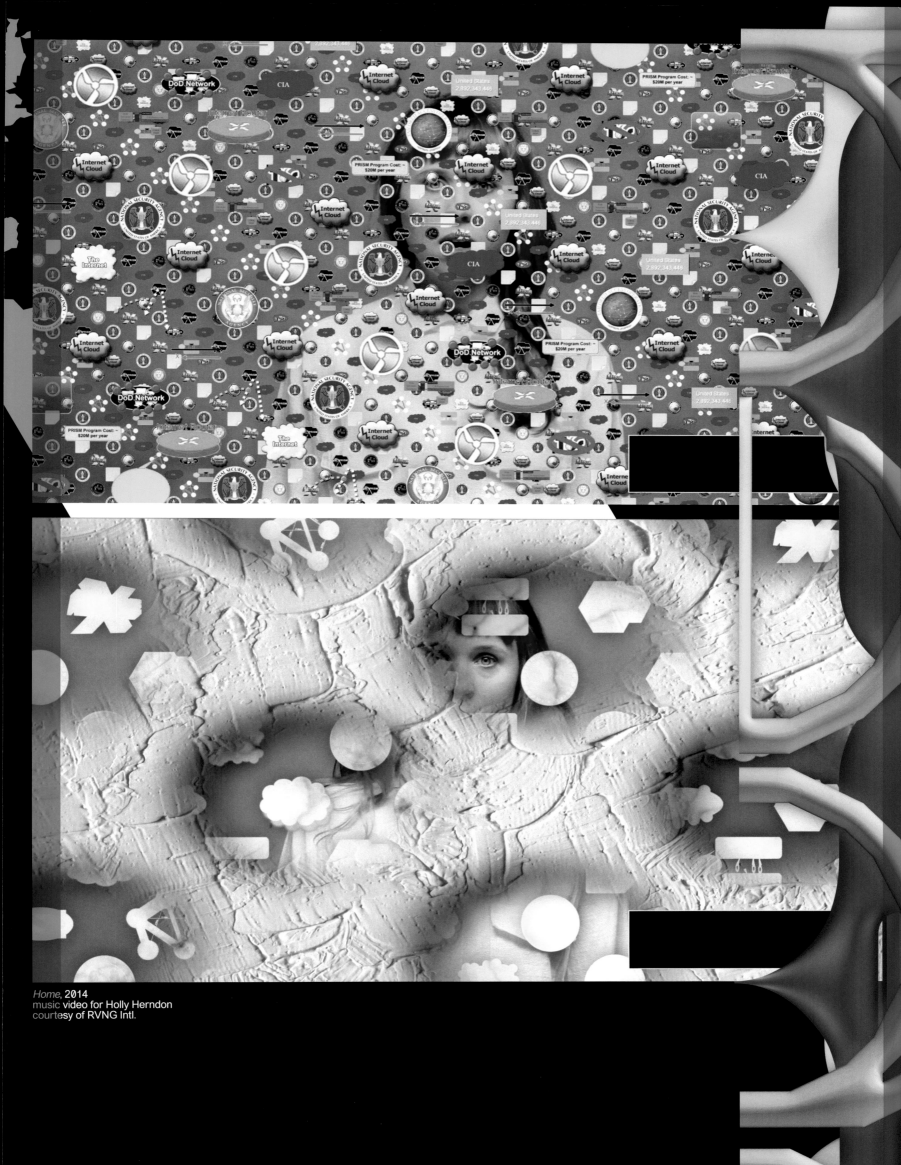

Home, 2014
music video for Holly Herndon
courtesy of RVNG Intl.

Home

Interference, 2015
music video for Holly Herndon
courtesy of 4AD/RVNG Intl.

Interferen

the eye of the storm.

new ways to love.

Interference

a platform.

Interference, 2015
music video for Holly Herndon
courtesy of 4AD/RVNG Intl.

we interfere,

Interference

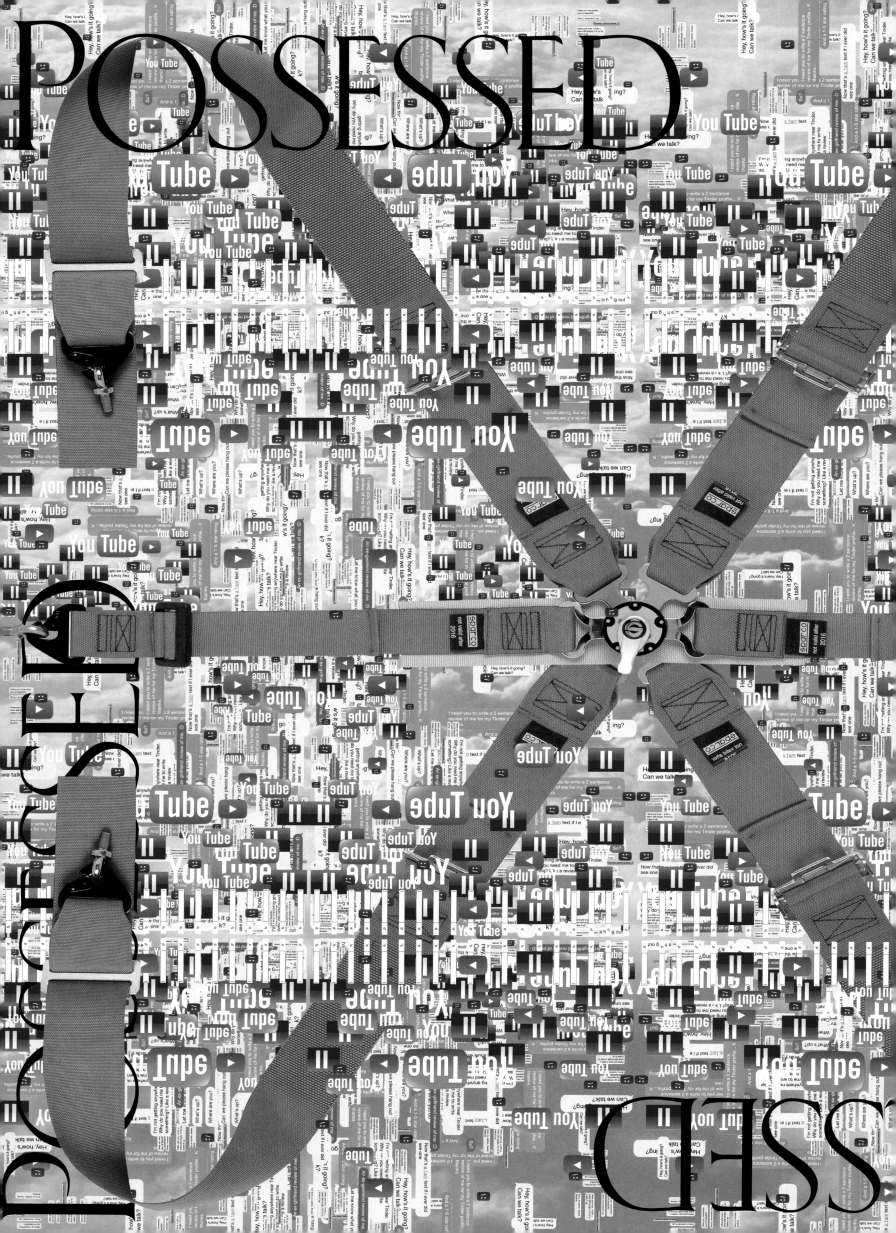

The Sprawl (Propaganda about Propaganda), 2015
fiction **documentary**, 70 min
Russian and Arabic with English subtitles

Possessed, 2018
scarf

next

REC

Art begins when one person, with the object of joining another or others

in one and the same feeling, invokes it once again in himself,

The Sprawl (Propaganda about Propaganda)

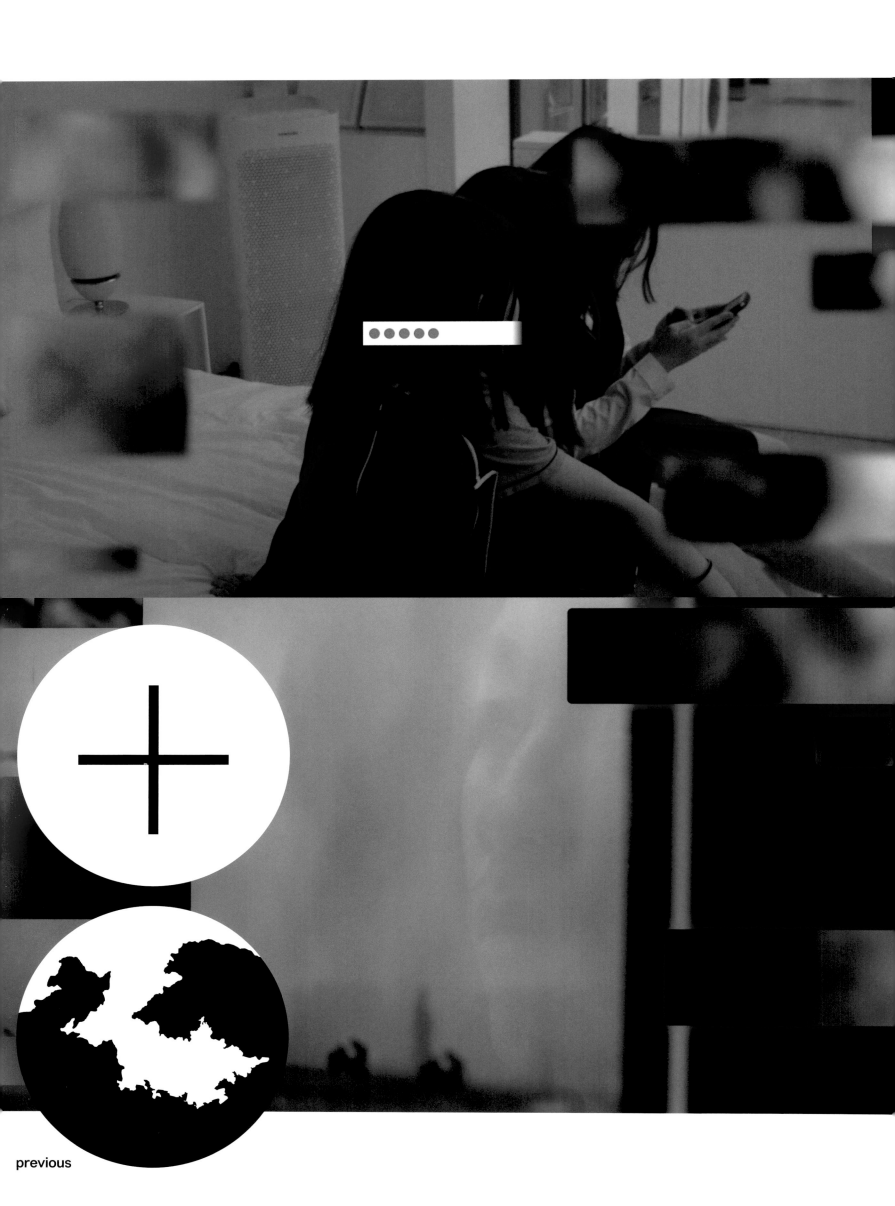

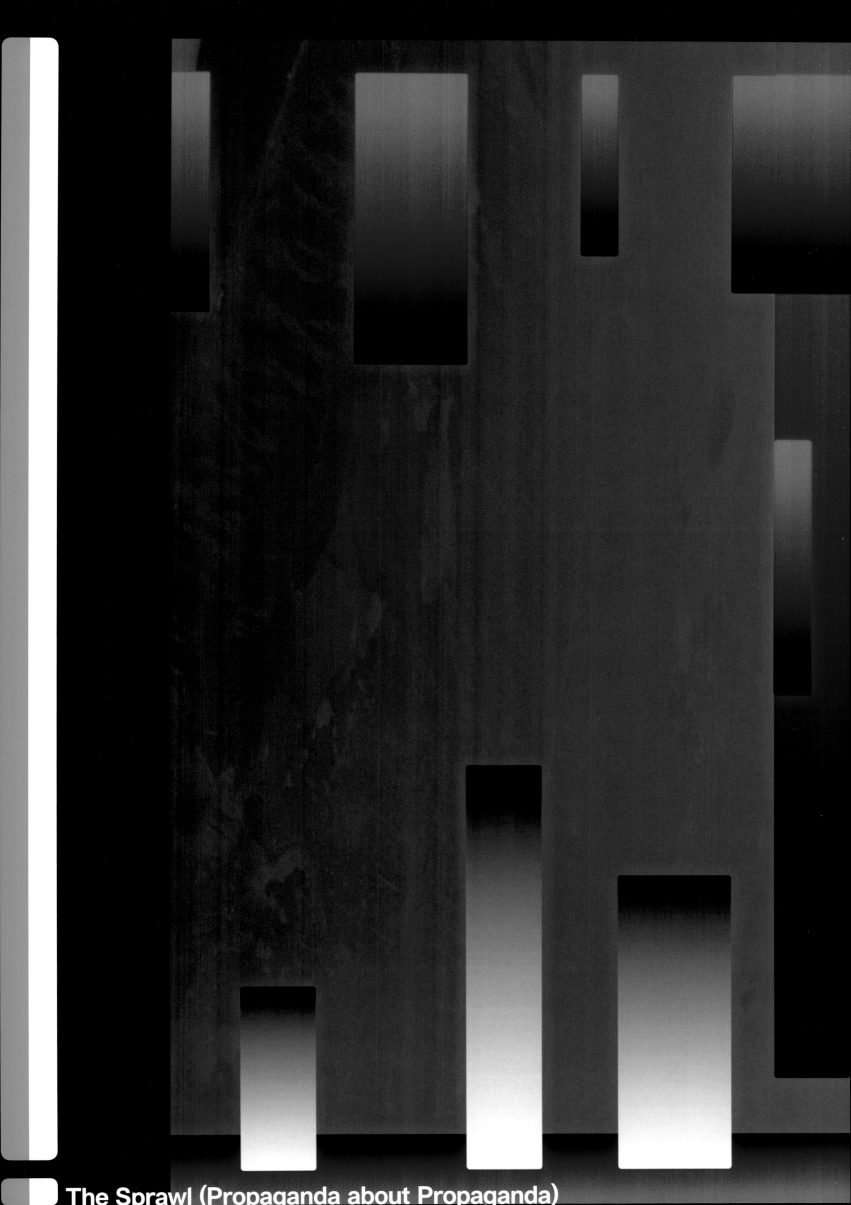

The Sprawl (Propaganda about Propaganda)

previous

THE DESIGN OF WHAT AND FOR WHAT
Benjamin H. Bratton ● Maria Lind ● MH
Stockholm, 2018

Maria Lind Metahaven, you have been responsible for the visual communication of Tensta konsthall since 2012. You have been seminal in shaping what could be called contemporary visuality. At the same time your artistic practice tries to capture and question our increasingly dire "now" in the most challenging ways, pointing to what might lie ahead. Benjamin H. Bratton is one of the most interesting thinkers today, whose book *The Stack: On Software and Sovereignty* (2016) has helped us think through planetary scale computation and algorithmic governance as key issues of the present and future.

The modern project involved a strong focus on the future, on futurisms of different kinds. However, for a while now, public discourse has been lacking in discussions on the future, and it's high time we bring it back. Yet we cannot conceive the future in the same way as we did in the past. Metahaven, what is your vision of the future?

MH History was the first subject that lent itself to post-production.

MH Today's politics run pre-modern, anti-internet, anti-liberal, and anti-diversity policies, exclusively on digital platforms.

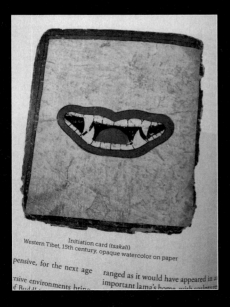

Initiation card (tsakalī)
Western Tibet, 15th century, opaque watercolor on paper

pensive, for the next age ranged as it would have appeared in important lama's home, with sculpture rsive environments bring f Rud

MH If Volkswagen and its diesel emissions scandal are the tip of the iceberg of the true contours of the Anthropocene—of cheating the regulatory frameworks around exhaust fumes, and thus eventually around man-made climate change itself—then Cambridge Analytica is simply a Volkswagen of post-truth.

MH The headings from a post by Foivos Dousos, "10 Tips for Content Producers in the Post-Truth Era" read:

1. Embrace alternative media outlets
2. Never use difficult concepts in your analysis
3. Avoid sourcing your claims
4. Construct an enemy
5. Implicate yourself in a tight dialectic with the Law
6. Indulge yourself in conspiracy theories
7. Invest in confusion
8. Show your weakness at every possible opportunity but at the same time never admit you are weak
9. Insist there is only one truth
10. Do not rely on stale memes
11. Sexualize working class masculinity
12. Forget cats
13. Lists, make more lists
14. Learn to Forgive
15. Drink Lots and lots of water.[1]

MH User-experience design in the "post-truth era" is about creating problems, instead of solving them. An interface's way of flattening realities, simplifying complexities, and antagonizing others, real, fake, or anything in between, translates into forms of "FOMO," and geopolitics alike. It translates into emotional States and a resurrection of the State, as a symbolic-fictional remnant of the idea of independence. The Council of Europe diagnoses the relationship between data and humans as an "Information Disorder,"[2] but we could equally call it a Comedy of the Interface.

Benjamin H. Bratton Indeed. First as tragedy, then as France. The rise of an ethnonationalist populism, we should understand, is a global phenomenon with global causes. And yet in each case, the locals either blame or congratulate themselves for their unique failure or accomplishment. But from Manila to Milwaukee, we see the same demographic voting patterns of urban, highly educated cosmopolitans, versus rural, less educated, monocultural nationalists or national monoculturalists. So even as globalization has been severing sovereignty from geography in uneven ways, we try to deal with the phenomenon one local eighteenth-century jurisdiction at a time. Yet, this is also when networks of city-states seem decisively detached from their national hosts. For those from the District 13s of our real life *The Hunger Games* (2012), the city itself may be seen as a source of arbitrary power, and in this way, urbanization itself is the focus of the populist backlash.

BHB The design of what and for what? *Tomorrowland* or *Mad Max*, *Wakanda* or *Elysium*?

BHB So while there are many reasons to hold in suspicion those whose main entitlement is to stand earnestly against the real on behalf of preferred folktales, we may do the same for those whose most important alibi is simple futurism.

MH Spiritual, sensual, dangerous, beautiful, pop, energetic, smile, continuum between past and future, sharp-toothed eye candy… The red moon rises in your mouth.

Hiatus
Malka Older

@lqwrkm#)_$*!
Hi all, just letting you know that I'm going to be going on social media hiatus for a few months.
> @a,lr24o,
> Have a good time, we'll see you when you get back!
> @,okrnzmr
> Nooooooooooooooooooooooooooooooooo you are one of the few things I love about this horrible website
> @btmwtm4zo
> Good luck! Breathe real air, smell real flowers, DO THINGS! Hugs!

@RaymondChandlerBot
We make the finest packages in the world, Mr Marlowe. The stuff inside is mostly junk.

@a,lr24o,
Does anyone know how to create columns in Word?
> @,okrnzmr
> here's something in format?
> @a,lr24o,
> Yeah but that makes consecutive columns not discrete
> @a,lr24o,
> I mean when you do that the end of the first one continues up to the top of the second one
> @,okrnzmr
> Ah. Maybe a table?

@btmwtm4zo
So I am in a strange city tonight, a city not completely unknown to me (or the rest of the world) but one that I don't know well. Let's call it NYC. I am here for a conference, and after it was over I walked alone to a restaurant I know.

@,okrnzmr
#Mood
Media unavailable. Please try again when you have access to up-to-date hardware.

@btmwtm4zo
It was almost empty and I sat at the bar and ordered. I was just ˜slightly drunk, there were cocktails at the end of the conference. I thought about how wonderful it is that I could sit there, a woman alone, some bar seats down from a man alone and another man alone...

@#jlwk53%
tfw you try to email someone you know #onhere and you can't remember their name and they recently changed their handle so you can't search

@NuruddinFarahBot
She wondered then if she had ever been on the right track. She had been reticent all her life, because it turned out that her opinions were different from what others expected. "That proves either that I am an exceptional idiot, or the reverse."

@a,lr24o,
Heading to Kiev tomorrow on a work trip anyone know anyone there?
> @r#%$˜
> You should read https://smile.amazon.com/Lazarus-Project-Aleksandar-Hemon-ebook/dp/B0017SV0IU/ref=sr_1_1?ie=UT-F8&qid=1528687080&sr=8-1&key-words=the+lazarus+project+book

@btmwtm4zo
...that I could sit there and not be particularly worried and not lose my reputation or even be concerned about it and no one thought it the least bit strange or wrong. I thought about walking alone in the streets of a strange city and about wandering alone #onhere
> TWEET DELETED
> Due to content that violates our use policy (see cf.124k:12) this tweet has been purged and expunged as if its vile content had never touched the unblemished layer of our interface.

TWEET DELETED
Due to content that violates our use policy (see cf.124k:12) this tweet has been purged and expunged as if its vile content had never touched the unblemished layer of our interface.
TWEET DELETED
Due to content that violates our use policy (see cf.124k:12) this tweet has been purged and expunged as if its vile content had never touched the unblemished layer of our interface.

@btmwtm4zo
I thought about the freedom this gave me. I didn't particularly want to strike up a conversation with the nearest man but I wasn't averse to it either, so I thought about what I would say if he did, what identity I might invent.
> TWEET DELETED
> Due to content that violates our use policy (see cf.124k:12) this tweet has been purged and expunged as if its vile content had never touched the unblemished layer of our interface.

 The linked image cannot be displayed. The file may have been moved, renamed, or deleted. Verify that the link points to the correct file and location.

Google
Search: Propaganda
Listed by most relevant

Dictator™Brand Hair Dye for Men! Get the autocratic mane you deserve!
> Promoted

FreedomPropaganda Your all-in-one service for burnishing your name and your fame!
> Promoted

News or Propaganda? How smart people evaluate their news sources.
> Promoted

Dictionary
prop·a·gan·da
präpə'gandə/ noun

1. derogatory: information, especially of a biased or misleading nature, used to promote or publicize a particular political cause or point of view. "he was charged with distributing enemy propaganda"
synonyms: information, promotion, advertising, publicity, spin, More

2. a committee of cardinals of the Roman Catholic Church responsible for foreign missions, founded in 1622 by Pope Gregory XV.

Famous Quotes:
"The propaganda that has here reached such a state of perfection covers all aspects of existence and constantly surprises one by finding new fields of endeavor. But once a new generation has grown up that has wholly emancipated itself from the tradition of a union between word and fact, the substance of the word will have been juggled out of it, and it will be like paper money which is nowhere backed by gold, and the propaganda itself will have lost its savor"
– Isak Dinesen

#VagueGram #Skies #Nodes

66

68

BHB The world itself is a model open to design and designation, not by false mastery, but because the planet uses humans and other things to know itself and to remake itself. We are the medium, not the message, you might say.

BHB Such a design should itself be understood as a kind of progressive alternative perspective to much of mainstream design culture, and as alternative to alternatives as well. Design is, among other things, some sort of magic way of thinking that involves sticky notes and Sharpies and colored bean bags. It's also a means by which pathological relationships to material culture are made more efficient and more delightful, and we are the worse off for it.

BHB This should not in any way suggest disengagement. The prevalence of techniques—for the modeling of ideal options, risk patterns, and plotted outcomes—underscores that speculation itself is not some supplemental or magical process. The global economy itself functions on speculative models of the near and long-term future. We are, in different ways, governed by models of the future already, and if so, what then?

BHB It is important to not confuse descriptive and predictive models. Heliocentrism as opposed to geocentrism is a descriptive model. We have predictive models that are more like those of Wall Street, which are meant to try to anticipate transformations of complex systems, and capitalize on those bets. Predictive models don't have to be true. They just have to work. Like a hammer doesn't have to be true, it just has to work.

BHB About a month ago I was doing an interview with a Chinese journalist and he kept interrupting me. He said, "I'm sorry to be Satan's lawyer, but could you explain this, this, this, and this?" I finally asked him what he meant, and finally figured out he meant devil's advocate.

BHB As I've said in relationship to other kinds of fast-food futurisms, such as TED: in our culture speaking about the future is sometimes a way to say things about the present—critical, utopian, projective, pragmatic—that would otherwise be unsayable. And too often it is, as we are all aware, an alibi for saying nothing at all. That future is where skateboards hover; ambient fields and graphical user interfaces are slightly slicker. It's a rhetorical sink where half-baked marketing plans usurp the place where actual ideas were supposed to go.

BHB Given this we might expect a design that is more intellectually and politically rigorous to resist or even eliminate futurity altogether as a key concept. Some would insist (wrongly) that design should focus instead on the most "at hand" immediate frames of spatial and temporal reference and so deal coming conditions largely through an ensuing survivalist aesthetics. "There is no time, and there is only this place," might be the rationale for this emergency interventionism. At worst, this also might be a primitivist disavowal of abstraction itself on behalf of an imaginary restoration.

BHB It has been hinted at that until recent times, cognitive maps and systemic unfolding might have been in conflict, but at least the ground underneath somehow felt solid. Design, as we know, can adhere to small, medium, large, and extra-large spatial scales: a single object, a large architecture, urbanism, and so forth. And you can also limit it to very short- or long-term durations: now, later, much later, etc.—suited to instantaneous user response, the next launch cycle, the life cycle of a city, the Anthropocene. But there can also be very small-scale projects with very long durations, and they're just as important in many ways as very large-scale projects that might have had much shorter lifespans than originally thought, like Kenzo Tange's megastructures.

BHB As a way to manage the vertigo of these detachments, we might imagine a matrix of spatial and temporal scales. It's not here and now versus there and then, it's also here and then and there and now.

BHB It takes a special kind of anthropocentric naivete to fully entertain the idea that making all design human-scale would be a long-term solution to anything other than the most pedestrian problems. Just as for astronomy, biology, and chemistry, the futures that are probably worth designing are those that exceed human phenomenology.

BHB Artificial intelligence (AI) can be a heterogeneous collection of sensing and signaling technologies that augment diverse and complex systems including distributed emergent cognition. It's more a synthetic rainforest than a robot teddy bear.

BHB One of the ways in which I've found it useful in talking generally about AI models, what they mean, and how they work, is to relate them to what we know of cinematic AI, for example, Jean-Luc Godard's *Alphaville* (1965), with Alpha 60 arguably the first cinematic AI and Andrei Tarkovsky's *Solaris* (1972). Both provide very different models of what we might think about AI. For *Alphaville*, AI is a city-state entity, personified with the cranky voice of a very heavy smoker. He is a centralized, meddlesome, single point of failure, personally contemptuous of the humans in his domain, a telepathic supervisor pulling the strings from above. It is a kind of new-wave influencing machine film for film noir schizophrenics. And he is a he, an ancestor of Siri and Samantha. As a model of urban-scale AI, Alpha 60 is a distracted dictator, capricious and vengeful, closer to the God of the Old Testament than any smiling assistant.

@btmwtm4zo
I decided I would be a pirate. Sure, why not. I am an actual pirate. (did I mention I was slightly drunk?) I sail the...Hudson? and steal shit from rich yachters. I just want to spin a story, I want to see if I can pull it off, for fun.

@btmwtm4zo
So I'm all ready with my pirate story. I mean I've got the monologue all thought out. I'm not going to force it on anyone, I'm not that drunk, but if dude turns to me and says "What do you do?" I'm ready.

@#914u23
#foodporn #virtualreality #tasteit
Media unavailable. Please try again when you have access to up-to-date hardware.

@#jlwk53%
Doing the thing #doing #affirmation

@btmwtm4zo
I'm psyched up, too. This is improv, this is creativity, this is fluid identities.

@3,oi539
Have you ever noticed how much ad copy DOESN'T ACTUALLY MEAN ANYTHING?

@AnnaAkhmatovaBot
We learned not to meet anymore,
We don't raise our eyes to one another,

@#jlwk53%
REGISTER TO VOTE This is so important.
http://*rwi1L4j*/ LatestOutrageousOverreach_longread

@btmwtm4zo
So he turns and looks at me.

@btmwtm4zo
AND I KNOW HIM.

@PeterDruckerBot
Most leaders I've known were neither born nor made. They were self-made.

@3,oi539
I had pickles for breakfast.

@btmwtm4zo
I fucking know him.

@ElizabethBishopBot
Then practice losing farther, losing faster:
places, and names, and where it was you meant to travel. None of these will bring disaster.

@,okrnzmr
WATCHING OUR VERY DREAMS http://*&$$$$.com/TheNewSurveillance-IsItBetterOrWorseThan1984_read

@btmwtm4zo
Not only that. I know him because I slept with his wife.
    @api3jk3l(.)
    Bihhhhh!!!!!
    @btmwtm4zo
    In my youth, comay.

@btmwtm4zo
This was a long time ago, actually before they were married but they were already dating, and...yeah.

    @#914u23
    #travelporn
    #oldschool
    #retrocamera
    #fronteras

@btmwtm4zo
That's right.
@btmwtm4zo
I AM A MFing PIRATE.

@*!(#(%)4 Hivemind: can anyone help me identify the person in this picture?

@a,lr24o,
Folks, I'm going on a social media heist for the next three months.

@a,lr24o,
*hiatus! social media hiatus! autocorrect wyd??
    @5,/lm3502-
    LOL I love the idea of a social media heist
    @,okrnzmr
    a /three month/ social media heist
    @1%N##!%
    Are you stealing their social networks?

@qp(96)2˜#m
You all ready for another border story?
    @,okrnzmr
    Oh no again? I'm so sorry
    @qp(96)2˜#m
    At this point I expect it but stilllllll

@qp(96)2˜#m
So I'm off a 16-hour flight, another 30 minutes to taxi around, get to the gate, and unload all three levels of the plane

@qp(96)2˜#m
Naturally it's a terrific line for immigration control, even after we've all split up for the kiosks after the biometric gates. I think I was standing there for about 45 minutes, bladder full, bag on shoulder, eyes blurry with dry airplane air and no sleep

@5,/lm3502-
[Emoji representing the emotion that there are no emojis to represent your emotion]

@qp(96)2˜#m
I think a lot about the architecture of these spaces, these monstrous halls subdivided into lines snaking like cramped & coiled intestines, the ways they signal control and order and promote meekness.

@5,/lm3502-
This shit that's going on now is unprecedented, unbelievable. Have you all seen this? They're watching us while we sleep
http://*&$$$$.com/TheNewSurveillance-IsItBetterOr-WorseThan1984_read
    @,okrnzmr
    OMG
    @ia,43m
    This is not for real
    @5,/lm3502-
    It very much is my friend
    @ia,43m
    Is not.
    @5,/lm3502-
    It is! Did you read the article? Completely Verified™
    @ia,43m
    Did YOU read the article? It's bullshit.
    @5,/lm3502-
    Is not.
    @ia,43m
    utter bullshit
    @btmwtm4zo
    I wrote the article. It's for real.

@qp(96)2˜#m
Finally I am gestured to the counter where a man sits high above my standing petitionary body, examining screens and readouts invisible to me and perusing the documents that, according to the State, legitimize my existence and physical presence in this geography.

@qp(96)2˜#m
"Been away for a while," he says, flipping through the pages emblazoned with patriotic ghosts. "What have you been up to?"

68

@vpi3jk3l(.)
Come on Sprats!

@btmwtm4zo
But that's not what I'm thinking as I look at him.

@#914u23
#FoodPorn #VR #JusticeForAllStadium #SpratsVsConks #GoSprats
Media unavailable. Please try again when you have access to up-to-date hardware.

@#jlwk53%
anyone else up late?

@btmwtm4zo
No. I lose all my mojo. I lose my entire invented identity. I lose all the confidence and badassery I have earned in the ten years since I've seen this man.

@btmwtm4zo
"Oh hey, hi, it's me, um, how've you, um, been?"

@btmwtm4zo
Legit nervous laugh and everything.

@RabihAlameddineBot
If you read these pages and think I'm the way I am because I lived through a civil war, you can't feel my pain. If you believe you're not like me because one woman, and only one, Hannah, chose to be my friend, then you're unable to empathize.

@ vpi3jk3l(.)
WHAT????

@sp@rtsB@!!
Watch @&$#%$'s incredible score #SpratsVsConks

@AntonioMuñozMolinaBot
Eres cada una de las personas diversas que has sido y también las que imaginabas que serías, y cada una de las que nunca fuiste, y las que deseabas fervorosamente ser y ahora agradeces no haber sido.

@#914u23
Grrrrrrr #Sprats

@btmwtm4zo
And he smiles and says some blahblah.

@P@3T@S
Stay invisible/Stay gapped/
Stay away/Stray maps/
Stray kids stray cats/

@btmwtm4zo
I don't even remember now honestly.

@WarsanShireBot
Look at all these borders foaming at the mouth with bodies broken and desperate

@vpi3jk3l(.)
ugh.

@btmwtm4zo
I remember that I didn't ask after her.

@#jlwk53%
Oh no what's going on?

@btmwtm4zo
And he didn't offer. Although there were a couple of awkward silences where one of us was about to automatically and then shut it down.

@Medi@LiteracyBot
Remember to check your sources and think through the logic of their claims

@8abrje#˜
Watching the news #PrayFor

@1%N##!%
Aw my little sib is hanging out with me to watch the game #Sprats #Sibs #Interactive #Wave
Media unavailable. Please try again when you have access to up-to-date hardware.

@vpi3jk3l(.)
LOL that commercial for cryogenics they really went there

@btmwtm4zo
I was so distressed I walked out on my bill. Totally unintentional but

@btmwtm4zo
I AM A MFING PIRATE

@#jlwk53%
When disasters happen, remember to be responsible about your social media usage #ThinkBeforeYouRetweet

@btmwtm4zo
but then when I realized I had to go back, lurk outside peeking in the windows until I was sure dude had left, and very apologetically pay up.

@vpi3jk3l(.)
Come on Sprats!

@cvr%˜&Yken#
You need this story right now http://˜#8%(.com/heart-warmingtaleof...

@qp(96)2˜#m
Reader, I sheherazaded his ass.

@qp(96)2˜#m
I told him about the river border I crossed on a ferry with immigration control in the center of the cabin and how I had to go back and forth on the river three times while I waited in line to cross the line in the ferry. I told him about

@P!K$˜#˜
What is even happening here?

@P!K$˜#˜
!!!!!!!!!

@qp(96)2˜#m
matching refugee camps meeting across the desert border marked only by GPS, which none of the residents could access because in both countries proof of citizenship was required to purchase a smartphone. About sunsets and sunrises seen from a mountain claimed by two nations.

@vpi3jk3l(.)
WHAT????

@G24rse¡an
I cannot even. How did they DO that????

@a¡lr24o,
I AM BACK FROM HIATUS JUST TO SAY HOW RIDICULOUS THAT SCORE WAS
　@5¡/lm3502-
　I knew you'd be back
@a¡lr24o,
I could not stand to watch this game without my tweeps! but then I'm gone again lol

@qp(96)2˜#m
The line behind me stretched longer and longer. Everyone from my flight had gone through, my suitcase waited alone in lost and found quarantine. More flights arrived, their passengers cleared customs, went home and slept and still I talked.

@P!K$˜#˜
FFS SPRATS!!

@qp(96)2˜#m
Finally I stopped for breath and he said "Welcome back"

@qp(96)2˜#m
Punctuated with a decisive page stamp

@vpi3jk3l(.)
ugh.

@ia¡43m
The shouting on my feed is almost enough to make me wish I cared about #sports
　@#jlwk53%
　sports fans have such
　exciting lives don't
　they

@G24rse¡an
Dang. WHY, Sprats??

@qp(96)2˜#m
I sailed through, head tilted towards the sound-proofing tile in the ceiling, and got flagged by customs under their proud flags

@qp(96)2˜#m
They wanted provenance papers on a plastic Mickey Mouse alarm clock with Mao hands.

@vpi3jk3l(.)
LOL that commercial for cryogenics they really went there

@qp(96)2˜#m
I told them I bought it on Wang Fu Jin at a shop with a thousand more identical ones, next to another shop with a thousand more, next to another shop with a thousand more

@qp(96)2˜#m
They confiscated it and waved me through.

@a¡lr24o,
Going back on hiatus, byeeee

@ia¡43m
oh this looks bad
　@P!K$˜#˜
　What's going on?

@5¡/lm3502-
Social media: I'm out of here. #Peace.

@¡okrnzmr I've decided after much reflection to take some time off from this website, maybe all websites. I don't have a specific length of time in mind, let's just say indefinite. Maybe enough time for things to get better. I hope to see you on the other side.
　@1%N##!%
　I hope it works out
　for you.

@q5n25*˜%)
Insomnia like
Media unavailable. Please try again when you have access to up-to-date hardware.

@P!K$˜#˜
What is even happening here?

@6order!ines
15 Gorgeous Border Regions Where The Line Is Uncertain http://6order!ines.org/15_Gorgeous-Border_Regions_Uncertain_Which-Side

@1%N##!%
You would think they would have learned what to do with the ball by now. #Sprats

@P!K$˜#˜
!!!!!!!!!

@7akla$#)$
YOOOOOOOOO!!!!!!

@sp@rtsB@!!
Watch @&$#%$'s incredible score #SpratsVsConks

@IsakDinesenBot
Truth, like time, is an idea arising from, and dependent upon, human intercourse.

@7akla$#)$
and OF COURSE they proceed to flake

@q5n25*˜%)
Can't stop thinking about this thing that happened on the subway today #twittertropes

@7akla$#)$
Life of a #SpratsFan

@P@3T@S
Stay invisible/Stay gapped/
Stay away/Stray maps/
Stray kids stray cats/

@90ARJ%*
I am having A DAY folks.
　@7akla$#)$
　Sending puppies
　Media unavailable.
　Please try again when
　you have access to
　up-to-date hardware.

@1%N##!%
DM me if you need to talk – it's been too long since we've chatted anyway.
　@90ARJ%*
　It HAS! DMing now.

@P!K$˜#˜
FFS SPRATS!!

@q5n25*˜%)
there was this woman standing on that space between train cars. I still am not sure if she was a performance artist or what

@Medi@LiteracyBot
Remember to check your sources and think through the logic of their claims

@90ARJ%*
There is a baaaaaad date going on a little farther down the bar where I'm drowning my extreme irritation

@8abrje#˜
Watching the news #PrayFor

@&˜Iskre(
#cooking #foodporn #healthy
Media unavailable. Please try again when you have access to up-to-date hardware

@q5n25*˜%)
She didn't seem to be hanging on, just swaying with the train. I don't think she had a sign, there was something written on her T-shirt but I couldn't read it.

@&˜Iskre(
Stay safe out there y'all

@7akla$#)$
LOOOOOL the #Sprats memes right now

@90ARJ%*
oh shit just saw the news ¡–(

@q5n25*˜%)
Then I turned around and she was gone. She wasn't in my car, and I didn't see her in the other. I've been refreshing the news all night to see if there was an accident on the tracks somewhere and nothing.

Malka Older
Malka Older is a science-fiction writer, poet, researcher, and humanitarian worker based in Washington, D.C. She is a PhD candidate at the Institut d'Études Politiques de Paris, where she studies the dynamics of multi-level governance and disaster response. Older has an undergraduate degree in literature from Harvard University, Boston and an MA in international relations and economics from the Johns Hopkins University School of Advanced International Studies, Washington, D.C. In 2015, Older was Senior Fellow for Technology and Risk at the Carnegie Council for Ethics in International Affairs, New York. *Infomocracy* (2016) is Older's debut science-fiction novel, the first in her trilogy "The Centenal Cycle," which includes *Null States* (2017) and *State Tectonics* (2018). Older's writing can be found in various magazines as well as in the poetry anthology *My Cruel Invention* (2015) and the anthology of writing by female aid workers *Chasing Misery* (2014).

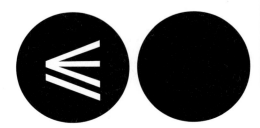

Malka Older

69

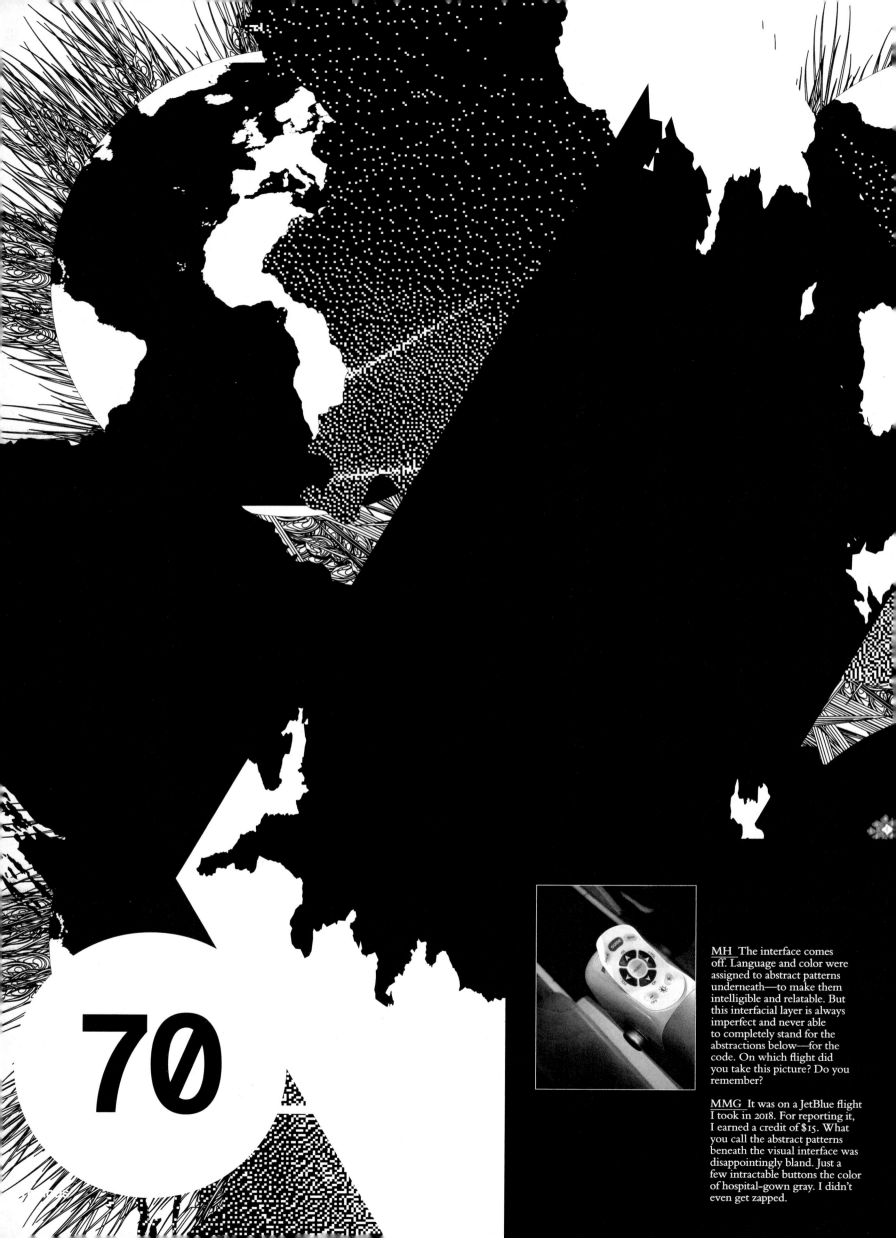

70

MH The interface comes off. Language and color were assigned to abstract patterns underneath—to make them intelligible and relatable. But this interfacial layer is always imperfect and never able to completely stand for the abstractions below—for the code. On which flight did you take this picture? Do you remember?

MMG It was on a JetBlue flight I took in 2018. For reporting it, I earned a credit of $15. What you call the abstract patterns beneath the visual interface was disappointingly bland. Just a few intractable buttons the color of hospital-gown gray. I didn't even get zapped.

Tuned to an Undead Channel
Ana Teixeira Pinto

"The sky above the port wa
of television, tuned to a dea
is the opening line of Willian
Neuromancer (1984).

Writing from his prison cell circa 1930, Marxist philosopher Antonio Gramsci described the crisis of his time as a political hiatus, originally translated from the Italian as: "The old [system] is dying and the new cannot be born. In this interregnum a great variety of morbid symptoms appear." The sentence was later translated as: "The old world is dying, and the new world struggles to be born: now is the time of monsters."[1] This rather loose rendition became wildly popular in the aftermath of Brexit and Trump's electoral victory because it seems to perfectly capture our present condition. But something got lost in translation, namely Gramsci's description of the crisis as a deadlock or impasse—a downtime if you will. In December 2016, German economist Wolfgang Streeck expressed a similar view in an interview with *The Guardian*.[2] Capitalism, he argued, is dead, but there is no political will to move its corpse out of the way. While the rot takes its course, the future hangs in limbo for what will likely be a decade-long sink. In Metahaven's film *Possessed* (2018), this downtime comes into sight as an atemporal form of temporality. An abandoned airport in Croatia— a space of hypermobility rendered immobile— populated by sleep-walking urban tribes and overgrown shrubs,

1
See Antonio Gramsci, *Selections from the Prison Notebooks of Antonio Gramsci*, ed. and trans. Quinton Hoare and Geoffrey Nowell Smith, New York: International Publishers, 1971, 75–276.
2
Wolfgang Streeck, interview by Aditya Chrakrabortty, "Wolfgang Streeck: The German Economist Calling Time on Capitalism," *The Guardian*, December 9, 2016, https://www.theguardian.com/books/2016/dec/09/wolf-gang-streeck-the-german-economist-calling-time-on-capitalism. Last accessed on August 10, 2018.
3
See McKenzie Wark, "Renotopia," *Harvard Design Magazine* 41 (Fall/Winter 2015), http://www.harvarddesignmagazine.org/issues/41/renotopia. Last accessed on August 10, 2018.
4
Ibid.
5
See Felix Stalder, "State Technologies: Data," lecture, *Now Is the Time of Monsters*, Haus der Kulturen der Welt, Berlin, March 23, 2017, https://www.hkw.de/en/app/mediathek/audio/55710. Last accessed on August 13, 2018.
6
Jonathan Crary, *Suspensions of Perception: Attention, Spectacle, and Modern Culture*, Cambridge, MA: MIT Press, 1999, 79.
7
Ibid.
8
See Alexander Galloway, "Are Some Things Unrepresentable?," *Theory, Culture & Society* 28, no. 7/8 (2011): 85–102.
9
Paraphrasing Fredric Jameson, "Cognitive Mapping," in Lawrence Grossberg and Cary Nelson, eds., *Marxism and the Interpretation of Culture*, Chicago: University of Illinois Press, 1988, 347–357.
10
Lauren Berlant, *Cruel Optimism*, Durham, NC: Duke University Press, 2011, 5.
11
Ibid.

MMG The unsupervised child and the uncaged bird, unleashed onto a world of abundant and cheap consumer items. I love this image. It raises many questions. Is there a coterminous range of intellect between a young child and a seasoned parrot? What are they thinking about what they see? How does their cogitating compare? Based on heuristic principles alone, and no scientific study I can point to, I wager that the child interprets what she perceives differently because of how she can reach for and use these objects. Parrots don't wear shoes or get their hair styled. That can prove a major impediment to interpretation. But at the level of perception, how wide is the difference really?

appears as something akin to the "Zone"—an enigmatic and somewhat sentient site whose access is restricted because the laws of reality don't apply there—in Andrei Tarkovsky's *Stalker* (1979). This impression of suspended animation is reinforced in the recurring image of a female character lying in a bed with a metal frame, and other cinematic idioms, which suggest a state of semi-awakeness, as if to signal that our stretched-out present is characterized by an epistemological—and by extension emotional—disorientation.

As media theorist McKenzie Wark notes, the "great socialist utopia that actually got built is service infrastructure."[3] Electrical grids, rail transport, municipal maintenance functions, and "one of the truly great, realized utopias: running water and sewerage," are the "lines that keep chaos and violence at bay."[4] The digital turn, on the other hand, seems to correlate with a "denial of the necessity for large, infrastructural utopias." It promotes, instead, what architecture theorist Keller Easterling termed "extrastatecraft," a plethora of non-state forces that have attained enough authority to be able to undertake the building of infrastructure, and what design theorist Benjamin H. Bratton—one of Metahaven's interview subjects in *The Sprawl (Propaganda about Propaganda)* (2015)—called "the stack," an "accidental" computational megastructure that, in addition to its technical functions, operates as a form of informal governance. Either fully privatized or semi-private (e.g., public-private partnerships or PPPs), these forces work in tandem, producing "zones" of financial accumulation and prosperous *technopoleis*, but also their obverse: vast areas of resource extraction, wholly deprived of infrastructural investment or life-sustaining resources.

In Metahaven's *Hometown* (2018) these increasingly stark contrasts take on the form of allegory. Filmed in Beirut and Kiev, *Hometown* is composed of two distinct but interlayered visual elements. Images of derelict facades infused with historical meaning, amidst urban decay, buildings left unbuilt and overgrown weeds and shrubs, are juxtaposed with a glossy interface-like surface, reminiscent of liquid crystals with intense pink, green, and blue hues. A story about a crushed caterpillar is told repeatedly. A young woman captures and briefly holds a butterfly in her hands before setting it free.

In insects and arthropods, as well as some amphibians and crustaceans, the embryo can develop into an organism dissimilar to its progenitors, before, in an abrupt and conspicuous way, molting to become a mature creature. Caterpillars and butterflies, one could say, occupy a position at, or on both sides of, a boundary or threshold—they are what one could call liminal animals. Liminality also has spatial and temporal dimensions. The characters in *Hometown* speak of a meeting, which will take place at dawn (between day and night) at a point at which there is a fork in the road (a liminal place, between two diverging paths). The protagonists of the film, two young women Lera and Ghina, are themselves in the midst of a liminal stage, as teenagers transitioning into adulthood. But liminality is not necessarily limited to one single entity or moment, it's a process that can affect a whole society—unlike the transition from childhood to adulthood—but there are no official rites of passage. The two cities, scarred by their recent history, blend into one ghostly urbanscape, where life seems to grind to a halt, and inhabitants are somewhat pensive or bereft of vitality. In contradistinction to the gritty, grayish tones of the captured footage, the graphic overlay seems eerily vibrant, pulsating with a promise of digital psychedelia and informational transcendence. In *Information Skies* (2016), another young woman, wearing a virtual reality headset, sits under an electricity pylon. The red and black computer-animated graphics look, at times, like rows of bricks. All the characters seem slightly dispirited or somber. In *Hometown*, curled, razor barbed wire looks remarkably similar to the coils of fiber cables, which overwhelm data centers. Sooner or later that which began as contingent tends to take on the quality of structure, and the tentative or intangible congeals into brick and mortar. As the nation-state withers, protocols —trade protocols, internet protocols— increasingly impose themselves as techniques of governance, the dominant forms of organization at the global scale. Unlike nations, they do not require monuments or grandiose narratives to frame social exchange. For media theorist Felix Stalder, protocols lie at the heart of the question to which cybernetics became the answer on how to govern society without recourse to politics. Protocols hold the promise of tackling problems of complexity in systems in which non-determinist actors are bound to one another through a continuous exchange of information. Trade protocols rule transnational capital flows and the market could be described as a giant information processor. Unlike laws, however, whose validity depends on the legitimacy of the sovereign—the consent, or lack thereof, of the governed—protocols come into force through voluntary adoption. Enforcement is decentralized and ubiquitous, but, once adopted, protocols become conditions upon which economic or social agents are constituted. In other words, protocols are enforced by the matrix of interdependencies they engender, as well as by the interactions they afford. But though the affordances of these protocols are initially beneficial (e.g., Facebook, the European Union, the World Trade Organization, Airbnb) it soon becomes clear they carry hidden costs. Leaving the space defined by the protocol is seldom an option, however, because the financial or social costs would be considerably higher than the costs imposed by the protocol into which one enters—in the case of Facebook, for instance, you trade privacy and integrity for loss of relevance and, by extension, loss of revenues. For Stalder this leads us to a psychological paradox: everybody is voluntarily doing what no one truly wants to do.[5]

In *Possessed*, a series of characters are seen taking selfies in ever more perilous circumstances. The voice-over narrator recalls how her parents always looked bewildered or camera shy, and laments her generation's groomed looks and studied poses, wholly detached from inwardness or introversion. The idea of the portrait is, here, paradoxically, turned inside out, into what Jonathan Crary describes as a "condition of externalization" rather than upholding a sense of selfhood or intimacy[6]; whereas the screen emerges as a biopolitical tool: at once "the object of attention and the object capable of monitoring, recording and cross-referencing attentive behavior."[7]

This emerging digital megastructure also seems to correlate with a crisis in representation: though equipped with a growing variety of optical media, we are increasingly unable to grasp the algorithmic totality that surrounds us. Data's primary mode of existence, as Alexander Galloway argues, is not a visual one,[8] and the twin forces of globalization and digitalization tend to widen the gap between individual experience and the economic structures that determine it. If one can find a common thread between Metahaven's several film projects, ranging from *The Sprawl* to *Hometown*, *Information Skies* to *Possessed*, it would be perhaps the questions they all seem to pose, albeit in different ways: what type of psychology emerges out of the present discontinuity between culture and structure? What happens to art when phenomenological experience—the raw material that aesthetics is made of—becomes secondary to information flows?[9]

In 1897, a historical moment, many have noted, that bears similarities to our present times, French sociologist Émile Durkheim popularized the term *anomie* to describe the absence of legitimate aspirations that results from the mismatch between personal goals and social guidelines. Excess individual discretion, Durkheim suggests, is tied to a fragmentation of identities and to an aimless or objectless expenditure of desire. The collective sense of the present time, according to cultural theorist Lauren Berlant, "presents itself first affectively." Holding together all the incoherence and contradictions between the "infrastructural activities of capital" and personal experience and subjectivity, goals, aspirations, or personal desires "help[s] or induce[s] people to navigate worlds whose materiality is overdetermined by many processes."[10] Though the social-democratic assurances of the postwar period in Europe, and the American Dream in the United States, have retracted, most people have remained attached to the now unattainable notion of the "good life"—with its promises of upward mobility, job security, and durable intimacy—despite mounting evidence that liberal-capitalist societies can no longer be counted on to provide opportunities for individuals to make their lives "add up to something."[11] Needless to say, these

Ana Teixeira Pinto

next

material processes cast a behavioral shadow. "Cruel optimism" is the term Berlant employs to describe a relationship in which the object of desire becomes an obstacle, an impediment to well-being. One might have a cruel attachment to food, to a certain body image, or to a vision of the good life. Most often, a cruel attachment involves a mediated relationship with a political project—typically capitalism, but one can also have a nostalgic attachment to the figure of revolution or of revolutionary struggle as it seems to be the case with the couple featured in Metahaven's *Information Skies*—that provides one with a compelling narrative or a means to organize daily life.

Metahaven, one could argue, make manifest that the historical present expresses itself as an emotional structure before it congeals into infrastructure. Durable intimacy is here tied to the question of who takes out the trash, not in the trivial sense of a couple's quarreling over household chores, but rather in the sense that waste management, as with all other types of public services and critical infrastructure, is fundamental for the sustainment of social and family life.

The young couple who appear in *Information Skies*, also apparently argue over unwashed dishes, though probably that happened before they joined the insurgency. Now, they seem to be locked together in an eerie choreography, in which proximity has come to displace intimacy. She speaks of heroism and of those who fell, romanticizing the life in the maquis, and says they "have a plot," which was formerly "a dream."

Halfway between a drama dealing with a strained relationship and a science-fiction

12
Paraphrasing Allen Feldman, "Appearing Under Erasure: Of Phobogenic Disappearance," lecture, *Dictionary of Now #7 FEAR*, Haus der Kulturen der Welt, Berlin, June 12, 2017, https://hkw.de/en/app/mediathek/video/56697. Last accessed on August 10, 2018.

13
Ibid.

14
Ibid.

15
Jameson, "Cognitive Mapping," 356.

16
Malaysia Airlines Flight 17 was a scheduled passenger flight from Amsterdam to Kuala Lumpur that was shot down on July 17, 2014 while flying over eastern Ukraine, killing all 283 passengers and 15 crew on board. Malaysia Airlines Flight 370 took off from Kuala Lumpur and was heading to Beijing with 239 people on board when it disappeared close to Phuket island in the Strait of Malacca.

17
See Emily Apter, "On Oneworldedness: Or Paranoia as a World System," *American Literary History* 18, no. 2 (Summer 2006): 365–389.

18
Journalist Peter Pomerantsev, interviewed by Metahaven in *The Sprawl*.

19
George E. Marcus, *Paranoia Within Reason*, Chicago: University of Chicago Press, 1999, 2.

20
Ibid.

21
Evelyn Fox Keller, *Reflections on Gender and Science*, New Haven: Yale University Press, 1985, 121–122.

22
Peter Knight, *Conspiracy Culture: From Kennedy to The X Files*, Oxford: Routledge, 2000, 2.

74

story, *Information Skies* is also composed of three visual layers, juxtaposing filmed footage with computer-generated graphics and anime-style animation. The Japanese-inspired soundtrack by M.E.S.H. glues these disjointed elements together, infusing the atmosphere with a spectral and somewhat disquieting pathos. They seem to live through times of perpetual yet low-intensity warfare. A thick fog covers the woods in which the protagonists dwell, pointing, perhaps, to a crisis of human emotion, or to a generalized dematerialization of force—what anthropologist Allen Feldman calls, "the violence of blanking out violence."[12]

Operating in a disjunction between "factuality" and "actuality," from which surplus political value is extracted, wartime, Feldman argues, is lived as a "time out of time."[13] From this perspective one could draw an analogy between the spatial out-of-place dimension of life in the maquis and the out-of-time dimension of wartime. Jacques Derrida referred to this temporal dimension as the *contretemps*, typically translated as a setback but literally pointing to an experience of time that runs counter to unidirectional progression or is essentially "out of joint." As the rhetoric of collateral damage (as accident or setback) suggests, the *contretemps* stands for the actions of non-action, and the rupturing of a single and organized temporality undermining our ability to "catch causality in the act."[14]

The frustrated attempts to catch causality in the act comprise the overarching theme of *The Sprawl,* a docu-fiction made in collaboration with cinematographer Remko Schnorr and electronic musician Kuedo, which thematizes, albeit obliquely, the current geopolitical fault lines, like the so-called Arab Spring (2010–2012) and ensuing Syrian Civil War (2011–ongoing), the Bahraini uprising (2011–2014), or the current conflict in Ukraine (2014–ongoing). These disparate events, however dissimilar, have a common denominator, *The Sprawl* suggests: they all occur under, and are informed by, an invisible yet ubiquitous "digital ceiling" that covers the globe. An upside-down highway is a recurring idiom, and oftentimes the

footage seems afflicted with digital blotches, similar to the oxidation or chemical damage suffered by silver-based emulsion photographs. According to Bratton, one of the intervening voices in *The Sprawl*, the regime of sovereignty established by the 1648 Peace of Westphalia treaty is "distorted and deformed" by the "accidental megastructure" that results from "planetary computation," the incorporation of networks on a global scale. Unlike the traditional model of sovereignty, tied to horizontally adjacent nation-states, the new regime of sovereignty is vertical and unmoored. But digital disruption is not only felt at an economic level, it also has an epistemic effect. As journalist Peter Pomerantsev argues in *The Sprawl*, the new forms of propaganda don't seem interested in persuasion, and are no longer tied to nation building, and rather seek to sow distrust, cynical detachment, and nihilism. Our fully interfaced digital environment is predicated on a paradox: the overabundance of information degrades its ontological status. Global capital remains a multidimensional force whose motions can only be grasped partially, as epiphenomena: rising house prices, racism, proxy wars, cheap appliances, discount sushi, etc.

Paranoia and conspiracy, Fredric Jameson argues, are the degraded ciphers for the failure to grasp the complexity of geopolitical vectors, marked by a "slippage into sheer theme and content."[15] The two ill-fated Malaysia Airlines flights—the first disappearing into the Strait of Malacca, the second shot down while flying over eastern Ukraine—seem to appeal to an overly suspicious psychology.[16] That psychology is held in place by the premise that "everything is connected," or by what professor of comparative literature Emily Apter called "Oneworldedness": a "delirious aesthetics of systematicity, vulnerable to persecutory fantasy, catastrophism, and monomania," which "envisages the planet as an extension of paranoid subjectivity."[17] Oneworldedness is a portmanteau of worldedness, the process of world production in literature and the notion of "One World," which stands for planetary integration. In *The Sprawl*, amateur digital forensics, which encircle or otherwise flag the putative anomaly, unearthing and indexing their "proofs," flash rapidly across the screen. Victoria Nuland, who was at the time the Assistant Secretary of State for European and Eurasian Affairs at the United States Department of State, is heard dictating the composition of Ukraine's government to be, while Russian officials speak of heroism, sacrifice, and motherland as they annex Crimea. Riddles are repeatedly interjected into the image flow, suggesting that the problem of post-truthism is a question of

figuration: a failure or inadequacy of the current conventions of representation to capture the casual chain connecting the "butterfly flapping its wings in China and a village in Birmingham going unemployed."[18]

But the disappearance of Malaysia Airlines Flight 370 could also be seen as a cipher for the geopolitical management of visibility and invisibility: for the Bahraini uprising—as writer Maryam Monalisa Gharavi suggests in her interview that runs throughout this book—rendered invisible by the news cycles that focus only on the parallel uprising in Syria, and by the psychopolitics of social media. As the process of de-westernization—that is, the ongoing geopolitical dispute over control of the capitalist matrix—goes virtual, the internet is increasingly becoming, in Metahaven's own words, a "weapon of mass disruption," amplifying conspiracy theories, paranoid ideation, and oppressive ideologies, rather than begetting freedom of speech and direct democracy.

Though it might seem counterintuitive, reason is not identical to sanity. As anthropologist George E. Marcus notes, paranoid ideation holds an ambiguous relation to rationality and logic and is often "mistaken for or identified with" reason.[19] Paranoia is not the opposite of reason, it is rather an exacerbated version of it.[20] The conspiracies *The Sprawl* maps, to paraphrase biologist and physicist Evelyn Fox Keller, do not "suffer from a lack of logic but from unreality." Paranoia is the psychology of declining hegemony: a style of interpretation, predicated on "subjective need—in particular the need to defend against the pervasive sense of threat to one's own autonomy,"[21] that is to say, the fear of submitting or surrendering control to others. Conspiracy theories are thus "less a sign of mental delusion than an ironic stance towards knowledge and the possibility of truth, operating within the rhetorical terrain of the double negative."[22]

Hence the shiny, glossy surfaces that digital aesthetics leans heavily into: these slippery, transient surfaces are a cipher for planetary instability. But precariousness is not challenged politically; rather, it is rendered lurid and recuperated into a libidinal economy. The result is a semiotic loop inside which emojis, wearable tech, crypto currencies, and stock images swirl and spin, while a multitude of heinous creatures feasts on the old world order's decaying flesh, adding a note of tension and terror to an otherwise lengthy and morose blight.

Ana Teixeira Pinto
Ana Teixeira Pinto is a writer and cultural theorist based in Berlin. She is a lecturer at the Dutch Art Institute and a research fellow at Leuphana University of Lüneburg. Her writings have appeared in publications such as *Afterall*, *Springerin*, *Camera Austria*, *e-flux journal*, *art-agenda*, *Mousse*, *frieze*, *Domus*, *INAESTHETICS*, *Manifesta Journal*, and *Texte zur Kunst*. She is the editor of *The Reluctant Narrator* (2014) and, with Eric de Bruyn and Sven Lütticken of a book series on counter histories forthcoming from Sternberg Press.

MH_ Is that a UFO in the sky? This is really intriguing. Is there maybe a puzzle you want us to solve?

next

Pirates, Parrots, Poetry
Eugene Ostashevsky ●MH

76

Metahaven We first learned of your work when reading about it in *The New York Review of Books* one evening in the summer of 2017. Since then, we've discovered your English translations of, among others, Daniil Kharms ("Play," 1930) and Alexander Vvedensky ("Snow Lies," 1930), and most importantly, your own recently published English poem-novel *The Pirate Who Does Not Know the Value of Pi* (2017).

Our work as filmmakers, artists, and designers has, for some years now, been influenced by the Russian children's poetry that you translated. In particular, that of Kharms, Vvedensky, and Korney Chukovsky, as well as the authorless Russian children's verses—sometimes referred to as "upside-downs" or "turnarounds"—have been of great inspiration to our films and our way of looking at the world.

We cannot fail to notice how central your role has been in introducing these works in the English language. Because we don't speak Russian—and we are well aware of the difficulties that can exist in its translation to other languages—we have been reliant on Russian friends and translations of this poetry in order to understand, and let resonate, the joy and meaning of this body of work.

Reading *The Pirate*, which you wrote in English, was thus a beautiful shock to us. It is an intensely moving, funny, and virtuosic epic that continues to offer new surprises. Apart from its structural qualities and specific aesthetics, it raises some questions that loop back to Kharms and Vvedensky, regarding poetry as a coping strategy and as a way of dealing with complex, contradictory, and unbearable realities. Lesia Prokopenko, a Ukrainian curator and critic, recently described these issues in an email to us:

I've been referring to absurdism, i.e., Kharms, a lot myself when trying to describe the present atmosphere. And you know of course, that these phenomena, especially in their partly anonymous form of nursery rhymes, are very typical of settings that struggle with ideological languages. […] This is typical both for Russia and for Ukraine at the moment, from different benchmarks, merging into similar narratives.

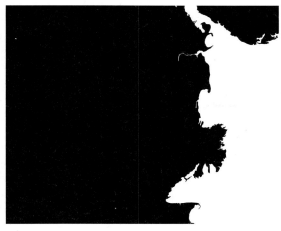

The Pirate works on several levels. Though the book is inexorably *whole* and departs from a single subject to which it remains loyal throughout, the writing plays with the storyline—with the words and rhymes as its own autonomous domain—as well as with overarching themes such as logic, (in)comprehension, and otherness, and the emotional hues that these themes cast onto the protagonists: the curious pair of the pirate and his parrot. We begin to care a great deal for both characters, even in the first pages of the book. This happens in spite of the fact that both characters are, at the same time, simply inventions that act as vehicles for the author to demonstrate his great ability to construct language games and create puns and rhymes. The refractions of the writing are so rich that the book can be experienced as highly versatile—depending also on one's own predisposition and mood. It can be experienced as an immersive emotional rollercoaster, or as an intense postmodern poetic guitar solo. The point is that the book is at least both. Early on, when the bond between the two characters and the reader is already firmly established, the parrot announces his intention to look up some ship names "later."

"Later when?" asked the pirate.
"When this book is over,"
said the parrot.
The pirate fell into deep thought.
"Will we exist when this book is over?"
he suddenly asked.
"If it's a good book," said the parrot.[1]

Perhaps not surprisingly, in a recent lecture you mentioned that *The Pirate* began as a children's book. Could you tell us about how it became a poem-novel?[2]

Eugene Ostashevsky I started writing *The Pirate* on a lark. My friends and I were acting silly, talking like pirates over dinner, and when I got home that evening I wrote the first poem—and then a few more the week after that. The book developed very slowly: it took nine years from the first poem to the final edit of the manuscript, and there are still passages I would like to rewrite. By saying that the book developed very slowly, I mean that the characters and their basic interactions took a very long time to discover, and that I discovered them through writing. I didn't conceive them first and write them down afterwards according to a plan. Kharms once wrote that he likes "writing poems and finding out different things from them"—a profound statement on art in general, if you take the time to think about it.[3] Similarly, for example, a key aspect of who the parrot is—that he is a non-native speaker of English—came to me after I already shipwrecked both characters. The pirate saying, "well, I am a native speaker and you're not," suggested itself. But it explains much about their interaction in the very first poems that I had written years before.

I did read a great deal about pirates and parrots while I was working on the book. I searched the Early English Books Online database for early modern opinions of pirates and parrots. I read the sixteenth-century colonial travel narratives compiled by Elizabethan intellectual Richard Hakluyt and ornithological texts by Ulisse Aldrovandi, professor at Bologna circa 1600. I read psychologist Irene Pepperberg's studies of Alex, her African grey parrot, and interviews with contemporary Somali pirates. As I read, all sorts of themes were coalescing: from colonialism—with the parrot as the speaking subaltern—to copyright infringement and the way modern businessmen (and pirates) see themselves, with the pirate as a radical free-market capitalist. And I stole from all the sources I read, because what's a book on piracy and parroting if it doesn't also perform piracy and parroting?

Everything I was reading was making its way into my text organically, without much foresight, because when I tried to produce rationally, according to plan, the results came out wooden and false. Outing the parrot as a non-native-speaker was thus a *satori* moment for me. As was the realization that their names, Pirate and Parrot, suggest near-complete identity according to medieval Jewish interpretation methods, since Hebrew represents words as clusters of three consonants, here: PRT. I got that only much, much later, maybe as late as when German poet Uljana Wolf started translating the book and complained she couldn't make the words *Pirat* and *Papagei* as similar in German. But maybe I "knew" all these things without being conscious of them… it's just that

next

if I were conscious of them in the beginning, I could not have written the book.

In general, I am a big fan of novels that seem to make stuff up as they go along. And also of heteroglossia, of Russian literary philosopher Mikhail Bakhtin's idea that a novel is the place where idiolects, sociolects, and even other languages collide—that the job of the novelist is to ironically join expressions taken from different walks of life, to parrot, rather than to commit to any particular point of view or discourse, even in announcements made qua author. My model is François Rabelais, who wrote in French in the 1530s and '40s. I've always loved Rabelais— he is a big, canonical author in Russia, where the *Gargantua and Pantagruel* novels are read by children, and Bakhtin wrote an important study of their style. Rabelais gave the Soviets (and Bakhtin in particular) a model of subversion against totalizing, ideological linguistic discourses, such as Stalinism (but not only Stalinism). Rabelais teaches you how to reduce to nonsense the things you are forced to repeat and believe. Admittedly this is a simplification, but it's nonetheless true. It is a bad sign that Rabelais is now almost forgotten, even in France.

Like *Gargantua and Pantagruel*, Cervantes's *Don Quixote* (1605-1615) was also canonized in the Soviet Union as children's literature. And this is as it should be, because—unlike adults—children actually read, possibly because real art is a form of play. These novels are episodic: the authors don't really appear to know what's going to happen next until they create that "next." Cervantes famously loses Sancho's donkey—he forgets that Sancho was riding a donkey—and then he has to make up for it. Rabelais is similar: as you read his books, new characters appear and an adventure happens, then others appear and another adventure happens. There are long-term transformations and changes, but they take place in all their randomness and contingency. The reader is constantly present at the author's discoveries. It's not the way we are supposed to write now; it's not the nineteenth-century-inspired psychological ideal and it is the opposite of a *Bildungsroman*, the educational coming-of-age novel. Or rather, it's a meta-*Bildungsroman*: it's a *Roman*, or novel, about the *Bildung*, or formation, of the *Roman*. This strong anti-mimetic tendency makes the early novel, paradoxically, more lifelike.

I regard what people call "absurdism" as a technique for skepticism, for putting a statement in doubt by indicating the role of grammar, vocabulary, phraseology, and—above all—pragmatics in creating our statements and opinions. People don't say things because they believe them, they believe them because they say them. But I don't know what it means to actually believe in something… I suppose it would mean you need to take your words

literally and perform them down to their inferences and implications. That, however, might not even be possible. If we assume that the world is rational, which is a tall assumption, language certainly is *not* rational. You cannot enact your words down to their very consequences because you would contradict yourself behaviorally over and over, like a Theaetetus who is flying and sitting at the same time.[4] But if the world is not rational, well… all bets are off, it's like dividing by zero! Even if you were to try to perform everything you say, doing so would not prove that you believe what you say, just that you want to *demonstrate* that you believe what you say. In real life there is no such thing as belief.

So what people call "absurdism" can come from taking words at face value: being a literalist rather than a pragmaticist—somebody who obtains things through successful social performance—precisely because sticking to literal meaning is how you demonstrate the utter impossibility of it being true. Sticking to literal meaning—and letting the chips fall where they may—is called, in philosophy, "deconstruction." An obvious example is seen in the conversations in *Alice's Adventures in Wonderland* (1865), a book whose author Lewis Carroll exercises his punctilious mathematician's ear for literal implication. Another example is the basic ideological presuppositions of the writings of Kharms and, especially, Vvedensky. In 1933 or '34, Vvedensky read *Pushkin Alive*,[5] a documentary biography of Pushkin compiled by Veresaev, who arranged testimonies in such

a way that a single event in Pushkin's life would be seen through the eyes of many witnesses. For example, Pushkin walks down the street and runs into two men, who then write to tell their wives about it. In that biography, relevant passages from their letters appear side-by-side under the date that they met Pushkin. So you see what ought to be the *same* event over and over from different points of view, but often there are irreconcilable differences, like in the Gospels. Vvedensky was deeply impressed by the biography's juxtapositions of testimonies, saying to a friend:

Interesting how witness reports contradict each other even where there can be no place for subjectivity. These aren't accidental errors. Openness to doubt, non-coincidence with our logical framework, are present in life itself. And I don't understand how there could have appeared such fantastical worlds with precise laws, worlds that do not resemble real life at all. For example, a committee meeting. Or, say, the novel. The novel describes life, time appears to flow there, but it has nothing in common with real time: there is no alternation of day and night, people remember their whole lives with ease whereas in fact it's doubtful one can remember even yesterday. Anyway, any description is just plain wrong. "A man is sitting, he has a ship overhead" at least has to be more right than "A man is sitting and reading a book."[6]

MH We wanted to begin by responding to your very precise definition of the political function of absurdist poetry, which you outline in discussing Rabelais. Absurdist poetry provides "a model of subversion for totalizing, ideological linguistic discourses such as the discourse of Stalinism (but not only Stalinism), […] Rabelais teaches you how to reduce to nonsense the things you are forced to repeat and believe."

The protagonist of *La vita e bella* (Roberto Benigni, 1997), in an attempt to shield his child from the traumatizing events of Nazi occupation in Italy, fictionalizes the deportation of his family. He transforms the ordeal into something that resembles an elaborate game. Language, art as play, poetry, and absurdism here function as coping strategies.

Though we can see the kinship that you feel with Rabelais, we also cannot help but notice how your work is distinct from his. The warmth in the exchanges between the pirate and the parrot, for example, hint at more functions for absurdism, beyond the masterful subversion of language:

What's so hard to understand? I don't want to be so hard to understand, parrot, I don't want my soul buried so deep inside me that there is, like, a nature preserve between it and these words, these worlds.[7]

Here we sense that something more than absurdism is at work. We sense a voice wanting, needing to be heard—a "soul" desperate to be seen. This "it" presupposes its own truth, or a belief in the existence of a soul outside of the realm of words, since there is a space, "like, a nature preserve," between "it" (the soul) and "these words, these worlds."

"This island is deserted,"
said the pirate.
"No, it's not," said the parrot.
"Do you know something
I don't?" said the pirate.
"It can't be deserted if we're on it,"
said the parrot.[8]

Here, the literal rather than the pragmatic understanding of the deserted island works to affirm the togetherness of the pair—they have each other, or at least the parrot expresses it as such. This exceeds absurdism, or even the grotesque.

"Where does happiness come from,"
asks the parrot.
"Where does *your* happiness come from,"
asks the pirate.
"I feel happy when I'm having an abstract thought," says the parrot.
"But that occurs very rarely."
"Why," asks the pirate.
"Because I'm not so intelligent,"
says the parrot.
"This is my Great Inner Grief."
"You're much more intelligent than me,"
says the Pirate Who Does Not Know
the Value of Pi.
"I know," says the parrot.
"But that's not enough."

They are sitting on the sand.
Palms are waving in the air behind them.
They are staring at the waves.
The pirate is holding a, what is he holding.

"My happiness," says the Pirate Who Does Not Know the Value of Pi, "mostly comes from the way some ray of light falls on some surface of water."[9]

Here, the pirate refers to a phenomenon of the physical world that exists outside of language. While you describe this phenomenon in a rather matter-of-fact way, another author could've used a more specific word such as "sunrise" or "sunset." You didn't do this, yet through this untraditional description the ray of light achieves an even more heightened, defamiliarized specificity. It remains "a beautiful thought," as is written later. But in terms of poetry, this is as close as it gets to an admission of being emotionally moved.

Some of the parts we just cited hint, in a way, at a break that occurs at some point between poetry and absurdism. They don't always run together, nor are they always joined, or are we mistaken?

Speaking to your reference to Stalinism, today we seem to be hitting into dystopian glam reincarnations of neo-totalitarian dictator chic with an internet (or better, Instagram) edge, and a resurgence of feudalisms and medievalisms. If absurdism could subvert Stalinism by taking its language literally instead of pragmatically, thereby exposing its internally contradictory and flawed nature, how can it—and does it already—subvert some of the neo-Stalinist glitter and filter bubbles that we see today?

EO Are you asking whether there is something else in my poems in addition to "absurdism," to skepticism, to the deconstruction of ideology by taking language at face value? Whether there is some sort of "positive" thing, some appeal to emotion, or beauty, or the soul—some kind of Poetry with a capital P? Yes, of course, "pirate," "parrot," "poetry"—the consonants are the same, so the meaning must be the same. But it's hard to talk about emotion, beauty, or the soul without commodifying them. It's hard to talk in general without commodifying what you say, without performing a power grab, without having your prime objective be the establishment and assertion of your power rather than a check of the veracity of your literal meaning. (Obviously I just invalidated anything I've said or will say in this interview, but I see no way around that.)

Already from Vvedensky's reaction to the documentary biography of Pushkin, we infer that absurdism is not just a deconstructive technique. (I hate the word "absurdism" because of all of the fluff associated with it, but since we have already been using it in this conversation, let's continue to use it.) It's not just a deconstructive or anti-totalitarian technique; it's not just a weapon against cultural dominance. It has to do with rationality, or rather, it has to do with the limits of rationality. Now, it's very hard to define rationality. Behaviorally, does rationality mean answering incentives or answering the *right* incentives? Am I acting rationally if I smoke? In medical terms: no. In economic terms: no. But aren't I answering *some* kind of incentive by smoking? A cultural incentive, for example: it lets me identify with film noir protagonists or with Eastern European intellectuals, or with my parents, or whatever. So isn't that behavior irrational in one way and rational in another way? Perhaps the problem here is that the "ways"—the frames through which we evaluate behavior—are incommensurable with respect to one another. What we call "absurdism" tries to indicate this incommensurability of frames and the irreducible manifoldness of motives and meanings.

But absurdism goes deeper than that. Even in relatively simple languages, such as those of mathematics, there will always be possible statements that are not rational according to the rules of that system, in the sense that they can be neither proven nor disproven from its axioms. This was demonstrated by Kurt Gödel's incompleteness theorems, which scuttled the attempt to translate arithmetic into the language of formal logic. I heard a lovely anecdote about the tremendous ramifications of Gödel's results. Supposedly, when Bertrand Russell—the philosopher who tried to translate mathematics into logic but failed because of Gödel's incompleteness—sent his grandson to kindergarten and the teacher tried to teach him that $2 + 2 = 4$, the grandson said: "My grandpa says this is something we can't really know!"

You ask about the soul. The soul is manifold, and an instance of bricolage. Or rather, "the" "soul" "is" "a" etc. No word is absolutely

next

precise about its referent. Of course, the soul contradicts itself! Of course, it's not rational! It depends on what you mean by "rational" but let's say that the soul is not "rational" in the sense that it's not consistent and not complete. There was a Neoplatonic tradition that held the soul is a number. The Neoplatonists, by which I mean people like Proclus, a Greek philosopher in late antiquity, thought that the metaphysical structure of the universe is based on relations among numbers. All of their ideas on number had to do with natural numbers: with one, two, three, and so on. They thought of natural numbers as individually held together bunches of ones, and they thought of fractions as ratios, as relations between those bunches. And they thought of God as rational, as the unity of unities of unities, etc., of ones. But the early Renaissance philosopher Nicholas of Cusa, in a book with the lovely title *Idiota de Mente* (The Layman: On the Mind) (1450), said: "God is not like 1, he is more like the square root of 2." Well, if the soul is a number—and of course the soul is *not* a number, it is just a concept, but let us try out some concept of number as an analogy to the concept of the soul (which also

means that the soul is *not* like a number)—it's an irrational number. There are all sorts of things in it, every number as a matter of fact, every possible sequence of natural numbers, if you express the irrational number as a decimal. It's a number that is incommensurable with the rational numbers—they have no common measure. This is why we call such numbers "irrational." But they used to be called "absurd numbers," or "surds," which also means "deaf" numbers, as a weird translation of Euclid's *alogoi*. Because you can't talk about the soul. Or rather, you *can* talk about the soul all you want, but you can't come up with a string of words—no matter how long—that would adequately express it. Neither in spoken language nor in sign language, either.

What I am trying to say is that you can't put up a fence between the absurd and the poetic: absurdism is not just a skeptical, deconstructive technique. Rather, it is a way of trying to speak about the things that matter without commodifying them, or, to be more precise—because non-commodification is impossible—to speak about them while at least trying not to commodify. Beauty is absurd. Love is absurd. Skepticism is a form of love and responsibility toward things that may or may not be there. But these are cheap formulas. They are really cheap and really worthless. They are cheap because I am sitting here soulfully typing about beauty and love, but what is the context in which I am doing so? *One* of the contexts is that I am an American citizen who used his passport about thirty-six hours ago to fly from Berlin, where my kids live, to Paris, where I teach. What does it mean to use an American passport? *One* of the things it means to me, as a former Russian, or rather as an ex-Soviet, is to participate in and therefore acquiesce to a political system that holds about two million of its own citizens in prison. As a child immigrant who was brought up on stories about the Gulag, *that* is what my adopted country has come to mean to me: a country that holds two million of its own citizens in prison.

Years ago, when I went to the Checkpoint Charlie museum in Berlin, it hit me in the pit of my stomach that the Stasi took children away from dissidents. I was a father already then. I knew about state-organized child thefts in Argentina, but at Checkpoint Charlie it really hit me emotionally as the most terrible aspect of the GDR's political system. Now, however, I am a free citizen of a country whose immigration services—ICE—separate asylum seekers from their children in prison. They are not, at least in intent, being separated forever, but the psychological technology of it feels fundamentally similar. They are separated for no practical reason, but to scare other parents out of seeking asylum. Let me rephrase this: the people that represent *me* are taking children away from asylum seekers—not even from dissidents, not from people who critique the US government, but from people who are powerless and who come to us seeking help. What goes on inside these ICE people's heads? I am asking a real question. What can possibly be the meaning of anything that I say about the so-called soul or beauty when I am one of the people in whose name children are taken

away from their parents? Living in Berlin you really feel how terrible it is that the US never got denazified. What is morality when you can moralize yourself into kidnapping children? That kind of morality is what enables people like those working for ICE to look themselves in the mirror.

I guess that already is my answer to your question about absurdism and contemporary totalitarian ideologies. All that nostalgia for power, manliness, and essence has resurfaced in our world of Putin, Erdoğan, Modi, Orbán, and other trumpeter swans. Does absurdism subvert totalitarianism in the age of Instagram? No, it does not seem to. On the contrary—and now I am speaking from my Russian experience mainly, although my American experience is quickly catching up—absurdism seems to also be part of the totalitarian package. This is because totalitarian ideologies need to subdue and disarm critical thought. They inoculate. They include the absurd in their propaganda, so that neither absurdism nor rationality can be used against them. Willful irrationalism, after all, was the Axis position in World War II: *natio* over *ratio*. The adherents of neither Putinism nor Trumpism are afraid of self-contradiction: rather, they appeal to their supporters by hitting precisely those buttons that are the most irrational and ambivalent, that mean both *a* and the opposite of *a*. Absurdism is powerless against such ideologues because they don't feel constrained by the rules of rationality. They don't even know what those rules are. After all, the rules of rationality are not the same as the rules of power.

1
Eugene Ostashevsky, *The Pirate Who Does Not Know the Value of Pi*, New York: NYRB Poets, 2017, 12.
2
See Ostashevsky, "Russian and Eastern European Cultures," lecture, Hunter College, City University of New York, New York, April 6, 2017, https://www.youtube.com/watch?v=VtlR7Hr24nw. Last accessed on August 29, 2018.
3
Daniil Kharms quoted in Leonid Lipavsky, "Razgovory [Conversations]," *Issledovanie uzhasa*, Moscow: Ad Marginem, 2005, 308. My translation.
4
Talking to young Theaetetus, the Eleatic Stranger distinguishes true from false statements by using the examples, "Theaetetus, whom I am talking to now, is sitting," and "Theaetetus, whom I am talking to now, is flying." Plato, Sophist 263a.
5
Vikenty Veresaev, *Pushkin v zhizni*, first edition published in 1926.
6
Lipavsky, "Razgovory," 407.
7
Ostashevsky, *Pirate*, 20.
8
Ibid., 76.
9
Ibid., 86–87.

Eugene Ostashevsky
Eugene Ostashevsky is a poet, professor, and translator based in Berlin and New York. Ostashevsky finished his PhD in Comparative Literature at Stanford University in 2000. He teaches humanities at New York University. As a poet he is known for his poem-novel *The Pirate Who Does Not Know the Value of Pi* (2017) and *The Life and Opinions of DJ Spinoza* (2008). He is the editor and primary translator of *OBERIU: An Anthology of Russian Absurdism* (2006), which contains works by writers Daniil Kharms and Alexander Vvedensky.

80

To argue is to look into the mirror.

In upside down reality, there can be no argument

There is no exit, as every new accusation is a reflection of another.

because the response is always: look at yourself.

The Sprawl (Propaganda about Propaganda)

Without beginning or end.

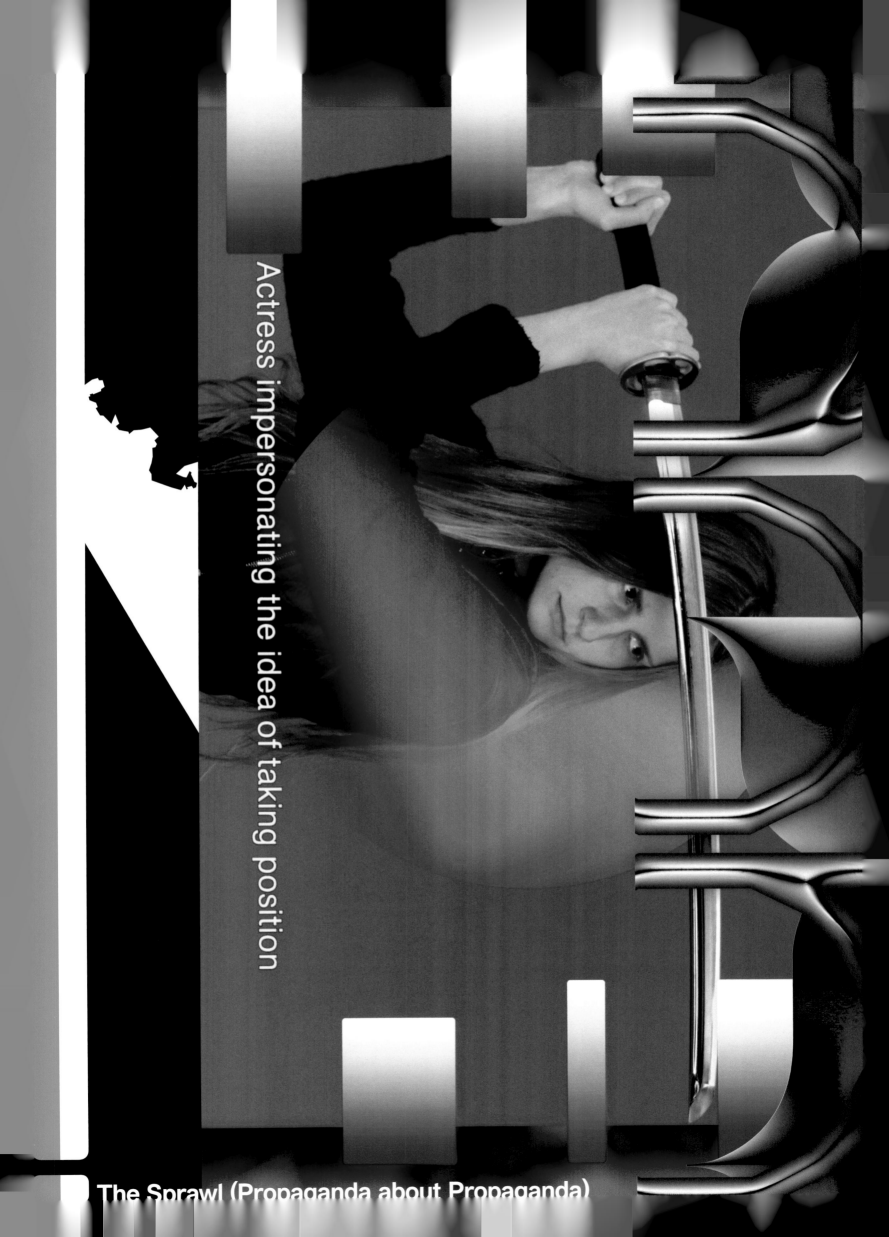

Actress impersonating the idea of taking position

The Sprawl (Propaganda about Propaganda)

SEEING
EVERYTHING

I live in the megastructure.

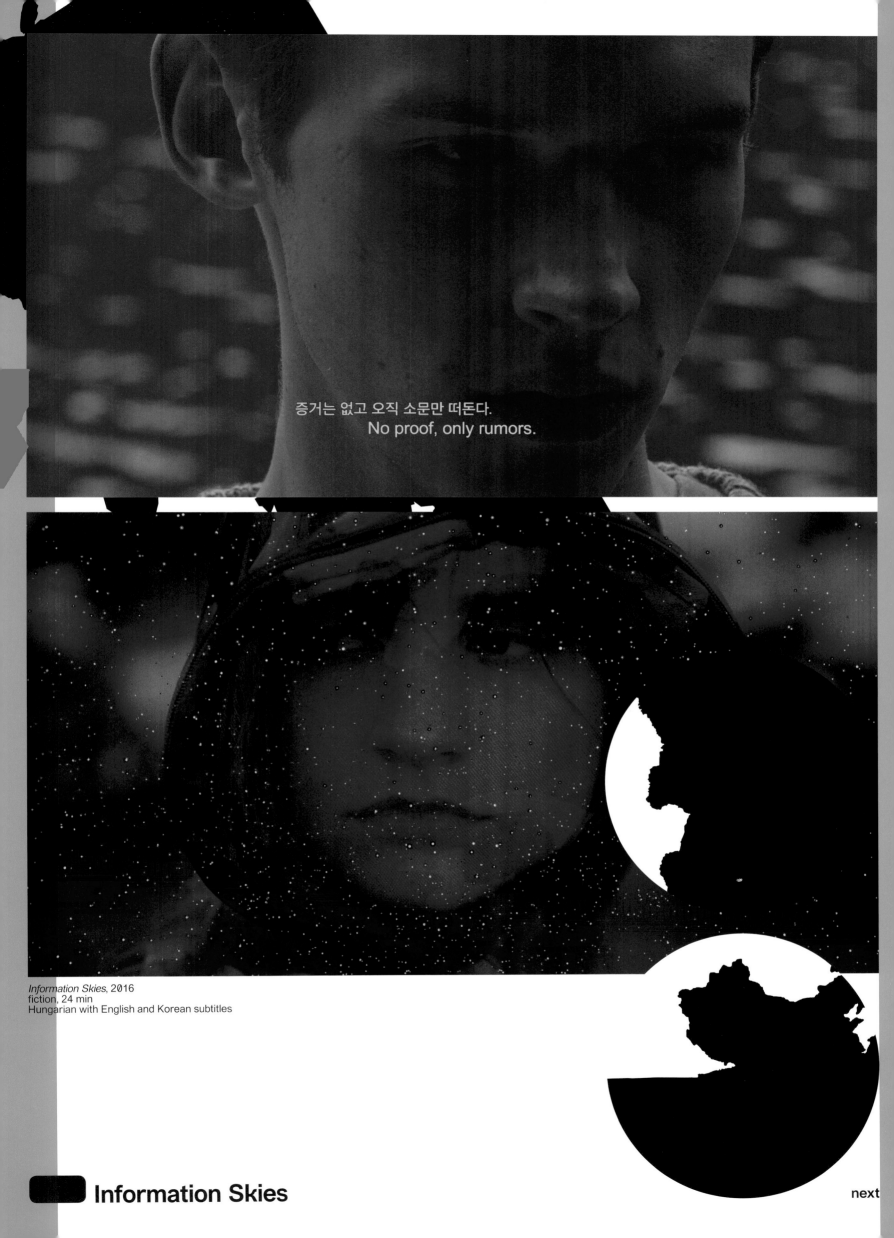

증거는 없고 오직 소문만 떠돈다.
No proof, only rumors.

Information Skies, 2016
fiction, 24 min
Hungarian with English and Korean subtitles

Information Skies

next

Information Skies, 2016
fiction, 24 min
Hungarian with English and Korean
subtitles

누가 무엇이 진실인지 알 수 있을까?
Who knows what's true?

Information Skies

Information Skies, 2016
fiction, 24 min
Hungarian with English and Korean
subtitles

Information S

색에 눈이 멀어버렸다- (제발 도와주세요) 갚을테니,
blinded by color. Please help me. I'll pay you
훨씬 나중에.
much later.

Information Skies

죽음은 가상현실이다.
Death is virtual reality.

오로지 끝없는 초원뿐일텐데 이것에 동의하는지.
An endless grassland with nothing there,

previous

لقد نشأنا ما بين الظاهريّ والاحتمالاتِ
والمُستبعد والأبواب الدوّارةِ والحوائطِ
العاكسةِ وطائراتٍ بدون طيّار.

أفضالٌ. خبزٌ وحليبٌ وسكرٌ. ملابسٌ من
صنع اليدِ. عملاتٌ من صنع اليدِ.

إن جدّي عالمٌ.

حين يأتي لاصطحابي من المدرسةِ

وقد ارتديتُ كنزتي الزرقاء

يقولُ أنها حمراءُ اللونِ.

يضمُّ يديَّ بين يديْهِ، ويعدُّ أصابع كلِّ
واحدةٍ. كمْ إصبع؟

يرسمُ يرقةً،

ويقولُ أنّها فراشةٌ.

كيف يا جدّو؟ أنت تمزحُ.

حينما تُمطرُ

لابد أن تسطع الشمسُ.

ستتكاثرُ الغيومُ مجدداً، النهارَ.

خطأً لغويٌّ. أحجيةٌ نقومُ بحلّها ونحنُ
نضحكُ.

الشمسُ تختبئُ في زُرقةٍ بلا قمرِ.

في قريةٍ صغيرةٍ، لا تتجاوزُ مساحتُها
أربعةَ بلدانٍ

على اتّصالٍ بالعالمِ، من دون هاتفٍ أو
شبكةٍ

ومن دون طائراتٍ تحطُّ في مطارِها
المزدحم

في هذه القريةِ التي ذاع صيتُها، ويجهلُها
الجميعُ

تعيشُ امرأةٌ متقاعدةٌ، بلغت عامَها الخامسَ
أو السادس

لستُ أنا هذه المرأةَ، إلا إن أصرّيتم.

هذه هي ملحمتُنا. لا تقلقوا، فهي ليست
بالطويلة.

إنها السرُّ الذي سمعَه الجميعُ.

قبل أن نستطردَ، فلنضبطْ ساعاتَنا

فساعةُ المحطّةِ العتيدةِ

قد أخطأَتْ، حينما أشارَت إلى انتصافِ
النهارِ
إذ جمَعَت بين الرقمين واحدَ واثنين،

فلنتّفقَ إذن:

إنها الساعةُ الثالثةُ.

111

والآن، تحت ناظريَّ الأقمارِ الصناعيةِ

ما بين نقاطٍ مُنّصلة تحتَ الأرضِ [فوقَ
الأرض]

ارتُكبَتْ جريمةٌ:
قُتلَتْ يرقةٌ بدم باردٍ.

أرجوانيٌّ داكنٌ، كالحبرِ.

لن نتّفقَ هنا: حينما يصيرُ واحدٌ وواحدٌ
ثلاثةً.

لأنني قلتُ هذا. لأنني أنا.

ولكن حينما يصيرُ واحدٌ وواحدٌ ثلاثةً
بحكمِ القانونِ

فهذه ليست أنا! - مَنْ ذا الذي قالَ بهذا؟

وهل ثمة فارقٌ بين هذا القانونِ المزعومِ

وبين قاعدةٍ تنّصُّ على أن واحداً وواحداً
اثنان؟

والآن، تحت ناظريَّ الأقمارِ الصناعيةِ

ما بين نقاطٍ مُنّصلة تحتَ الأرضِ [فوقَ
الأرض]

ارتُكبَتْ جريمةٌ:
قُتلَتْ يرقةٌ بدم باردٍ.

أرجوانيٌّ داكنٌ، كالحبرِ.

97

EURASIA
SCENES / SHOTLIST

FRIDAY JUNE 8, 2018

SCENE 09A
—Moment with good light.
KARABASH SLAG MOUNTAIN
TIMUR TYPING A POEM
Keyboard is hidden hidden in the slag
CLOSE
The black soil, camera from low

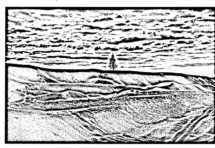

TIMUR is reaching out to the black SLAG, going on his knees. Under the soil appears to be a KEYBOARD-like structure. He starts slowly typing "I know the truth" by Tsvetaeva.

Я знаю правду! Все прежние правды — прочь!
Не надо людям с людьми на земле бороться.

Смотрите: вечер, смотрите: уж скоро ночь.
О чем — поэты, любовники, полководцы?
Уж ветер стелется, уже земля в росе,
Уж скоро звездная в небе застынет вьюга,
И под землею скоро уснем мы все,
Кто на земле не давали уснуть друг другу.

+*Silentium!* also
+VERSION with SENTIENT GLITTER on HANDS.

SCENE 10A
—Good light conditions (late in the day)
KARABASH — DRONE
THE "INSANE RIVER" — "THOUGHTLESS RIVER" —
"бездумная река"

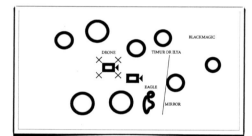

SCENE 12A
—Good light conditions (time of day not specific)
KARABASH
THE "INSANE RIVER" — "THOUGHTLESS RIVER" —
"бездумная река"
VERY WIDE, EPIC LANDSCAPE SHOT
TIMUR walks, stands, then crouches next to the INSANE RIVER.
He SEEMS TO drink the water from the INSANE RIVER.
(not real!!!)))
VERY SLOW, CEREMONIAL MOVEMENTS
+ one version with ONLY LANDSCAPE (and no TIMUR)

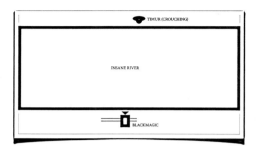

SCENE 14A
—Daytime
KARABASH COPPER-COLORED FOREST
CAMERA AND EAGLE. The CAMERA (on TRIPOD) FILMS ITSELF AND THE EAGLE in a MIRROR, which leans against a TREE. FRAME OF MIRROR NOT VISIBLE! Caretaker of eagle NOT VISIBLE.
NOT TOO WIDE! (50mm?)

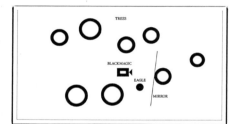

SCENE 14B
—Daytime
KARABASH COPPER-COLORED FOREST
COMPLEX SHOT of CAMERA (on TRIPOD) AND EAGLE with BOTH ACTORS and DRONE. The CAMERA FILMS ITSELF AND THE EAGLE in a MIRROR, which leans against a TREE. FRAME OF MIRROR NOT VISIBLE! Caretaker of eagle NOT VISIBLE.
MORE COMPLEX version of scene 14A.
NOT TOO WIDE! (50mm?)

SCENE 14C
—Daytime
KARABASH COPPER-COLORED FOREST
The BLACKMAGIC stands alone on a TRIPOD in the COPPER FOREST, filming everything in DEEP FOCUS, away from the CREW. The DRONE flies through the FOREST, seeking the camera.
NOT TOO WIDE! (50mm?)

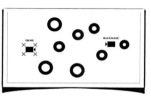

SCENE 14D
—Daytime
KARABASH COPPER-COLORED FOREST

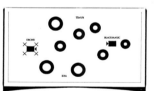

previous

“Who You Love is a Fact”
Richard Birkett ● MH

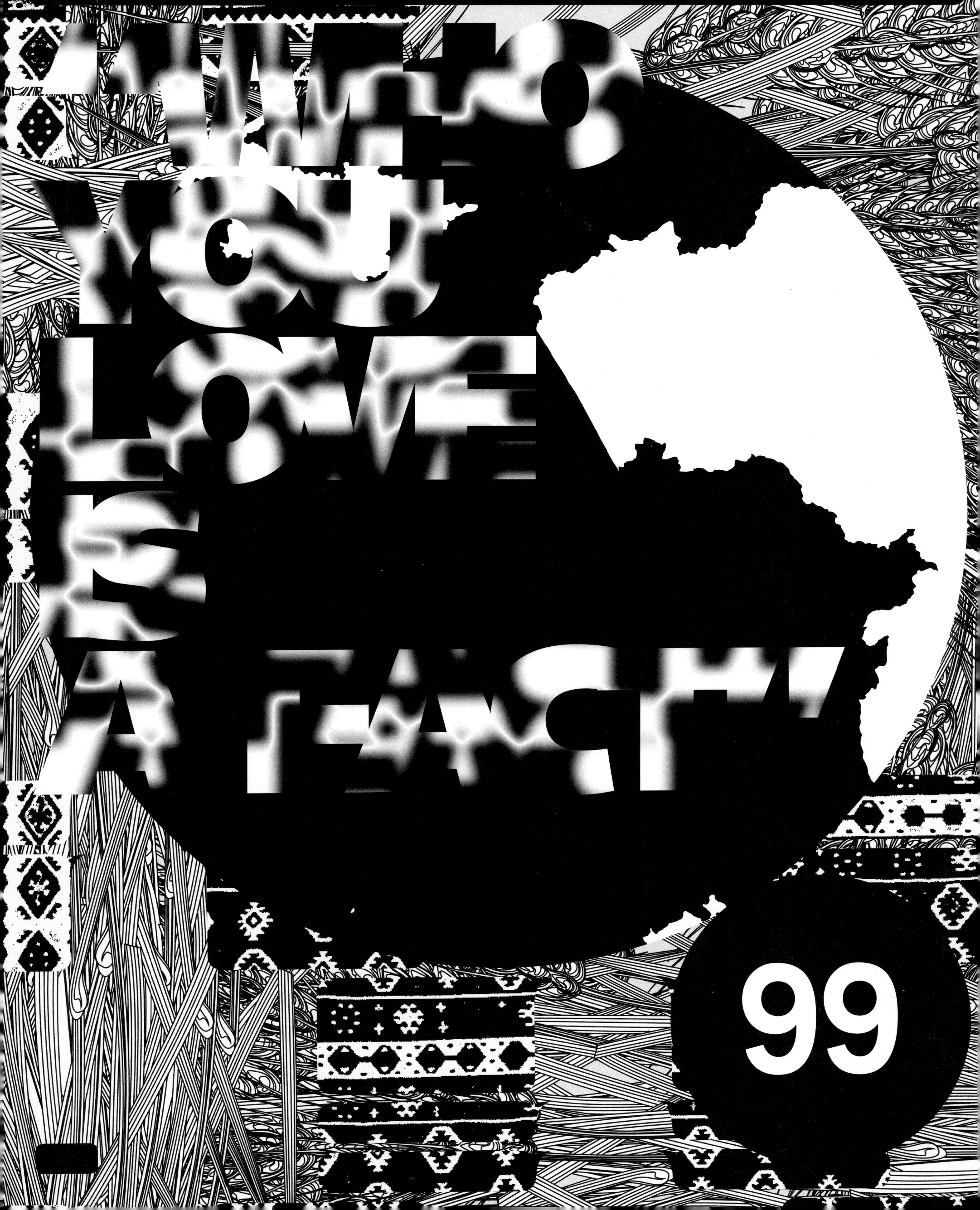

Richard Birkett I have been thinking about your use of the poem "I know the truth" (1915) by Marina Tsvetaeva in your film *Eurasia (Questions on Happiness)* (2018), and the excerpt from Anna Akhmatova's poem cycle *Requiem* (1935–1961) in your first full-length film *The Sprawl (Propaganda about Propaganda)* (2015).[1] Akhmatova and Tsvetaeva were contemporaries in early twentieth-century Russia who both experienced the disappearance of loved ones during the Stalin era. The first section of *Requiem* describes, in prose, how Akhmatova, standing in the queue outside Kresgy prison in Leningrad (now St. Petersburg) awaiting news of her son, meets a woman who whispers in her ear, "Could you describe this?"[2] to which she answers, "I can." The first line of Tsvetaeva's poem is, "I know the truth—give up all other truths!" In both poems, there is an imperative to witness from deep within a collective condition of opacity and loss, but also a distinct ambivalence around what it means to speak for the experiences of others. How do you see the space carved out between their voices and their function in relation to one another? In what way do you find resonance with these particular personal/historical forms of voice?

Metahaven In the Akhmatova excerpt in *The Sprawl*, we hear about the quietly flowing river Don and a house that sits under a yellow moon. It seems relatively peaceful at first. The moon is not full; it wears a tilted "cap." It does not merely shine; it "sees." It gazes into the house, where it sees a lonely woman. She is desperate. Her son is imprisoned and her husband dead. "Pray for me," the poem follows, an embodiment of the abyss of loss. The moon, an actor in the scene endowed with vision, is used similarly in our film when it becomes a huge red sphere with "REC" written on it—the moon is a witness.

In "I know the truth," Tsvetaeva shows a

1
The Akhmatova poem excerpt can be read in the script of *The Sprawl* on page 137.
2
Or in some translations: "Could one ever describe this?"
3
Marina Tsvetaeva, "The Poet" [1923], in *Selected Poems*, trans. Elaine Feinstein, London: Penguin Books, 1994, 48.
4
Ibid.

harsh reality: despite the fact that we will all soon be dead, we do not let each other live in peace; we do not let each other sleep, even though we will soon all sleep beneath the earth's surface. This, for her, is the one truth that should make us give up "all other truths." There's a quieting in the middle of the poem, where the wind stops and the stars are still in the sky, and everything seems almost peaceful. It is hard for us to elaborate on this poem as it is conclusive in and of itself. There are a lot of differences between Tsvetaeva's and Akhmatova's work. Even in "I know the truth," Tsvetaeva begins with enthusiasm, ending the first sentence with an exclamation point. By comparison, the voice of Akhmatova appears more controlled, if equally uncompromising. Tsvetaeva wrote a collection of poems for Akhmatova, whom she greatly admired. When considering the connections between Tsvetaeva's life and her poetry, the sincerity of her work comes to the fore even more.

It took us only a split-second to decide to work with these poems in each case; there wasn't a lot of reflection involved. Even though they were written in czarist Russia or in the Soviet Union, they create a strong connection with listeners outside that context.

What do you think or feel when you read these poems? How do you feel about their use in moving-image work?

RB I agree that there are notable and insightful differences in tone and feeling between them, despite both dealing with mortality and lyrically summoning up earthly and cosmic natural forces. My experience is of uncompromising and deeply affecting appeals, voiced distinctly by women, toward and against violence and death perpetuated in actions and language: Tsvetaeva's line, "*what* do you speak of, poets, lovers, generals?" is particularly powerful. However, Tsvetaeva's poem has a universal declamatory tone relatively absent of personal loss when placed in contrast to Akhmatova's, which is comparatively rife with it. Your description of Akhmatova's poem as an "embodiment of the abyss of loss" is incredibly fitting.

There is of course a direct correlation with the personal and historical circumstances under which the poems were written: "I know the truth" was written in 1915, a year after Tsvetaeva's husband volunteered for the Eastern Front of World War I, but two years before the Russian Revolution transformed their lives through famine, exile, and their eventual persecution on return to the Soviet Union; Akhmatova wrote the section you excerpt from *Requiem* in 1938, following the death of her first husband and the year of her only son's arrest and incarceration by the KGB in the midst of the Great Purge.

In your moving-image works, these poems carry a lyrical and affective texture: they are part of a layering of textual and visual symbolism, operating alongside different modes and rhythms of voiced address, as well as imagery that is graphic, documentary, and cinematic. Within this weave of materials, the poems are immediately striking in their generation of mood and atmosphere, and work in concert with your underlying musical themes. This emotive aestheticism, that is to say, a conveyance of felt experience through an alignment of words, images, and sounds, is to me quite rare within moving-image work seen in the context of contemporary art—a now global "genre," but one with an infrastructure and set of logics still

heavily oriented toward Europe and the United States. I understand your choice to use the poems was not overthought, and that reducing them to critical tools is not productive. Yet I am interested in how their presence alongside other elements in your films performs a crucial role in relation to the witnessing and writing of history that is central to your moving-image works since *The Sprawl*. You focus on Russian and Soviet history and recent geopolitical shifts. But you also examine the position of speaking within a complex of political and ideological forces, and the conceptual and emotional relation of these forces to different forms of linguistic and/or media production. How do you think about poetry as linguistic texture in placing it in relation to the moving image? How does a line like, "I know the truth—give up all other truths!," speak from history and into the present and future?

MH Poetry is a way to express what can't be expressed any other way. The work of Tsvetaeva and Akhmatova speaks of necessity, first of all. It is also *field reporting*, which, somehow, in an emotionally gripping and linguistically precise way, betrays circumstances around the time of their writing, forging a permanent link between the past and our current lived experience through rhyme, meter, and motive. Neither the starting point for Tsvetaeva's nor Akhmatova's work is similar to that of avant-garde poetry. Their work is rather lodged in a narrative-poetic tradition that flourished during the so-called Silver Age of Russian poetry. It is then enacted in the context of the Soviet Union, itself a continuation of the czarist era in some respects, and current Russia is also a continuation of these preceding epochs. The perception or experience of flagrant injustice can lead one to critique systems through writing, image, and action; the lyrical form both poets use to enact their critique doesn't give in to sloganeering or propaganda—it is an antidote to these. We find that Tsvetaeva in particular is a kind of filter who lets the listener (or reader or viewer) co-experience a startling reality mediated through the poet's personal experience imbued with unsentimental warmth. The difference between subject matter and its treatment becomes strikingly apparent; and there is a dynamic range of emotions that can be addressed within that difference. The persistence of her sense of "love"—can we call it that?—is what gives her work its inescapable directness, especially when describing the most dire circumstance. At the same time, as she writes, "the way of comets [...] is the poet's way."[3] The poet is like a train that everybody "always comes too late to catch."[4] This is almost the inverse of Baudelaire's romantic idea of the poet as a majestic albatross, chained to the deck of a ship, prevented from flying, and mocked for its clumsy appearance. The self-pity in Baudelaire's poet is missing from Tsvetaeva's, who even in the harshest of circumstances, is the comet, at the vanguard of possible feelings.

Making *The Sprawl* made us dive more deeply into all of this, prompted by the overly reductive way in which Russia was talked about in much of the Western media. We found that we ourselves shared the same sense of epistemic uncertainty as Tsvetaeva, Akhmatova, and even Tolstoy in *What Is Art?* (1897). Coming to terms with this convergence through a texture, a mesh of emotions, is what we try to do in much of our work since *The Sprawl*.

It makes no sense to deny the content of

facts, or their existence. For Tsvetaeva, however, versions of the truth coexist, and in spite of this splintering it is possible to put what is shared into words and images. Poetry always speaks to necessity, saying things impossible to state as facts that nonetheless need to be said. Given current debates about truth—and the hyper-fragmentation of the political and social landscape due to mutual exclusion among the fundamentalisms that arise from it—the epistemic uncertainty we've been thrown into likely won't go away soon, even if certain pivotal figures vanish from the scene.

RB Hunting for poems online involves navigating a web of Tumblrs, Google Books citations, and often, with original non-English language poems, a dizzying number of translations. Happily, this particular Google search for Tsvetaeva's "The Poet," from which the line "the way of the comets" is taken, took me to poet and writer Jackie Wang's fantastic Tumblr *Giulia Tofana the Apothecary*, and from there to Hélène Cixous's 1991 essay, "Poetry, Passion and History: Marina Tsvetayeva [sic]." In an early passage, Cixous describes a world consumed by "more and more sonorous […] noise machines." If the "milieu of the media," where "people are entirely governed by the obligation to create scandal," embodies this invasion into every aspect of life, then equally, Cixous states, "even an organization like Greenpeace is just another noise machine from which one cannot imagine that justice or truth will appear."[5]

In opposition to this condition, Cixous turns to the desire to "plant some paths, some slowness, some trees, some thought and silence," and to Tsvetaeva's texts that "work on this inside of an outside, on an inside-outside." Cixous extols how "underneath a worldly surface, we can find in [Tsvetaeva's] oeuvre a woman full of wealth, an extraordinary tapestry, a writing gathering thousands of signs."[6]

For me, this last passage really resonates with the texture, "mesh of emotions," that you pinpoint as a central aspiration in your work since *The Sprawl*. Particularly, "a writing gathering thousands of signs," suggests an oppositional movement between the "hyper-fragmentation" and occlusion that accompanies the "noise of machines," and the gathering of signs is a means to generate a shared orientation within this epistemic uncertainty; as you say of Tsvetaeva's poetry, it is a form of *field reporting*, within and outside history. This might be a somewhat literal transition, but I want to ask you about the interface as a key instrument within a contemporary economy of signs. Defined within critical research as "interface politics," the nature and design of interfaces as mediating and discursive makes them central to establishing trust—and suspicion. In your moving-image

work there is almost an overload of converging and layered modes of visual, linguistic, aural, graphic, and symbolic communication. The moon in *The Sprawl* is a good example of this as an image and a linguistic signifier (spoken in Russian and written in English), a graphic motif that also stands for the red "REC" symbol, and a recurring drawn circle as both free-floating graphic and a functional "circling" of image evidence. In any of these aspects, the allegorical use of the moon as a witness in Akhmatova's *Requiem* remains operative. How do you see poetry, a "writing gathering thousands of signs," as equating to and functioning within this system of interfaces that your work employs?

MH In our understanding, an interface is a graphic representation of a digital platform, tool, or machine, meant to enable the user to interact with and operate it. And, as platforms work at reality, interfaces enable users to do this on their own terms to, according to the Oxford English Dictionary Online:

follow/unfollow, block/unblock, see/unsee.

But that is only the beginning. Interfaces can mediate the world on their own terms. Interfaces are political because they are reductive; their buttons carry words that categorize and force choices. They are—must be—reductive to have any real effect on the world. Interfaces condition us to believe things about reality while acting on it.

Poetry uses language for the opposite effect. Buttons with words on them for you to click, do not currently exist in poetry in the same way as in interactions with machines. Poetry disrupts the relationship between the use and ends of language; it disrupts the straightforward use of language. So, on some level it can be seen as running counter to the interface. This is not to say that interfaces cannot have poetry.

We just wanted to add something from "Lyrical Design," a lecture we gave at the Design Museum in London in July 2018:

Especially amid all things post-truth, there are things that are beautiful, and there are things that are true, and there are things that need to be said. Lyrical design, as we see it, is simply this. A return to the bare necessity of what needs to be said in the way that it is sensed, and cannot be said in any other way.

RB I was thinking of the term "interface" as operative within your moving-image works more broadly: on one level, your work gestures toward the language of the user interface—graphic shapes as generic buttons or frames float unmoored in layers of moving images as artifacts of "representations of choices"; on another level, the generic interface as "a point where two systems, subjects, organizations, etc., meet and interact,"[7] a shared boundary where conditioning occurs in both directions, appears in your work in multiple meeting points between communicative, linguistic, and symbolic systems.

MH Yes, they are representations of dialogues and log-in attempts. They are the signs and signals of an unspecific floating OS.

RB In contrast to your production of an online platform such as *The Sprawl*, the direct functionality of a user interface is absent in your moving-image works created for galleries or film festivals, yet the viewer is still called on to navigate moments of confluence and interaction, a designed space of mediation. For instance, in the two-screen film *Hometown*

(2018) the binary nature of the image (sometimes one image that is split in two, sometimes two separate images that at times mirror each other) is echoed in the relationship between two spatial locations, Kiev and Beirut, and the two young women around which the film revolves. There are also two principal registers of imagery: filmed footage, and interstitial sequences of 2D animation. There are distinctive meeting points generated in these visual binaries, but the work also generates points of semiotic confluence. Within the poetic text, the lyrical and absurdist analogy of a caterpillar "murdered in cold blood" is read once by each character, in Ukrainian and in Arabic. I would say that a form of interface exists in this figure of the caterpillar (that also appears in rudimentary graphic form in one of the sequences of 2D animation, and is alluded to in a shot where one of the women catches and releases a butterfly), wherein different systems of representation (linguistic, cinematic, graphic) meet and a multivalent form of symbolism is generated. What also comes to mind is your use of several languages within your work, and the interplay between different writing systems in subtitles.

MH One could draw a four-square diagram in which technology is aligned according to one axis leading from invisible to visible, and another from past to future. Technology feels at its most advanced, and most interesting somehow, when it is in the future, and when the machine itself appears absent except for its effects—when technology's presence is implied and overarching and at the same time understated and ephemeral. Obviously, technology is not invisible: its absence in one space is always connected to its presence in another. The absence of fossil fuels in a Tesla car implies a massive, resilient electrical grid, for example, to charge it anywhere; it implies batteries, the factories where these batteries are made, the mines where their parts are won, and the places where they go after use. Every invisibility implies a very physical food chain behind it. But what we are interested in is how the specter of technology—in the widest sense—can be implied in everyday things. That is, both in the sense of distributed and decentralized intelligence—sensing landscapes, "steppe of pixels"—as well as in ordinary objects that cannot be addressed, not part of an internet of things, and by that virtue connected to us by emotion, memory, or desire, more than communication links. In 2012, futurologist Venkatesh Rao asked: "what if all surfaces are potential screens?"[8] It is a good question, especially when taking into account that a surface no longer technically needs to *be* a screen as soon as we are intent on *seeing* it as one.

RB If a conditioning is occurring within the form of interface that your work points to, beyond "communication links," it seems to displace a belief-based notion of reality with a "gathering of signs." Within "lyrical design," how do you approach combining registers of signification? How does this speak to versioning and as you mention earlier that "in spite of this splintering it is possible to put what is shared into words and images"?

MH Maybe it's partially about continuously developing ideas around rendering equivalences between data and space. For example, what currently interests us is the spatial (lack of) logic that we are trying to build in *Eurasia*. We filmed in the heavily polluted basin of the Sak-Elga

River near Karabash in Chelyabinsk Oblast, Russia. It is an ecological disaster zone where everything in the surroundings has a reddish hue and is polluted with metal, predominantly copper. There is a copper smelting facility there straight out of *The Lord of the Rings*. Our contemporary gaze looks at this kind of zone as an aberration that needs to be corrected.

But we realized that multiple historical time periods co-exist in the same space, overlapping each other. Most of the time to cope we "unsee" these simultaneous other versions of reality, which becomes impossible when another version suddenly appears as the predominant one.[9] We like to think that progress is our benchmark, but the membrane of our progress is very thin. We are in non-linear time where the "now" feels exceedingly complex and thick but matters less.

Data plays a crucial role in this (and hence its architecture). Data is not just the "material" that keeps this landmass conceptually "as one" (through satellite data, geo-sensing, surveillance, 4G networks, communications and logistics infrastructure, etc.), but it is also the material that sustains the belief system around each of the "versions" of reality that are being seen and unseen. In data, you can live inside a coherent bubble of beliefs. In physical space—such as in Karabash—you can find yourself trapped in the version you were unseeing. The shared is what we were unseeing from each other.

RB I greatly appreciated my epistolary engagement with you during the *Eurasia* shoot you describe above in Karabash and the surrounding area, receiving the daily shot lists and image updates via email in London, getting a vicarious sense of the intensity of your encounter with the landscape. What felt most compelling about these

5
Hélène Cixous, "Poetry, Passion and History: Marina Tsvetayeva," in *Readings: The Poetics of Blanchot, Joyce, Kafka, Kleist, Lispector, and Tsvetayeva*, Minneapolis: University of Minnesota Press, 1991, 111, https://loneberry.files.wordpress.com/2016/08/cixous-on-tsvetaeva.pdf. Last accessed on August 13, 2018.
6
Ibid., 112.
7
Venkatesh Rao, "Public Computing and the Screens World," talk, *The Conference*, Malmö, August 23, 2012, https://videos.theconference.se/venkatesh-rao-publiccomputing-and-the. Last accessed on August 29, 2018.
8
Tsvetaeva, "The Poet," 48.
9
See Rao, "Public Computing."

missives was strangely not the images, however, but the simple diagrammatic representations of particular shots that appear in your shot lists. These schematizations of the cinematic gaze seem appropriately logistical, yet somewhat surreal when imagining them mapped onto an environment so otherworldly and inhospitable.

In one particular diagram, the icon for the drone camera is positioned above a solid red strip, simply marked "INSANE RIVER." A caption reads: "DRONE (CAMERA POINTING DOWN)." The accompanying description of this scene provides an interpretation of the diagram: "The DRONE is hovering over the red waters and is TRYING to see itself, filming itself." I see within this the idea of the sensing landscape: the river actively receives and returns the gaze of the drone camera; equally, there is the attempt of the sentient drone—a technology entwined with both the present-day violence of remote "logistical" warfare and futurist predictions of technological singularity—to be visible, to be witnessed. It's a scene that in my imagination is simultaneously horrific and poetic. It resonates deeply with the sense in both Tsvetaeva's "I know the truth" and Akhmatova's *Requiem* of the landscape, the cosmos, as witnesses beyond history and language. In Tsvetaeva's "The Poet," the line, "For the way of comets […] is the poet's way," is followed by, "And the blown-apart […] links of causality are his links."[10] This phrasing seems to beautifully render both a state of epistemic uncertainty, and a sense of being within non-linear, non-teleological time.

I wonder if you could elaborate on your words above, and say more about the role of data (as much a material spatial architecture as a digital one), in relation to this poetic concept of "the blown-apart links of causality"? It seems to me that we are talking here less about willful occlusions of the "truth" enacted by nefarious state or extra-state forces—and therefore the forensic work required to reestablish broken links—than an active process of "seeing" and "unseeing" written into conceptions of reality and heightened by technologically enhanced cascades of information.

MH We love to get asked questions that contain their own answers! We could just copy-paste that last paragraph in here and be finished.

First, we have realized that disinformation is always there, but slightly differently situated within our epistemic landscapes; second, we are developing forms of literacy around it; and third, we are beginning to accommodate it in our lives, coping with the "nefarious" state and extra-state pollution of discourse as part of the real. Andrew O'Hagan's long piece on the Grenfell Tower fire in 2016, exploring the lives of the tower's residents and victims, the fire's aftermath, and the institutional, social, political, and policy frameworks around the tragedy, begins as follows:

It was a clear day and you could see for miles. From her flat on the 23rd floor, Rania texted one of her best friends from back home and they talked about facts. Who you love is a fact and the meals you cook are facts. When the sun shines it is a fact of God and England is a fact of life. Rania always said she had preferred living in Mile End because the markets were better over there, but at least Westfield was near her now in White City. She was 31. "I was born in Egypt 11,426 days ago," she told one of her neighbours, pleased with the new app on her iPhone that could count days.[11]

O'Hagan establishes the scale at which an event is real, and the scale at which it is reproduced in the lives of those directly affected. The piece collapses all versions of actual and possible realities into a single point, where everything is true. All lives lost or changed, hopes crushed, and futures cancelled are as true and real as the fire, its cause, the need for its explanation, and the fallacies that occur in the story that gets told about it. As O'Hagan writes, "who you love is a fact." Likewise, Tsvetaeva and Akhmatova are not defending some kind of abstract, universal love. In their writing, they embody real limits. They embody a struggle and sacrifice for concrete objects of love, set inside a distressed episteme.

The understandable counter-response to post-truth, and especially to some of its identifiable perpetrators, is the desire for a reality that is purged of all ambiguity. We should defend a world in which facts matter, and in which the rule of law gives equal rights to all. But we should not strive for a dictatorship of the Real.

Richard Birkett
Richard Birkett is chief curator at the Institute of Contemporary Arts (ICA), London where he was curator from 2007–2010. In the interim he held curatorial positions at Artists Space, New York and Yale Union, Portland, OR. He has curated exhibitions with artists and groups such as Bernadette Corporation, Chto Delat?, Lukas Duwenhögger, Forensic Architecture, Aaron Flint Jamison, Morag Keil and Georgie Nettell, Laura Poitras, Cameron Rowland, and Hito Steyerl. His curated group exhibitions include: *Materials and Money and Crisis* (with Sam Lewitt), mumok, Vienna, 2013; *Radical Localism: Art, Video and Culture from Pueblo Nuevo's Mexicali Rose* (with Chris Kraus and Marco Vera), Artists Space, 2012; and Nought to Sixty, ICA, 2008.

10
Tsvetaeva, "The Poet," 48.
11
See Andrew O'Hagan, "The Tower," *London Review of Books* 40, no. 2 (June 2018), https://www.lrb.co.uk/v40/n11/andrew-ohagan/the-tower. Last accessed on August 8, 2018.

104

MMG French quality at Bulgarian prices. German quality at Hungarian prices. Italian quality at Vietnamese prices. British quality at Malawian prices. Japanese quality at Mexican prices. The Beer Price Index says that in 2018, in US dollars a beer in Cairo costs $2.39, a beer in Istanbul costs $4.71, a beer in Oslo costs $5.57, and a beer in Lausanne costs $9.51.

Maryam Monalisa Gharavi

Maryam Monalisa Gharavi is an artist, poet, and theorist. Her work explores the interplay between aesthetic and political valences in the public domain. Gharavi's work has been shown at venues including: Nottingham Contemporary; Pioneer Works, New York; Serpentine Cinema, London; Framer Framed, Amsterdam; Museum of Fine Arts, Boston; Art Dubai; New Museum, New York; Pacific Film Archive, Berkeley, CA; and Sonic Acts, Amsterdam. Her writing has appeared in publications such as *Triple Canopy*, *Women and Performance: A Journal of Feminist Theory*, *The White Review*, *Art in America*, and *The Literary Review*. Gharavi has a PhD in Comparative Literature and Film and Visual Studies from Harvard University, Boston and an MFA in Film/Video from Milton Avery Graduate School of the Arts at Bard College, Annandale-on-Hudson, NY. She held a Fulbright U.S. Scholar/Visiting Professorship at Birzeit University, West Bank, and was a lecturer at Harvard from 2013 to 2017. Book publications include *Bio* (2018), a translation of Waly Salomão's *Algaravias: Echo Chamber* (2016), and the poetry volume *The Distancing Effect* (2016). She was editor at *The New Inquiry* between 2012 and 2017, and is author of the open text *South/South*.

next

Post-Fact and Virtual Reality
Kate Cooper ● Lil Internet ● MH

POST-FACT
AND
VIRTUAL
REALITY

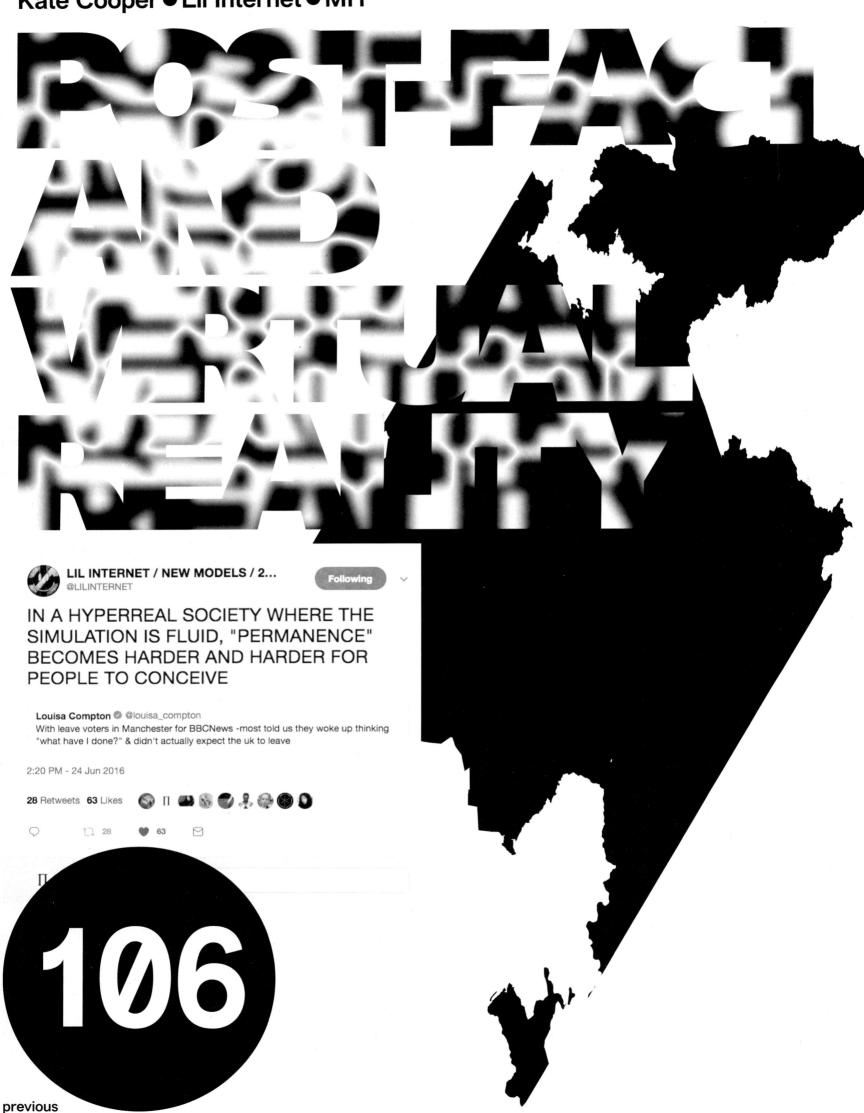

LIL INTERNET / NEW MODELS / 2…
@LILINTERNET

Following

IN A HYPERREAL SOCIETY WHERE THE
SIMULATION IS FLUID, "PERMANENCE"
BECOMES HARDER AND HARDER FOR
PEOPLE TO CONCEIVE

Louisa Compton ● @louisa_compton
With leave voters in Manchester for BBCNews -most told us they woke up thinking
"what have I done?" & didn't actually expect the uk to leave

2:20 PM - 24 Jun 2016

28 Retweets 63 Likes

28   63

Π

1Ø6

wrote that "the purpose of conjuring, at least most of it, is to entertain audiences by pretending to violate natural laws." He believed that, "in a curious way, this has something in common with how the universe behaves. When a person is mystified by a good magic trick it is because he can't figure out how the magician did it. When a physicist is mystified by an unexpected observation it is because he can't figure out how the universe did it."[1]

In our times, the impact of statements sometimes seems inversely dependent on their truthfulness, meaning that the least truthful statements often become the most effective. Through what journalist, author, and producer Peter Pomerantsev calls "disinformation cascades," post-fact wildfires control news cycles, seemingly commanding attention much better than facts do.[2] Even refutation first requires repetition. Part of the attraction of post-fact is that, like the conjurer's magic tricks, it seems to endow certain people with the capacity to defy reality. Moreover, once people have become convinced of a post-fact and license it through their vote, it can quickly *produce* reality—and create new facts. Sociologists William Isaac Thomas and Dorothy Swaine Thomas theorized this dynamic, known as the Thomas theorem, in 1928: "If men define situations as real, they are real in their consequences."[3] Or in terms of the context of the above tweet: the statements about the European Union on which Brexit was based, were mostly false. But Brexit as an outcome is an actuality.

Lil Internet's tweet addresses a hyperreal society of fluid simulation, and refers to the brutal wake-up from this VR dream, in which a decision was made that was not supposed to produce real consequences. We can also imagine the inverse—experiences in VR making increasing claims to being (legal) reality. Legal scholar Jack M. Balkin writes that the proliferation of legal truth is important because it:

> shapes, directs, and constrains how people live their lives. It produces incentives and disincentives for people's conduct. [It] shapes people's beliefs and understandings. Law has power over people's imaginations and how they think about what is happening in the world. Because law's truth is not the only truth, and law's vision of reality is not the only reality. Law's power to enforce its vision of the world can clash with other practices of knowledge, and with other forms of truth. […] Law continuously creates a form of knowledge—legal knowledge. As soon as law creates a category or an institutional structure, it is possible for things to become true or real in the eyes of the law whether or not they are judged true or real from another perspective.[4]

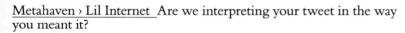

Metahaven › Lil Internet Are we interpreting your tweet in the way you meant it?

LI Yes, you are reading my tweet correctly. Here are a few thoughts and hypotheses that currently inform some of my societal analyses:

— As societies spend more and more time immersed in VR, the schematic of VR engagement can become preferable to what is experienced in analog time and space, and people start to demand this schematic of analog reality.

— The ultimate freedom this post-fact era offers, is the freedom from being wrong—like VR, it's the freedom to conform reality to your subjective "truth," as opposed to a totalizing consensus or democratized "truth."

— In VR we inhabit echo chambers to avoid cognitive dissonance. Post-fact enables these illusory "safe spaces," such as chat rooms filled with like-minded people, to exist in objective reality.

— Smartphones have reduced the separation of reality from VR, making the two realities nearly seamless. VR begins to function as an augmentation of reality, rather than a separate space—we are the closest to true hyperreality (in terms of the elimination of a divide between reality and simulation) that we've ever been, and Trump, post-fact, etc., are all growing pains of society's transition from reality to this hyperreality.

— The danger arises from there being no permanence in VR. While we've already done away with fact in order to bring reality closer to our self-curated VR experience, we will never be able to do away with permanence. There will be no "post-permanence" reality. Only through drastic (and likely violent) reminders of the permanence of reality will society realize that VR-informed decisions like the Brexit vote have much higher stakes when enacted in real life.

— There is an immediate pedagogical imperative to teach people the structural and operational differences that exist in VR space as compared to analog, organic space: to teach them how empathy is lost through online communication, how anonymity—relative or complete—leads to an increase in sociopathic engagement, how the algorithm-directed attention economy rewards communication differently than in analog communities, and so on… Mere awareness of the dissimilarity in structure provides a frame through which people can more cautiously engage in online VR space.

— Access to all data, to every fact, has not lead to a more enlightened, objective society but to one where each individual's subjectivity is based on *feelings* (validated by the echo-chamber-like algorithms of the feed and self-curation) that *demand to become reality*. No matter if this demand is used for left or right, socially liberal or conservative politics, we now live in an era of unprecedented selfishness, in which billions of individuals each insist reality conform to their own subjective experience—because that's *how it is in VR.*

MH › LI It is interesting to see this "demand that feelings become reality" as a full side effect of the technological stack, of which VR is only one part. It is remarkable that as recently as only a few years ago the term "VR" seemed like an antiquated concept associated with low-resolution fantasy worlds. And in a way, when you limit the concept to an individual illusion taking place inside a headset, it still feels that way, with the exception that the screen has brought us so close to the retina that it has come to exclude everything else.

We could then think of a "VR-less VR," a mental condition where the presence of the gadget is no longer needed to instill the disorder. Can VR's effects be achieved by other means? VR wouldn't be so powerful if it didn't adjust itself to our preexistent desires and tendencies, if it didn't respond to our hopes and fears, only to then shape them. The demand to have an infinitely shapeable reality that obliges individual emotions is a marketplace for the technological stack and its shareholders.

But what if we take the headset and VR out of the equation and apply this demand to reality itself? Design theorist Benjamin H. Bratton equally brought this up in our film *The Sprawl (Propaganda about Propaganda)* (2015) in his description of "cognitive fundamentalism" and "subtitling the real." It isn't just about supplanting the real with desire, but also about subtitling or interpreting reality so that everything becomes ideologically flattened. It seems that with the lead-up to the Brexit vote, the Leave camp used exactly these tactics.

Your imperative to teach people the difference between VR and reality is interesting—would this be instead of a "media literacy," a sort of "reality literacy" class? What would the exercises look like?

LI_ I want to be clear about my use of the term "VR"—I'm using it literally, as in any simulated experience that is meant to be perceived as "reality," or is assumed to follow the same rules as analog, organic life. I think of social media as VR. I cannot allow myself to equate the simulation of the internet—no matter how social—with its organic counterpart, and often think about social media as simply an MMORPG: a massive multiplayer online role playing game like *World of Warcraft*. When I first thought of this analogy—social media as an MMORPG as opposed to some sort of mirror for our "real" social lives—something clicked. I realized that the rule set of online space is extremely simplified when compared to "natural" space, not to mention the fact that the simulation itself takes place on a flattened plane.[5] If a majority of society ends up spending a majority of their (societal) time online, and if the online space is gamified and motivated by an attention economy, you end up with a society ultimately directed by the game, as both the "virtual" and the "reality-based" society is thought of as being one and the same. This MMORPG, this VR of social media space has begun to affect our cognitive and perceptual framework when in "natural" space. We think more computationally, we believe that even in the natural world (sometimes referred to as "meatspace") rule sets apply. It's the difference between looking at life as something understood through heuristics and one that behaves according to algorithms. I believe this confusion between these two types of "firmware" has led to the resurgence of identity politics on all sides of the political spectrum. Determine an identity, define that identity, denote a rule set for this identity, work out the metrics and data for each identity, and demand "reality's feed" adjusts. Of course, all of the inequalities addressed by activists are valid, except I believe that in analog life identities operate with much more nuance and much less clarity than the algorithmic framework and rule sets suggest. The very idea of applying rule sets to the natural world is a sign that humans are beginning to mimic the operations of the simulation they spend a big part of their lives within.

I used to consider contemporary society as being truly hyperreal, but I recently started thinking of it as augmented reality, with the MMORPG layer organizing and determining people's actions in organic, analog space. When it comes to "media literacy" today, I think most importantly the structural distinctness of simulated and organic social life needs to be taught: "Hey kids, today we will talk about how the internet and social media operate differently from real life." The entire internet operates on an availability bias since only the novel has any chance of maintaining a signal in the noise. Young people are hurled into an augmented reality society that treats imitation and authentic as equal, without much knowledge of its social effects. We are plunged into something that affects every part of our lives without much awareness of its consequences. It's like the David Foster Wallace parable of the fish who asks, "what the hell is water?"[6]

MH_ In his influential 2003 essay "Are You Living in a Computer Simulation?," philosopher Nick Bostrom argues that a main product of our civilization is advanced computational power. One of the functions of these computational resources, if sufficiently powerful, might be to run simulations of the past. "Then it could be the case that the vast majority of minds like ours do not belong to the original race but rather to people simulated by the advanced descendants of an original race," Bostrom writes.[7] This goes as far as saying that life itself, as we experience it, becomes a function of computational power.

It feels like our Twitter feed is a constant stream of conceptual artworks: for example, Turkish President Recep Tayyip Erdoğan's FaceTime appearance on CNN in July 2016 after the failed "coup d'état."[8] They are not artworks as *objets trouvés* but as constant demonstrations of operative concepts, where the attempt to understand, unravel, and dissect every occurrence in and of that complex, stack-like computational architecture results in more weirdness—yet, weirdness with a clear capacity to shape reality. Nothing is clarified, and we only get pulled in deeper and deeper.

KC_ In our current condition we comprehend time differently; our short-term memory is reset every few weeks. I think this is due to the speed with which we receive new information, images, and news. How do we begin to think long-term?

With Brexit, the systems of power and organizational structures at play are beyond comprehension. Even the politicians involved are unable to grasp the situation. We know we are going to leave the EU, but somehow this was beyond our control or understanding in light of the processes involved (for example, in the work of Cambridge Analytica).

MH › KC_ In his 2015 testimony to the US Congress about "Russian disinformation," Peter Pomerantsev said "our global order is based on a reality-based politics." We featured this fragment in *The Sprawl*, with the intent to break it down—to show how absurd it sounds—since the project of *all politics* is to shape the perception of reality in order to act on it.

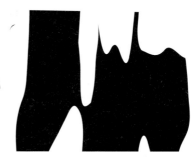

KC_ There is a breakdown between the infrastructure that shapes our experience of reality and the images we are presented with. The authenticity of an image, as well as its production and distribution, are no longer readable through our traditional methods of critique. For example, when I present an artwork of computer-generated imagery (CGI), there is often a complete misunderstanding of how it is made and the labor involved. This same misconception also surfaces in relation to events like the 2008 financial crisis or Brexit, where explanations are too abstract, which allows for different parties to reframe the circumstances of these events and create new narratives. Lies are increasingly becoming the norm within this current political condition—instead of showing how things work, it is designed to directly cater to how we feel.

I wonder how this reality relates to images; if, for example, we can't visualize offshore finance, it becomes hard to understand why it is wrong, even more so when the judicial framework creates a space in which such practices are legal. It's difficult to visually relate this abstract world to the real consequences it might have. If you can't see it or grasp its framework, how can you oppose it?

The notion that withdrawal is the most privileged position, fosters a discounted understanding of reality. I want to link this to Lil Internet's idea of a new media training and what that might look like. I'm thinking more widely about a concept called "ground truth," a term used in various fields to refer to information provided by direct observation, but in machine learning specifically it refers to an original image that is considered to be true and that the resulting copied images always refer back to. But the "truth image"—or source image—can itself be fabricated. It's almost the counterpoint to post-truth. Despite its source function, ground truth can be fictional: the image feed on which all consecutive "facts" and known truths are based, can be informed by something fictitious.

Ground truth can also refer to a particular sense of closeness—like photos taken on the ground in military training compared to aerial views of a space. The concept is used in the military to indicate that a source is literally close to the soil, so aerial photographs don't possess this truth, nor can they be used as evidence in the same way. I wonder if our proximity to reality also has a connection to our physical proximity to "the lens" or a situation or event, which begs questions pertaining to what this means for artistic practices and the way we produce work.

The meaning of a given truth within a system of cultural codes has become completely contextual—there are so many layers of meaning in politics at this moment in time.

MH › KC It's interesting that you mention CGI and its use in your work, as this is a computational procedure that supplements the "reality-based" photographic imagery produced by camera optics. Are you comparing CGI and finance on the level of their computational abstraction? How can we understand this new VR condition—what are the rules and conditions? How do we equip ourselves and as › LI suggested, what kind of training do we need? VR is a singular experience, and one that is concerned with affect. How does this relate to your moving-image work?

LI A future based solely on fictional narrative building—where the media space is the primary theater of war—is exhausting to me, particularly as someone who works as a video director for a living. All I can think of is my job becoming militarized, a fight for existence itself—could I make a compelling enough piece of media to steer opinion, regardless of facts, away from something like genocide? This incredibly high-stakes media-based narrative warfare is already here,

as seen in Trump's use of a faux-trailer for a Hollywood-produced film about North Korea's future and potential peace during the 2018 summit in Singapore (production company name: Destiny Pictures). That moment was a hyperreal slap in the face that gave me uncanny valley vibes about reality itself. It's already here, and I already fear my job may become militarized.

The fact that the pop culture world I work in is becoming increasingly politicized, that bold political statements like Childish Gambino's "This Is America" (2018) can top the charts and be extremely profitable, is another sign that World War III has already begun in the media theater.

The big question for me (in apprehension of an exhausting militarized music video future) is whether the crossing of this hyperreal threshold is reversible. Perhaps social and informational life on the internet will prove too disorienting, taxing, and tiring for many people and there will be a mass "log-off" movement. Perhaps one day the hot topic will be related to an imperative for a new media literacy. But more likely than not, I'll find myself in the trenches of a new war, where I'll think less about truth and more about how to make the reality I prefer seem the most real.

KC The main question is how you galvanize this insular experience to encourage forms of shared empathy or meaning. Images often serve as a reflexive space where artists attempt to critique reality, either from a position within this reality, or only slightly removed from it: this feels unproductive to me. That's why fiction is so important when creating images.

Being able to move between different positions, perhaps even truths, is important for an artist, especially in relation to questions and ideas surrounding essentialism. As artists we want to have conversations with diverse and complex voices, but none of these voices should be restricted to *only* speak from one position. Sometimes identities can limit us, but at the same time they are important, if only because we don't want someone in a position of privilege to use the "other" as cultural capital. But when identities become fixed, we get stuck and our positions can be used against us. As Lil Internet says, in mainstream media images have become "weapons" and the stakes are high. Understanding the infrastructure around this reality is so crucial: how algorithms work, how Cambridge Analytica was able to produce propaganda in such a targeted and precise way, and on such a large scale.

In terms of the value of "moving-image" work, I think art has become a derivative of all the other things we have to perform within a practice. Where is the space of moving image and where can it be most productive? In my own work, I'm interested in the construction of images, especially in the ability of images to embrace inauthenticity. Within the position of fiction, there seems to be more space that is useful.

Returning to the idea of a "new media training," understanding and teaching others to understand how ground truth works could be a path forward. I think it is important for people to learn to recognize the embedded infrastructure around images—it's certainly crucial to my own work.

1
Martin Gardner, *Science: Good, Bad, and Bogus*, New York: Prometheus Books, 1989, 91.
2
See Peter Pomerantsev, "Why We're Post-Fact," *Granta*, July 20, 2016, https://granta.com/why-were-post-fact/. Last accessed on August 7, 2018.
3
W.I. Thomas and D.S. Thomas, *The Child in America: Behavior Problems and Programs*, New York: Knopf, 1928, 571–572.
4
Jack M. Balkin, "The Proliferation of Legal Truth," *Harvard Journal of Law and Public Policy* 24, no. 1 (Winter 2003): 103, https://papers.ssrn.com/sol3/papers.cfm?abstract_id=383400. Last accessed on August 1, 2018.
5
See Norah Khan, "Empty Models, Flattened Language," edited transcript of talk at *WorldHack*, BabyCastles, New York, February 17, 2018, https://noranahidkhan.com/2018/02/17/empty-models-flattened-language/. Last accessed on August 7, 2018.
6
See David Foster Wallace, "This Is Water," commencement address, Kenyon College, Gambler, OH, May 21, 2005, https://web.ics.purdue.edu/~drkelly/DFWKenyonAddress2005.pdf. Last accessed on August 30, 2018.
7
Nick Bostrom, "Are You Living in a Computer Simulation?," *Philosophical Quarterly* 53, no. 211 (April 2003): 243, https://www.simulation-argument.com/simulation.pdf. Last accessed on August 7, 2018.
8
During the so-called coup d'état in Turkey in July 2016, Turkish President Recep Tayyip Erdoğan addressed the nation via FaceTime: *Reuters*, "Erdoğan addresses Turkey via FaceTime amid attempted coup–video," *The Guardian*, July 16, 2016, www.theguardian.com/world/video/2016/jul/15/erdogan-face-time-turkey-coup-attempt. Last accessed on August 17, 2018.

Kate Cooper
Kate Cooper is an artist based in London and Amsterdam. Cooper's work explores modes of representation and female forms of labor through recent developments in computer-generated imagery. Selected exhibitions include: *Freedom of Movement*, Stedelijk Museum Amsterdam, 2018; *Art in the Age of the Internet, 1989 to Today*, Institute of Contemporary Art, Boston, 2018; *Suspended Animation*, Les Abattoirs, Toulouse, 2017; and *Commercial Break*, Public Art Fund, New York, 2017. She is the director and co-founder of London-based, artist-led organization Auto Italia and attended the Rijksakademie, Amsterdam.

Lil Internet
Lil Internet is a writer, producer, and creative music director based in Berlin. He has worked with artists such as Beyoncé, Diplo, and Iggy Azalea, and is a co-founder and director of content for New Models. Lil Internet also produces pop and electronic music. His writing has appeared in publications such as *Artforum* and *Texte zur Kunst* and is often focused on platforms, hyperreality, narrative, and pop culture.

BHB In Tarkovsky's *Solaris*, this sentient ocean of the surface of the planet in Stanisław Lem's 1961 novel is a kind of cloud polis model of AI. Here, everything, all things at every scale and tempo, every memory and mote of dust, is part of a comprehensive nebular and numinous totality.

BHB As the hardware and software for artificial neural networks gets much, much smaller, and much, much cheaper, AI can be built into smaller and cheaper things. It becomes an internal quality of things more than an external supervisor of them. Things learn. Inanimate objects learn in ways independent of their supervision. Imagine it more like hundreds or thousands of little AIs in the room with you.

BHB This model is then more akin to a forested field of plants and insects, some mammals, some birds in the air, photosynthesis, organic cycles of seeding and decay, and like the bees and flowers whose couplings evolved over millions of years. It's an animated churn of different forms and formations.

BHB So, what else do we know? What else are we good for? If as in Lem's *Solaris*, the surface of the planet's ocean was sentient, planet Earth's strategy toward sentience includes layered networks of neurons in the folded gray matter of animal brains, particularly but not exclusively, the cerebral cortex of primates—namely humans. And we are, like cosmist Nikolai Fyodorov wrote over a century ago, the medium through which the planet thinks. By having folded some of its matter into the shape of brains, and then waiting a few million years for these blobs to sort it out.

BHB Earth has very recently learned its own age. Earth is about 4.6 billion years old. This confident figure for the age of the Earth came as late as 1953. This was the same year that Samuel Beckett premiered the play *Waiting for Godot*. We, the Earth's digestive residue, were able to discover and know the planet's own duration, which is quite an impressive thing, since for most of our existence, we thought the planet ran on our time.

BHB Was this project, in which Earth formulated from itself a biochemical intensity—that is, humans who would prove capable of knowing how old Earth is—worth the cost? Was discovering this fundamental truth worth exhuming hundreds of millions of years of pre-Mesozoic biomatter for two centuries of fuel supply and the inauguration of mass extinction? Perhaps a better question is: what would make it worth it? Must the price of the accomplishment of Copernicus—moving the human off-center—be to destroy, or at least threaten, that which it knows? The answer of course is not given in advance; it's something that must be designated—here and then, there and now.

MH You always go well past what people might assume is your final position, comfortable straddling lesser-known abstractions and narrating these with artistry and humor. We are attracted to the ultimate return to sense as a way to know. What connects us—maybe—is the idea of the accident as included in the design, not as some sort of exception that is a function of the system and central to its logic. Design is not merely a tool, but also a lens. We currently see this lens becoming stronger and stronger; it's becoming a telescope.

BHB I agree on design as something that must not only be comfortable with ambiguity, but with accidents. There are certain ways in which particular notions of design telescope down to eliminate ambiguity, to make things that are so intuitive and obvious that it "has to" be that way. While I'm thankful for doorknobs that work the way I imagine they will, I think taking this as a universal principle has, in the long run, also brought its own accidents and its own problems.

Human-centered design (HCD)—from Steve Jobs to Don Norman and the rest—deals with the moment at which an object's interface explains complex and contradictory systems to users. One way is to try to understand the folk ontologies by which users imagine the system must work, and to design interfaces that correspond to these mythologies—something Apple has done well. The other is to design interfaces that increasingly demystify and disenchant those kinds of objects; this has proven harder to do. I think one of the things that has occurred to us is that the interface itself has become this dream world of self-perpetuating, self-reaffirming intuitive mystification. It's not surprising that the ultimate ramifications of HCD applied to global infrastructures is a dangerous geopolitical imaginary, narrowing worldviews through an infinite mirroring process that occupies a place previously held by politics.

BHB I think part of the question might be to explore further the kinds of diversification for this to function. As part of a next subversion of these questions around the stack, I have been working on the development of global China as a dominant player within stack geopolitics.

لقد نشأنا ما بين الظاهريّ والاحتمالات
والمُستبعَد والأبواب الدوّارة والحوائط
العاكسة وطائراتٍ بدون طيارٍ.

أفضالٌ. خبزٌ وحليبٌ وسكرٌ. ملابسٌ من
صنع اليد. عملاتٌ من صنع اليد.

إن جدّي عالمٌ.

حين يأتي لاصطحابي من المدرسة

وقد ارتديتُ كنزتي الزرقاء

يقولُ أنها حمراءُ اللون.

يضمُ يديَّ بين يديْه، ويعدُ أصابعَ كلِ
واحدةٍ. كمْ إصبع؟

يرسمُ يرقةً،

ويقولُ أنها فراشةٌ.

كيف يا جدو؟ أنت تَمزَحُ.

حينما تُمطرُ

لابد أن تسطع الشمسُ.

ستتكاثرُ الغيومُ مجدداً، النهارُ.

خطأٌ لُغويٌّ. أُحجيةٌ نقومُ بحلّها ونحنُ
نضحك.

الشمسُ تختبئُ في زُرقةٍ بلا قمرٍ.

في قريةٍ صغيرةٍ، لا تتجاوزُ مساحتُها
أربعة بلدانٍ

على اتّصال بالعالم، من دون هاتفٍ أو
شبكةٍ

ومن دون طائراتٍ تحطُ في مطارها
المزدحم

في هذه القرية التي ذاع صيتُها، ويجهلُها
الجميعُ

تعيشُ امرأةٌ متقاعدةٌ، بلغت عامَها الخامسَ
أو السادس

لستُ أنا هذه المرأة، إلا إن أصرَّيتم.

هذه هي ملحمتَا. لا تقلقوا، فهي ليست
بالطويلة.

إنها السرُ الذي سمعه الجميعُ.

قبل أن نستطردَ، فلنضبطُ ساعاتِنا

فساعةُ المحطّة العتيدة

قد أخطأتْ، حينما أشارَت إلى انتصاف
النهار
إذ جمَعَت بين الرقمين واحدَ واثنين،

فلنتّفقَ إذن:

إنها الساعةُ الثالثةُ.

والآن، تحت ناظريّ الأقمارِ الصناعيةِ

ما بين نقاطٍ مُتّصلة تحتَ الأرض [فوقَ
الأرض]

ارتُكِبَتْ جريمةٌ:
قُتِلَتْ يرقةٌ بدم باردٍ.

أرجوانيٌّ داكنٌ، كالحبرِ.

لن نتّفق هنا: حينما يصيرُ واحدٌ وواحدٌ
ثلاثةً.

لأنني قلتُ هذا. لأنني أنا.

ولكن حينما يصيرُ واحدٌ وواحدٌ ثلاثةً
بحكم القانون

فهذه ليست أنا! - مَنْ ذا الذي قالَ بهذا؟

وهل ثمة فارقٌ بين هذا القانونِ المزعوم

وبين قاعدةٍ تَنُصُ على أن واحداً وواحداً
اثنان؟

والآن، تحت ناظريّ الأقمارِ الصناعيةِ

ما بين نقاطٍ مُتّصلة تحتَ الأرض [فوقَ
الأرض]

ارتُكِبَتْ جريمةٌ:
قُتِلَتْ يرقةٌ بدم باردٍ.

أرجوانيٌّ داكنٌ، كالحبرِ.

MH In recent years, stemming from a recognition of the mapping perspective, we have been thinking about the level at which to narrate the contradictions and consistencies being produced. We now think about what we call the perspective of the inhabitant rather than that of the map. It's not so much at the human level. It's much more about the level at which the sensual meets the sci-fi.

BHB A particular kind of sensuality, yes.

MH We were thinking of the film *Arrival* (2016), for example. It's based on a book called *Story of Your Life* (1998), which deals with non-linear time and our gradual discovery that the language that is used does not differentiate between past, future, and present. This is something that teaches the protagonist, a linguist, to deal with traumatic loss. The film, however, is also half *Independence Day* (1996), and…

BHB …and Terrence Malick.

MH Yeah, and Terrence Malick. And there's Brancusi as well; he designed the spaceships. So there are all these ways in which the film does not embrace the full extent of its own consequences. This might be because the assumption seems in order for the story to remain relatable to an audience, it must stay away from these consequences. *Arrival* never really engages with either end of the spectrum of non-linear time. If you render this idea of non-linear time fully into language and understanding of events, you end up with poetry, and not with aliens functioning as a self-help group for the human protagonist. On the other hand, the main feat of the aliens is that they "come in peace."

The inhabitant's perspective was a very helpful one for us to engage with in thinking beyond models, and how to then start producing work. Perhaps we can talk a little bit more about the inhabitant, whether it's a person, an avatar, or even a story.

ML But isn't the inhabitant also a model?

BHB I would say that it is. I guess I would qualify the point about "experience." This interest does not disqualify the importance of the experience or empathetic identification. One of the things I really appreciate about the work that you make is the way in which it engages with cinema as a medium in flux, as it has become "interactive." This is more than form vs. narrative, it is an enactment and demonstration of ways of conceptualizing circumstances and relationships that we cannot see, both from the outside and the inside, both technically and experientially at once.

MH It is important to work toward narrative in order to be able to reject it. If you are only going for a disjointed experience of which the incoherence is the very point, maybe that won't work. It seems more interesting to build things from a mode of narrative that you can then also resist and work against.

BHB I agree. I would resist the notion of some fundamental criteria on which these "experiential" processes must depend. In your work, "interactive" experience is a phenomenon we stand outside of, perceive, and deal with on its own terms. It is an analytic object: the objectivity of affective interaction.

ML One thing that is clear in Metahaven's films: they are much more about presentation than representation. The forms of articulation are always foregrounded somehow, making the films experiential. They are about the situation in which you have an experience, often through atmosphere, rather than one that involves a traditional clear narrative. Let's pick up on the notion of empathetic identification, which you have spoken about. For you futurity does not depend entirely on identification, that is, in terms of how we've learned to engage in things by identifying with them. But within the realm that you present, identification is almost impossible. What are the implications of that?

BHB I'm not sure that identification becomes impossible or undesirable. My critique is more that identification need not be the precondition for a viable futurity, even if it feels as though it should be. We are used to speaking about identification as an interior experience, but there are also ways to think about identification as a process of exteriorization. I'm arguing on behalf of this exteriorization, of outsideness.

1
Foivos Dousos, "10 Tips for Content Producers in the Post-Truth Era," *Medium*, March 4, 2017, https://medium.com/@foivosdousos/10-tips-for-content-producers-in-the-post-truth-era-9e7fb6daee39. Last accessed on August 30, 2018.
2
See Claire Wardle and Hossein Derakhshan, "INFORMATION DISORDER: Toward an interdisciplinary framework for research and policy making," report, Council of Europe, September 27, 2017, https://rm.coe.int/information-disorder-report-november-2017/1680764666. Last accessed on August 24, 2018.

Benjamin H. Bratton
Benjamin H. Bratton is Professor of Visual Arts at University of California, San Diego. His writing spans philosophy, design, and computer science. Recent books include *The Stack: On Software and Sovereignty* (2016) and *Dispute Plan to Prevent Future Luxury Constitution* (2015). He is also program director of the The New Normal think-tank at the Strelka Institute of Media, Architecture and Design in Moscow, Visiting Professor at SCI-Arc in Los Angeles, and Professor of Digital Design at the European Graduate School in Saas-Fee, Switzerland.

Maria Lind
Maria Lind is a curator, writer, and educator based in Stockholm. Lind studied art history, Russian, the history of ideas, semiotics, and feminist theory at Stockholm University, and attended the Independent Study Program at the Whitney Museum of American Art, New York. She is the director of Tensta konsthall, Stockholm. She has previously worked as director of: 11th Gwangju Biennale (2016); graduate program, Center for Curatorial Studies at Bard College, Annandale-on-Hudson, NY; Iaspis, Stockholm; and Kunstverein München, Munich. She is a professor at the Oslo National Academy of the Arts, and received the 2009 Walter Hopps Award for Curatorial Achievement. Lind's writing appears in *Selected Maria Lind Writing* (2010). Recent co-edited publications include *Art and the F Word: Reflections on the Browning of Europe* (2014), *Contemporary Art and Its Commercial Markets: A Report on Current Conditions and Future Scenarios* (2012), and *Performing the Curatorial: With and Beyond Art* (2012).

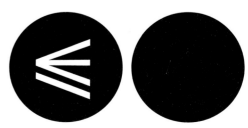

113

A puzzle. Laughed – Solved!
Головоломка. Розсміявся – Розгадав!

Dark purple, ink-like.
Темно-пурпурово, чорнильно.

Hometown, 2018
fiction, two-channel, 30 min
Arabic and Russian with English and Ukrainian subtitles

Hometown

next

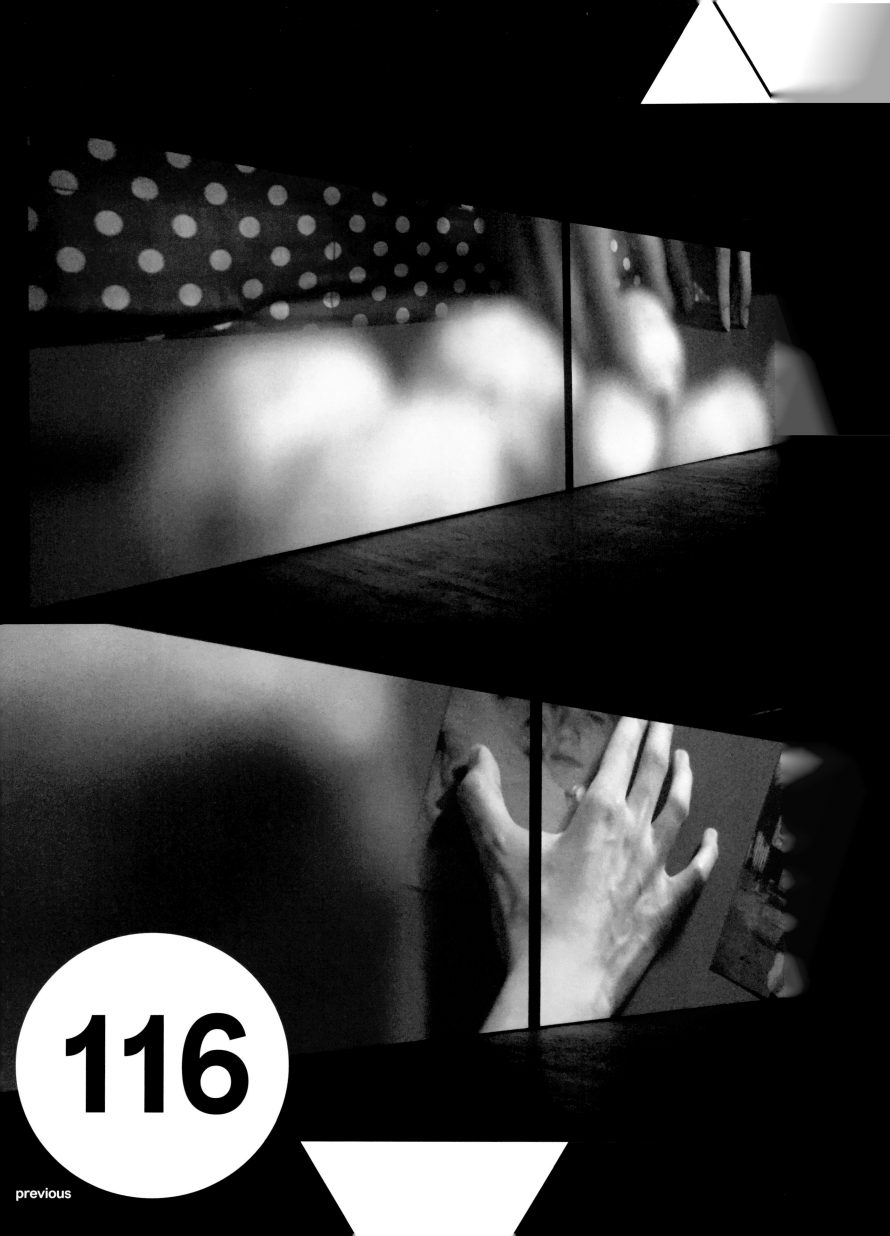

116

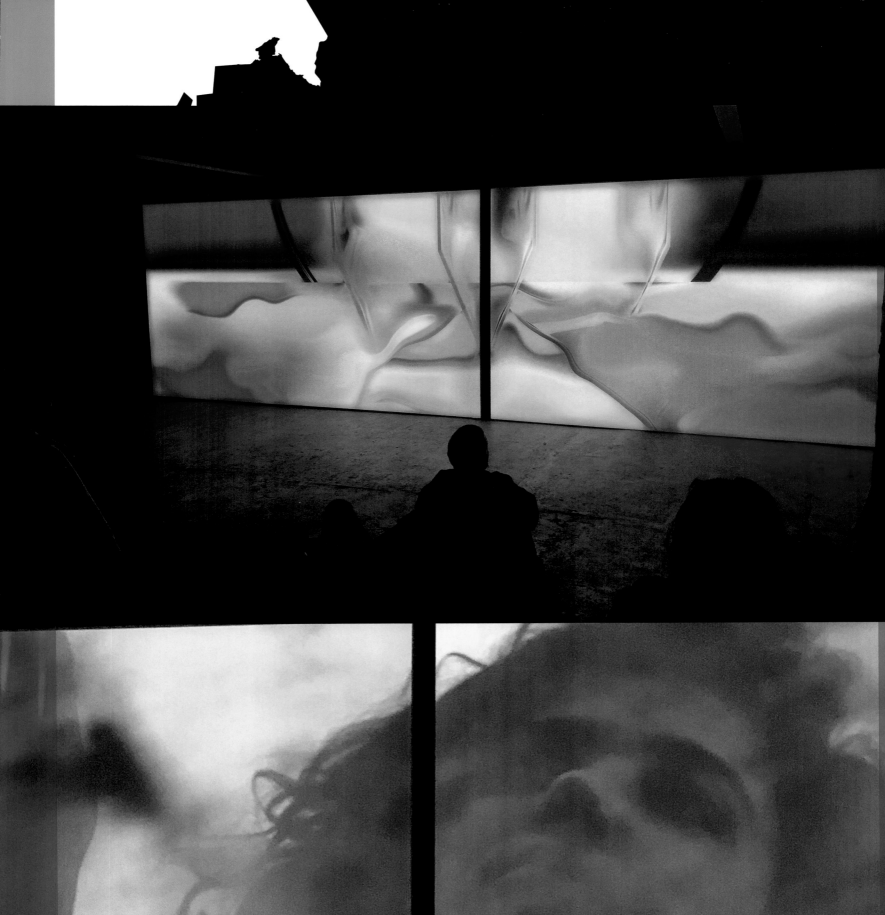

tastes s of fruit, the orchard, of our ancient s
Смак фруктів із саду, нашої давньої землі,

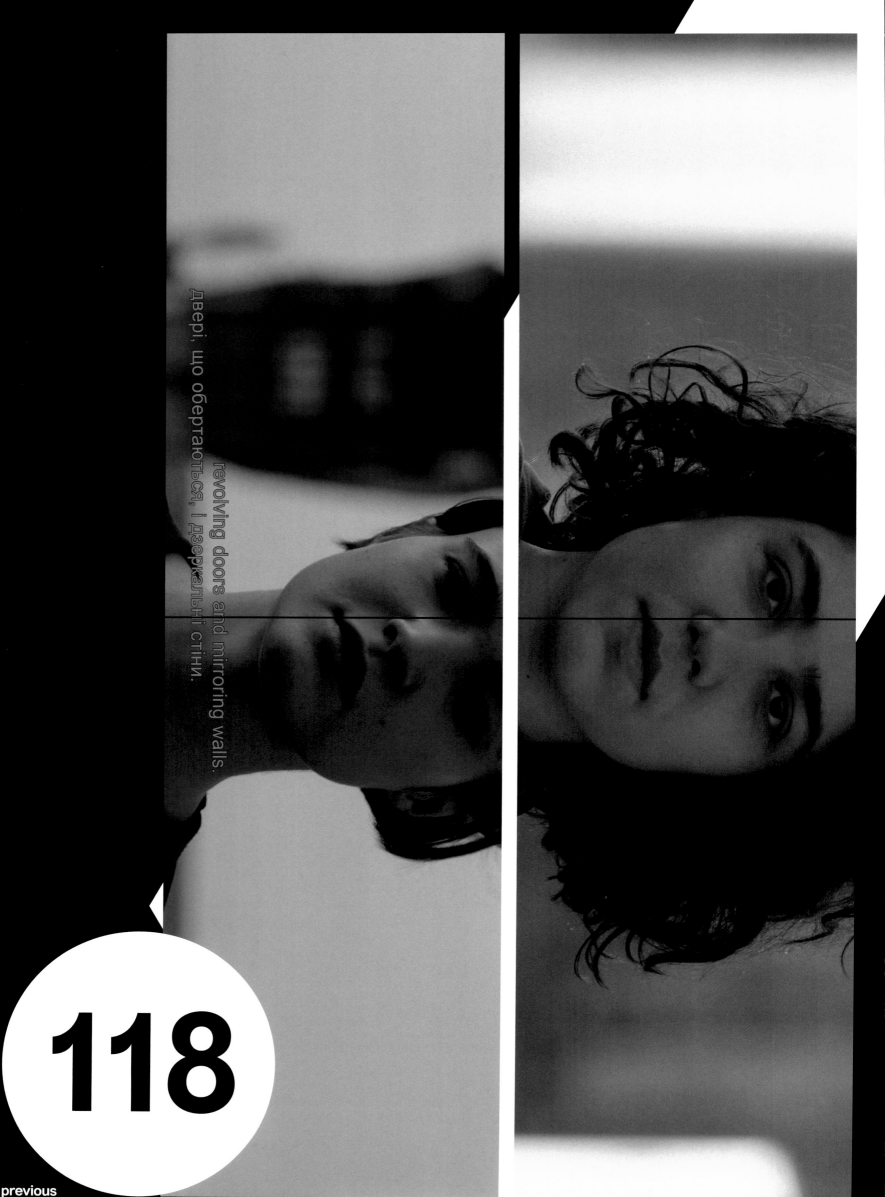

revolving doors and mirroring walls.

двері, що обертаються, і дзеркальні стіни.

118

a crime happened: a caterpillar got murdered in cold blood.
скоєно злочин: гусінь холоднокровно вбито.

сонце — симуляція,

sunrise — :simulation,

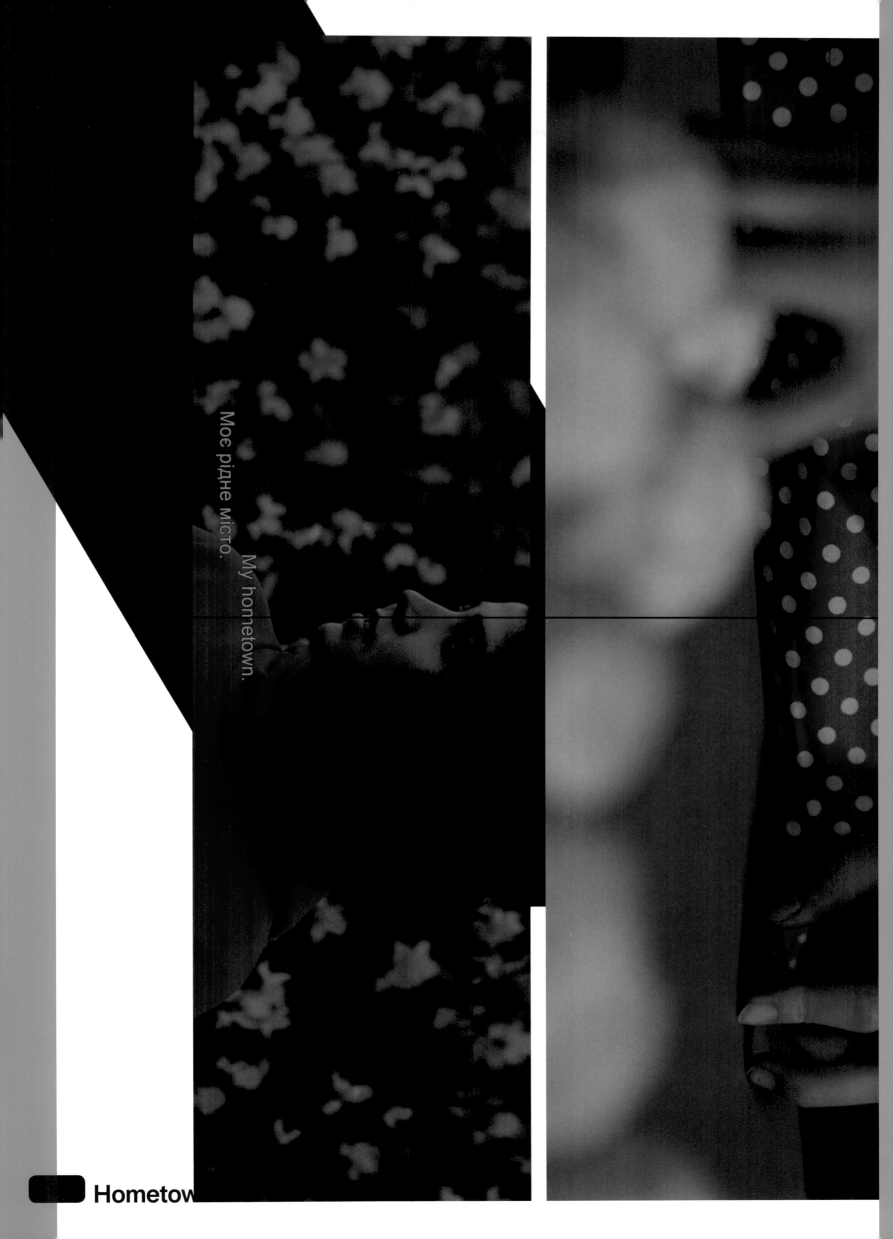

Моє рідне місто. My hometown.

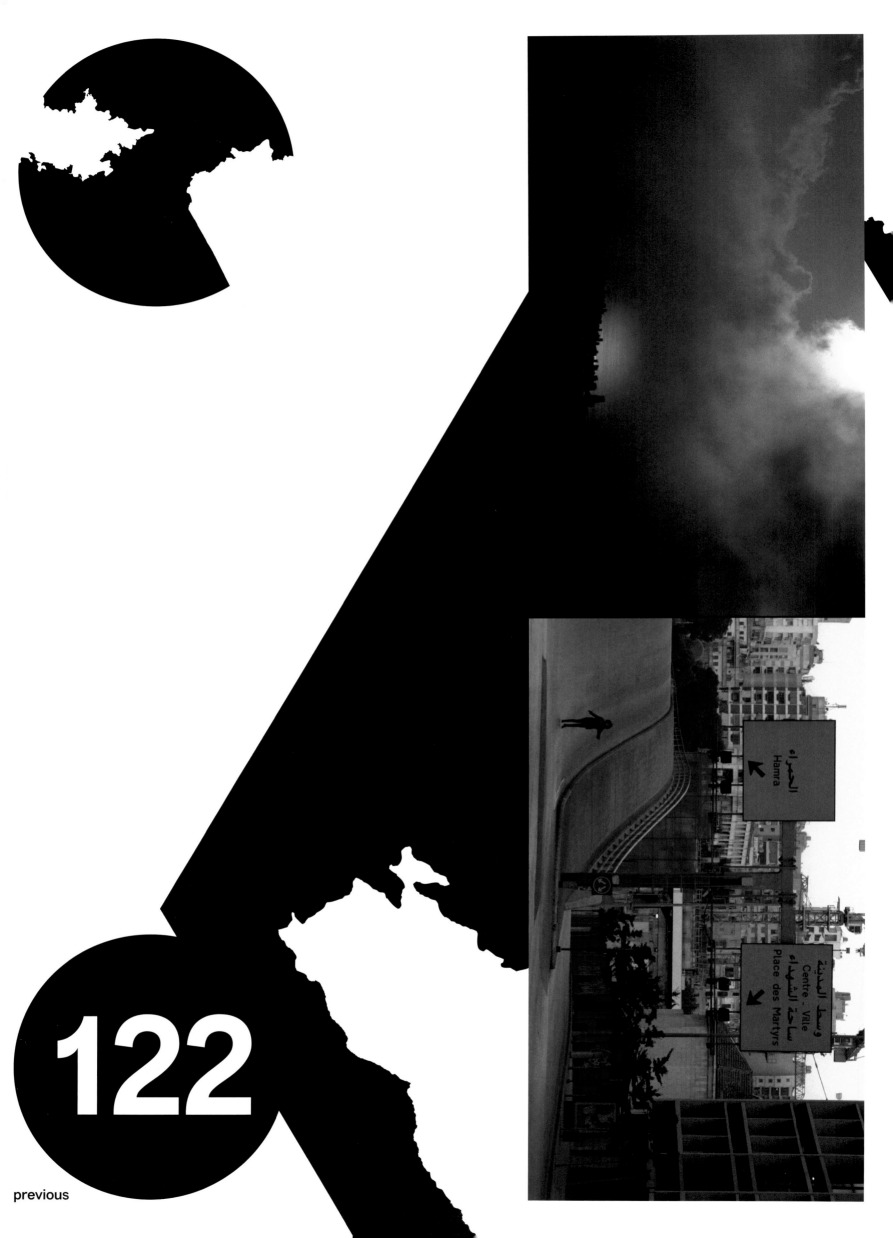

Possessed, 2018
fiction documentary, 63 min
English
co-directed with Rob Schröder

next

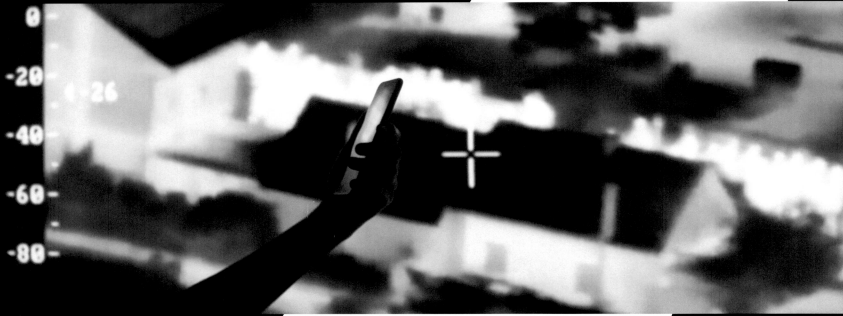

124

Possessed

next

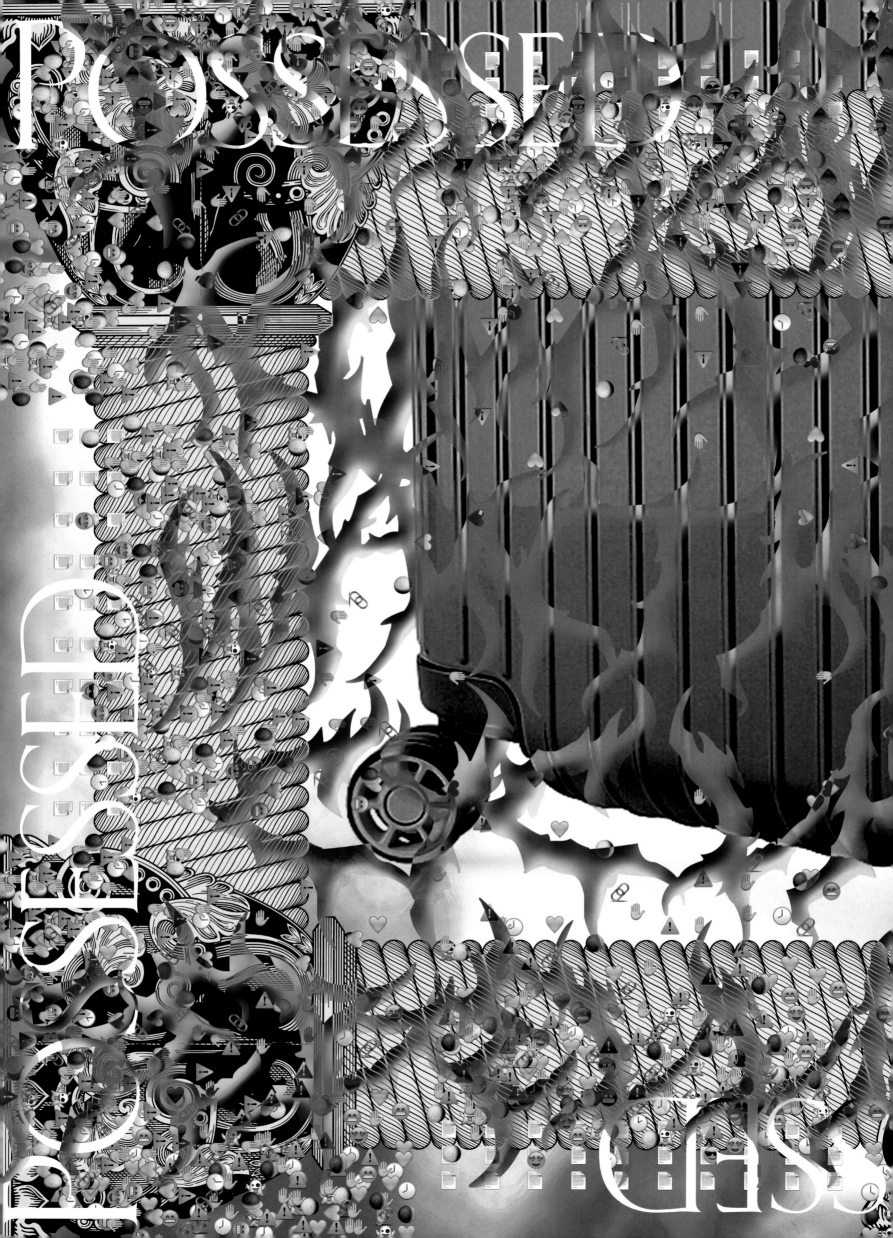

Metahaven Like us, you use fiction in your writing. Not so long ago we discussed, in this regard, the wonderful feeling of being liberated from making truth claims and, in a sense, being a critic. But it's more complicated than simply avoiding a reality-based discourse, it seems. What is the logic of moving away from criticism? What does "fiction" liberate us from, given that we both engage fiction to relate to reality? With too much to critique, and critique always catching up too late, has the vocabulary of criticism exhausted its relation to its subject?

Brian Kuan Wood I do think that a few very large-scale systems that managed to faithfully stabilize objective truth claims are giving way to something else. Epochal sea changes are of course felt throughout history—and even as an individual person passes through different stages of life—but for some time now, we seem to be inside of a long adjustment of what can be expected from the nation-state. Suddenly that which formerly set the foundation for civic life and duty, life-enhancing infrastructure and technology, acceptable uses of force and military organization, looks like one big synthetic family among a number of others arising in less official or private domains. While this in itself can have quite dangerous consequences, it is accompanied by some kind of bursting abscess of narratives of arrival or becoming that don't play well with electrical grids and efficient tramlines. On the level of grand narratives the term to describe these may be colonialism, but on the level of the individual they can give way to a phantasmagorical redistribution of allegiances more willing to incorporate ethnicity, kinship, memories of conquest and flight, or identitarian self-exoticization. It often seems like the oldest truth-fiction is really history itself—whose power is as true and necessary as it gets, while at the same time being a sublime narrative machine, inscribing events into consciousness as much as consciousness into events.

Young people today understandably find themselves caught between taxonometric regimes organizing otherness. They are attracted to technologies for registering aberrant behavior patterns left over from Victorian ideas about gender or European eugenicist ideas of race. A term like "intersectionality" has a centripetal architecture that tends toward a center, harmonizing and neutralizing aberrant otherness into the cozy cosmopolitanism of the Western liberal metropolis. It's no surprise that with the rise of right-wing politics, European countries are perhaps interested in issues of structural equality than in United States-style diversity. European countries are perhaps stuck in a state of never-ending amazement at the appearance of foreign-looking faces on its streets and imagines the US to have a much more robust model for metabolizing these differences. In fact the US has always dealt with differences by replacing notions of equality with notions of diversity, which can only mean a constant, albeit meticulously managed, race war. Many of my curatorial students at the School of Visual Arts in New York—the majority of whom are not from the US—are concerned about "post-truth" and "fake news." I try to remind them that the real horror lies in trying to find "real news" or "truth-truth"—a kind of ancient teleological mindfuck that only philosophy and religion seem capable of addressing. But I also try to point them to some of your early projects, such as *Stadtstaat* (2009) and *Brand States* (2008), which have been important for my own understanding of these dynamics. These projects consider tourism logos as having more visual currency than state flags. In *Brand States* fiction is used operatively: states see their existence entangled with their image and attractiveness as a destination, their ability to market and narrate themselves beyond being a place where people and buildings most likely exist, but may or may not be much more. The need to attract tourism and foreign investment renders the nation an image, and it must be an immersive one. But how can a nation create the depths necessary for this immersive image? *Post-Borat* Kazakhstan, for instance, is investing heavily in gamified tourism—a kind of Pokémon Go meets Lonely Planet. The need for a nation to become an immersive image is a political and economic reality that has led to catastrophic or near-catastrophic conditions, particularly in countries with the wealth to have once invested heavily in public infrastructure—the dismantling of which is no whimsical speculative fiction. So in the long tail of Cool Britannia and creative-class rezoning experiments from the 1990s onward, *Stadtstaat* showed that the desperate use of design and branding to corporatize domains previously thought to be private—not only the private business sector, but also the private lifeworld—becomes so absurd that it switches us on to a much more ecstatic domain where state and corporate fictions and private fantasies together erupt into some strange wavelength of historical time. This was also around the time when a lot of critical and theoretical work was discovering what a warm nest the catastrophic or apocalyptic mode could be to write in, with the forward march of capital impossible to stem. You, on the other hand, approached the same conditions in a structural pop mode: with the weak demagoguery of a certain critical mode out of the way, the equally weak mechanisms of corporate governance could actually be approached in all their desperation as open-source and available for intervention. It's still a terrifying political prospect, but you managed to make it into (at least to my mind) an immensely inspiring artistic provocation to start trying to identify other registers to plot what was happening, both around me and within me, as these epochal shifts continued.

MH What about the form to present and embody such artistic provocations? Our 2009–2010 period work, which you call "structural pop," such as *Stadtstaat*, used graphic design to give these fictions some level of credible interface. *Stadtstaat* played on a long overdue transformation from walled city to infrastructural corridor, sovereign entity to network node, and centralized power to self-surveillance hub. It suggested both a new social network, titled "TRUST," and a new brand of fast food, called "Pizza Dystopia." The latter resonates with the accumulation of more-or-less globalized tastes in European public space, fading between East and West, pizza and dystopia, Poland and Belgium, social housing and capitalism, Montepulciano and Vapiano, and so on. Keeping these sensorial impressions on the level of structural pop prevents them from

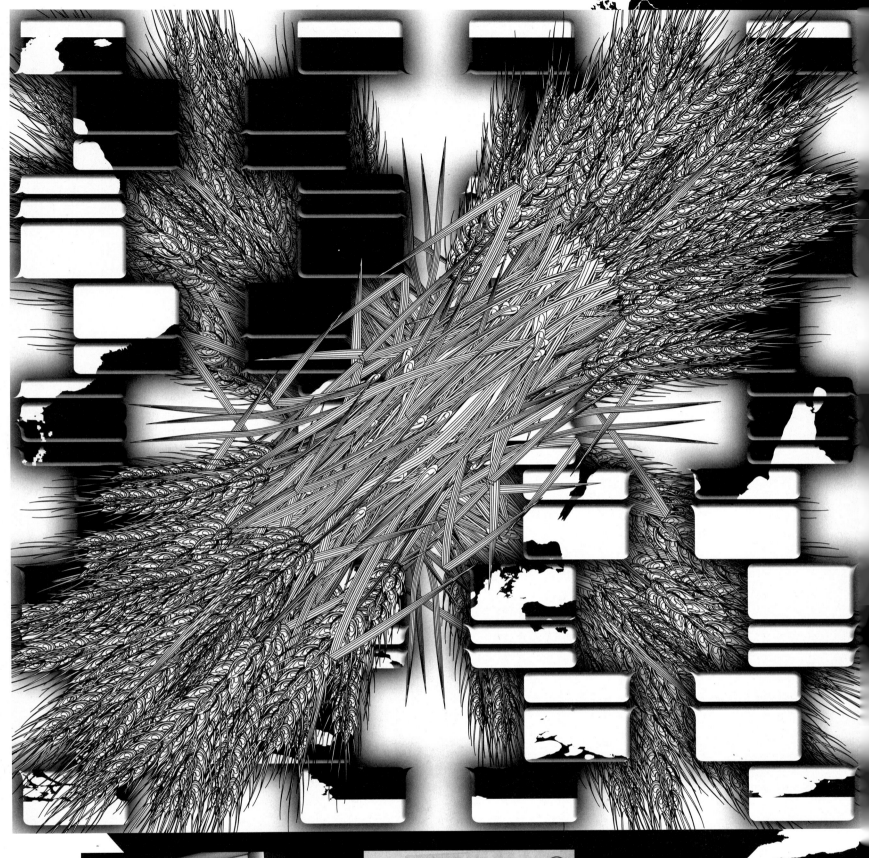

BU25-00/S1

Colloquium on Fake News
and Disinformation Online

13:30 -> 18:00

27/02/2018

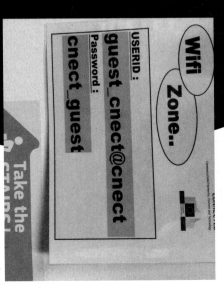

WiFi
Zone..

USERID :
guest_cnect@cnect
Password :
cnect_guest

Take the
STAIRS!

freezing into dystopian theory or creative industries startup lingo. If *Stadtstaat* were to exist today, it would call itself *disruptive*. It would have sun-tanned executives in BMW electric cars saying things like "Ciao bella!" and "one Aperol Spritz, please!" in smart-grid startups and pop-up gin bars. It would have solar and wind power. Its homes would have intelligent washing machines. But it still would have slums, Lidl, teenage runaways, right-wing populism, and Post-its. It would have innovated and patented its own color of Post-its. It would be at the nexus of major European drug trade routes.

Graphic design as the visual form of *change by which everything stays the same is*, on some level, interchangeable with a written narrative. Yet, design changes the feeling between things, and the descriptions of things. "Pizza Dystopia" can be narrated in words. It can also be typeset in stretched Futura capitals, by which it becomes a thing. To create structural pop you need to experience the "thingness" of the story: the pop-yellow RAL-color of the painted dry-port container cranes, the cracks in the mirroring foil of a hairdresser's window display, the dark-blue sans serif font of the "EURO ASIA" supermarket sign—which is actually a version of a major prepaid SIM card provider's logo.

The interoperability of visual and narrative forms resonates with your short story "The Story of Peter Green Peter Chang"[1] and the invention of "Bubble Rubble." It's quite imperative for our readers to know what Bubble Rubble is, because it is delightful.

BKW I wrote "The Story of Peter Green Peter Chang" to organize what I was sensing was happening to me around what we might call "reverse diaspora." What happens when we are called to return to a place of origin when that call arrives through anonymous flows of global capital? Perhaps something in the logistical operations of those flows reaches out and claims you as a long-lost beneficiary of some ancestral inheritance be it a galaxy or a pile of dirt. The territorializing apparatus of the global market gains a temporal axis: coordinates on a flat map are suddenly engorged with my own history. For instance, the coordinates of a vacation to Six Flags or a holiday in Thailand, suddenly lands me in front of my great-grandparents' vacant home that no one in my family has spoken of—in front of Six Flags or on a Thai beach. Or you invent a tool and then outsource its manufacturing to China, where it turns out they've already been manufacturing it for centuries. And you had forgotten that your grandparents are from there. Glitches appear in the very possibility of a global market, first in the assumption that all places can be abstracted onto a unified plane of equal relevance and modular interchangeability, and second, in the possibility of certain places being so loaded with meaning that their economic transactions become null and void.

People whose families experienced historical ruptures are full of gaps and cracks, sensitive to places that offer clues to those missing pieces. For "The Story of Peter Green Peter Chang," I wanted to have some fun with Chinese-American amnesia. Peter is a kind of virtuosic gentrification architect attracted to new markets in China who finds himself attempting to upgrade a property in his ancestral hometown, essentially trying to extract profit from something that already belongs to him. The trick came in moving energetic matter through time and perhaps in him. He develops his own technologically advanced building material called "Bubble Rubble."

He nicknamed it Bubble Rubble for paradoxically combining the weightless properties of bubbles with the fragmented material properties of decayed or derelict infrastructure. The trick came in moving energetic matter through time in a way similar to a financial trader, although we can never be certain, as the research remains undocumented and the technology mostly hearsay. According to the rumors, this Bubble Rubble borrowed from both the economic aspirations of historical communities of the land on which he built and the material decay of existing structures at his disposal. This combination, as the story goes, makes possible a kind of hyper-material that resolves apparently conflicting temporal axes into a single plastic substance—concretizing both the desires and disappointments at either end of a building's lifespan and cloaking them within the retro-modern vernaculars favored by gentrifying building developers. What appeared to be mostly baked together out of prefab floorplans and made-to-order ventilation systems were in fact buildings whose very existence was spectral to the point of being holographic, while at the same time absolutely materially present.

MH Perhaps something *Stadtstaat* forgot about, what with its single-minded focus on "European values," was Asia. Central Asia is becoming further integrated in economic infrastructures together with China and Russia. The One Belt, One Road Initiative is an infrastructural axis from eastern China to the United Kingdom that delivers indirect structural influence for China in Central and Eastern Europe through massive investments in these regions. For some, the initiative is the wave of a magic wand bringing the idea of Eurasia to life; for others, it unwelcomely re-centers world Schmittian geopolitics on the "world island." Somehow, the New Silk Road—even if it isn't directly political—has the effect of a Sadim touch, with several countries falling into structural authoritarian rule: Turkey, Hungary, Poland, to name a few. The "negative soft power" of authoritarianism is also a purported stability in the face of a West that has confirmed, time and again, that its future is only as good as the stock market. This power is in charge of controlling "truth" itself, if we take truth to be various flows of empirical data. What happens next is akin to something you elaborate in your 2014 essay "Is it Love?"—inspired by Haddaway's 1993 Eurodance hit "What Is Love?"—in which the liquid social fabric of affect and love bears the brunt of massive economic uncertainty, leading to a soup-like subsistence in seas of "capitalist realism"—using the term coined by the late Mark Fisher in his book of the same name.

BKW One thing we have in common is a modulation of scale: if you say galactic, I say hairstyle; if I say God, you say font kerning. Not only is there creative play and fun in this dance of throwing the ridiculous against the eternal to see what sticks, and vice versa, but it is also the game one plays with and against truth, like a heuristic process or a logical test.

The question of love and Eurasia makes me think of your term from the *Brand States* period: "super-state abyss." The question of Eurasia could be said to be similar to that surrounding the emotional economy of our favorite super-state model: the European

The European Commission (EC) has started several initiatives to combat Fake News. In a series of public collo-quia, the EC discusses the threat of fake news and online disinformation, and what it should do about it. Showered in acronyms and good intentions, it is not always clear to what actions these meetings amount, and if and how they understand the interplays between computation, social construction, and shifting shapes of power.

photo Metahaven, 2018

131

Union, as a kind of post-national or super-national form of belonging and exploded version of the nation-state with different ethnicities, provinces, languages, etc.[2] The nation-state is a rather odd and unstable protocol for containing these different groups of people. We still see this federation of federations as a promise for world peace, whose failure we lament, as we do that of the United Nations. If it's really such an abyss—the political horizon of bankrupt European-style social democracy on the one hand, and savage US-style corporate governance on the other—it's no wonder the far-right is taking over.

We are faced now with a fascinating question: who can be invested with the moral authority to broker transactions, fundamental to money or contracts on any scale—the third party with the objectivity and power to enforce in case of any breach? This basic form of abstraction allows for an agreement to be captured and moved to a different place while carrying the same value.

Money is backed by national central banks or the US military industrial complex. The blockchain model offers a new world-historical option, with software able to record transactions with minimal volatility. Between friends and family, it's trust—the history and the relationship itself—that ensures promises are kept, or compensated when they're not. My essay "Is it Love," which you used for your film *City Rising* (2014), experiments with overplaying the slide from national or state governance into the private domain. Rather than understanding the private as corporate domain, which has arguably no objective moral authority whatsoever, I wanted to consider the domain of private life: the precarious worker or entrepreneur as the exemplary hero of neoliberal economy. As with your *Stadtstaat* "Trust" currency, I wanted to explore the nightmare of all public services operating through love between people. Love becomes a structural hegemon ruling the world. At the same time, plumbing the lower depths of Western humanism was a dead end and intellectually disingenuous. Many of these processes led me to feel uncannily at home in China, Hong Kong, and Taiwan. I visited more often and discovered answers there. Part of this probably had to do with realizing that

when left alone in the world—structurally, institutionally, financially, working on a laptop in some café—it is wise to address the historically constituted parts of the self that healthy institutions usually fill in one way or another, in an honest encounter with what they really are and where they are from.

Funnily enough, Xi Jinping, China's General Secretary, has spoken often of China's "civilizational" project, and the One Belt, One Road project makes no secret of China's expansionist ambitions. The "reverse diaspora" I mentioned earlier is by no means just about return—it is about a pendulum of global power swinging from the place you moved to, to the place you moved from generations before. Many are quick to point out that China is unsophisticated in dealing with cultures other than its own—yet it contains over fifty ethnic groups, while having lost millions of people to waves of emigration in the country's many upheavals throughout the modern era. I must have partially been "summoned" by a civilizational turn in China's neoliberal policy, as if it was seeking contact with its long-lost children.

Neoliberalism is volatile, with sudden reallocations or redistributions of resources. Successful state branding might entice you to move toward the place you are originally from; the terms of diaspora can suddenly become inverted. Since the nineteenth century, China has been ravaged to hell in the Opium Wars, the civil wars, famine, the Cultural Revolution, and onward and onward. Now it controls immense financial and technological power, proclaiming itself beautiful and vital. Yet it also sees itself as on the losing side of colonial history, a rare view for a country in such a strong position. China's vast power could place technology in the service of something quite different than the old deterministic Hegelian view of progress or the creepy libidinal fervor of "disruptive tech." When major parts of the memory are missing, technology might also serve to reconstitute those parts and heal the organism. With these movements somehow backwards and forwards into strange new forms of foundationalism, or new ways of grounding the self and sense of place in the world, I watched your latest film

Hometown (2018) with great interest. With all of your projects, every single time I've been surprised by the way that you approach the subject. I'd be interested in knowing what you had in mind in making *Hometown*, since we never really spoke about it. In a way, I felt we didn't need to—I knew that in your family you had experienced birth as well as death, and this made me think it was an important film for you. I may have even wondered, tongue-in-cheek, whether the film wanted to move more to the "haven," and away from the "meta" side of things.

MH Aside from the subject matter, the impetus for *Hometown* is to develop a vocabulary that shifts away from critically proper, to a lyricality that embodies it. The impetus to glorify aspects of existence can then shine a more truthful light on the problems of and around it: you glorify something under circumstances that aren't so glorious, opening up a space where this gap is exposed. Two very particular examples of writing embody this, which we quoted in *Digital Tarkovsky* (2018).

In March 2000, journalist Anna Politkovskaya reported from inside a tent school for refugees in the destroyed Chechen capital Grozny. The children are assigned to write a glorifying text about their country. Politkovskaya cites the writings of a young pupil, Marina Magomedkhadjieva, to expose the trauma of loss:

My city Grozny always radiated beauty and goodness. But now all that is gone like a beautiful dream and only memories remain. The war is blind, it doesn't see the city, the school or the children. All this is the work of the armadas from Russia, and therefore not only our eyes are weeping, but also our tiny hearts.

Now we have nowhere to go to school, to play and enjoy ourselves. Now we run back and forth and don't know what to do. But if they asked us we would say: "That's enough bloodshed. If you do not stop this senseless war, we should never forgive you." Soldiers! Think of your children, of your own childhood! Remember the things you wanted in childhood and what your children want, and you'll understand how sad and difficult it is for us. Leave us alone! We want to go home.[3]

1
Antwood—"Sublingual" (Planet Mu, 2017)

Juha van 't Zelfde "I work directly with brands," says an anonymous voice, addressing an imaginary audience, "and only brands that I like, that I personally would use and that I think you guys would actually care about."

I wanted to start with something that I imagine to be quintessentially Metahaven: an ultra-HD sensibility for political radicalism, aesthetic experimentation, and internet wit. Producer Tristan Douglas, also known as Antwood, made this album *Sponsored Content* (2017) as an exploration of the idea of subversive advertising. He writes: "In the past year, I found that autonomous sensory meridian response (ASMR), which I had previously used as a source of Foley in my music, was a fairly effective sleep aid. I'd been using the videos in this way for a few months, when I noticed a popular ASMR YouTuber announced a plan to incorporate ads into her videos; quiet, subtle ads, woven into the content."[1]

The *Blade Runner* of punchlines DOT JPG? Antwood offers a pretty witty jibe at the kind of identity performance so typical of late capitalism.

Metahaven Ha! Maybe the *Blade Runner* of polkadot.com? First of all, we are friends, and collaborators, and you commissioned our first long film, *The Sprawl (Propaganda about Propaganda)* (2015), when you were the artistic director of Lighthouse in Brighton, before becoming the course leader of the Shadow Channel MA program at the Sandberg Institute, Amsterdam. Throughout our exchanges we have talked about music. Hence this playlist: it is somehow, a battle of the bands, but also, hopefully, a list that highlights some of our common favorites. But it is also edited, and manipulated. Its formation is both enabled and tainted by platforms like YouTube and Spotify, and things such as earphones, hectic days, and crowded cafés. As for *Sponsored Content*—that's somehow not completely how we feel right now. We feel much less internet these days. Has there been a time-lapse of sorts?

JZ Perhaps this song is more the Metahaven of *Uncorporate Identity* (2010), and less so of *The Sprawl*. For that Metahaven, there is another track on the album that may fit better: "FIJI Water." Music that will make your brain tingle.

2
Antwood—"FIJI Water" (Planet Mu, 2017)

MH The track itself—OMG! Especially in the moment where the synths are more hidden.

3
Henry Purcell—"When I am laid in earth," *Dido and Aeneas*, Act III, Véronique Gens, Les Arts Florissants, William Christie (Erato, 1995)

MH We respond to your initial entry with something that is the opposite of internet, and closer to our current mood. Are we experimental? Maybe not. Are we radical? That's a good question. Are we political? If so, in what way? Are we internet? Sorry.

JZ For some reason I have stayed away from opera for most of my life. Perhaps it is the class and price barrier that prevented me from going, but I have tried on various occasions (I even worked at the Royal Concertgebouw in Amsterdam for two years, which is close to the world of opera). This is obviously a very beautiful yet alien musical dialect for me. But the cello triggers my next selection, by a wonderful trio of artists.

MH Entire operas are on YouTube. We know people who spent large parts of their lives home-taping operas from vinyl records, and never saw one live. Opera as an art form speaks to many other things than class, including artistic, cultural, political, and literary factors, and obviously, emotions as well.

JZ No need to defend the art form. I meant the context in which it is presented: opera houses. The same goes for classical music and concert halls. But every art form has its crowds and its barriers, and those of opera and classical music are just the ones I find the most challenging. I prefer dingy basements I guess.

4
Jóhann Jóhannsson with Hildur Guðnadóttir and Robert Aiki Aubrey Lowe—"End of Summer Part 2" (Sonic Pieces, 2015)

JZ This is my DJ-muscle memory: I heard the cello from Purcell and in my mind faded into the one from Hildur Guðnadóttir in this saddest of pieces from this trio. Jóhann's passing is such a loss for the world. His scores, for *Sicario* (2015), *Arrival* (2016), and *The Miners' Hymns* (2010) just to mention a few, have added so much to cinema. He had only just started. This piece for me really reveals the intensity and gravity of work.

MH It's stunning!

5
t.A.T.u.—"All The Things She Said" (Universal Music Russia, 2002)

MH The video is captioned as follows: "Music video by t.A.T.u. performing All The Things She Said. YouTube view counts pre-VEVO: 5,405,015. (C) 2002 Universal Music Russia." That says pretty much everything about t.A.T.u. We are huge fans for their flaws, precisely because they are also the Milli Vanilli of the post-Soviet space: an entirely staged act produced by the male gaze, playing to all the preconceptions of its presumed audiences. Note: at the opening ceremony for the Sochi 2014 Winter Olympics, a version of t.A.T.u.'s *Nas ne dogonyat* (They're Not Gonna Get Us) (2002) was playing when the Russian athletes entered the stadium.

JZ I remember t.A.T.u., and at the time I wasn't wise enough to read it like this. To counter this, here's a sincere music video—wait, it's almost an opera!—from an entirely self-made, do-everything-yourself, and zero-fucks-given artistic polymath: Mykki Blanco. Shot in the German countryside in 2016 by *Control* (2007) cinematographer Martin Ruhe, the video is a theatrical short film about outsiders, forbidden romance, and violence. "I had once thought Europe was my safe haven from American white supremacy, and how wrong I became," Blanco told *The FADER* in an interview in 2016.[2]

The combination of his powerful poetry, musical intensity, and bewildering performances makes Blanco one of the most important artists—not just musicians—of his generation, and his Instagram and Twitter feeds should be part of every art school curriculum.

6
Mykki Blanco—"High School Never Ends" (Dogfood Music Group, 2016)

MH In terms of musical construction, just magical. Thanks for refreshing us after t.A.T.u.!

7
Napalm Death—"You Suffer" (Earache, 1987)

MH Before we move back into more recent music, may we remind you that this song is 1.316 seconds long and, for that reason, revolutionary? We're talking the United Kingdom under Thatcher, clouds of Chernobyl striking Europe, Cold War Reaganomics, and hardcore punk in the vein of Discharge merging with death metal with questionable musicianship in the dreary north of England. The lyrics are "You suffer… but why?"

JZ Solidarity! Love this. Needed this. Thank you. This is so much better than Brian Eno telling stories about how he composed the 3.25 second startup sound for Windows 95.

8
Kuedo—"Visioning Shared Tomorrows" (Planet Mu, 2011)

MH This is beautiful and somehow also quite atypical Kuedo. This track could kick in at two-thirds, or toward the end of a yet-unmade Adam Curtis film, in which it would accompany several shots of dancing people. In the voice-over, Curtis would say that the stories that Western politicians invented to keep their societies together, did the very opposite of what they were intended to do, and fragmented the political spectrum into ever smaller factions of "us" and "them." And here's something that he actually said: "The Left has left talking about power to *Game of Thrones*."[3]

JZ Bring out the Adam Curtis Bingo Card.

MH Yes! Curtis has to come up in every conversation that's vaguely about what we are talking about.

JZ "Visioning Shared Tomorrows" is such a good title too. This track is hope *sonified*. Pure paradise music. At the time, it not only introduced his new album—for me it also ushered in a new sound of high-definition trap fiction, picking up frequencies such as Lex Luger and Southside (working with rappers Waka Flocka Flame and Future) left off. I think Planet Mu label founder Mike Paradinas is owed credit here too, with familiar follow-up releases of futurist artists such as Jlin, Sami Baha, and Silk Road Assassins.

9
Eduard Artemyev—"Meeting on the Milky Way" (Melody, 1995)

MH We are moving closer to the present again. This is a recent experiment by the composer of the score of Andrei Tarkovsky's *Stalker* (1979). But listening to this track gets you into a Eurovision math metal Frank Zappa synth-harmonic reinterpretation of *Stalker* with the production value of a sound studio specializing in Fiverr commercials, as played in a Slovenian taxi cab. No-holds-barred MIDI mayhem.

JZ Sounds about right.

10
Laurel Halo—"Carcass" (Hyperdub, 2012)

JZ Let me see your electronic exaltation and raise it with Laurel Halo's eXistenZial expressionism. An acidic, phosphorescent yearning. "Carcass" is what I imagine the Social Media Rapture to feel like.

MH A really haunting track that grows on you. It's hyper-emotional, hard to pin down, hard to listen to, and hard to turn off. It has Halo's floating poetics. And yes, the Social Media Rapture.

11
Galina Ustvolskaya—"Symphony No. 2: 'True and Eternal Bliss,'" Yekaterinburg Philharmonia, Oleg Malov (Megadisc Classics, 2000)

MH Try and listen to this without shivers running down your spine and/or tears running down your cheeks. This Ustvolskaya symphony—which has also been performed by Reinbert de Leeuw and the Asko-Schönberg Ensemble, and has been portrayed along with its composer in a short documentary, *Scream Into Space* (2005) by Josée Voormans—is so powerful and all-encompassing, like a huge blow to the heart. It is so unbelievably straightforward in its delivery. It is also very loud, and yet, it has this incredibly beautiful inner space to it.

JZ I read somewhere on YouTube that "the symphony is written in a single movement presenting itself as a sound ritual without having much to do with the definition of the classical symphony." I am listening to it on headphones in a café in Amsterdam, which doesn't help with "feeling" the work. Would love to hear this live, the stomping instruments would surely scare the hell out of the audience. The voice reminds me of Keiji Haino in Nazoranai.
Beautiful intensity change halfway through.
The end. A spellbinding symphony.
These have been the longest 22 minutes this year. Leave it to classical music to challenge my attention span.

12
Nazoranai—"Feel The Ultimate Joy Towards The Resolve Of Pillar Being Shattered Within You Again And Again And Again" (Nazoranai, 2012)

JZ Ustvolskaya made me want to listen to Keiji Haino, the Japanese haunted weather god. Having worked with both musicians Oren Ambarchi and Stephen O'Malley, when they asked me in early 2011 if they could try out their new trio Nazoranai with Haino in Amsterdam some time, I was thrilled Koen Nutters of DNK could help organize their show at OCCII a few months later

133

Brian Kuan Wood

Brian Kuan Wood is a writer and editor in New York. He is an editor of *e-flux journal* and Director of Research at the School of Visual Art's MA in Curatorial Practice in New York.

Politkovskaya's university thesis was about poet Marina Tsvetaeva, who is understood to be one of the warmest and most lyrical twentieth-century Russian poets. When her daughter was three or four years old, Tsvetaeva wrote the following:

> There are clouds about us
> and domes about us.
> Over the whole of Moscow
> so many hands are needed!
> I lift you up like a sapling,
> my best burden:
> for to me you are weightless. [4]

This idea of burden, or best burden—what you love the most—is in a sense also the obstacle that keeps you from being totally free. That's very important. Criticality doesn't happen in a neutral space; it happens in a vulnerable space, where care for others is always on the same plane with the idea of judgment of the world. In Tsvetaeva, there's a lot of shifting between lyricality and darkness. This would amount to a description of her life. Another influential author for *Hometown* is Svetlana Boym. Her book, *The Future of Nostalgia* (2001), talks about a longing for something imagined that was never there. She quotes a poem about someone who returns home, finding a table there, covered with a white-and-red checkered cloth. This signifier tells them: "home." But if you think about it, it makes no sense. Was it even there? "Home" is built out of elements that are partially generic. In our film, the hometown is made out of footage of Beirut and Kyiv.

BKW A few days ago I went to a church in Berlin to see my old friend Hassan Khan, someone who's very important for my thinking and development. He was working with five choral singers on his new piece *tainted* (2018). I should clarify that I really hate being in any church—I grew up going to Catholic school, I had had enough of it then already. But I was surprised at how content I felt sitting in this particular church, realizing that nine or twenty blocks away in any direction, you would probably find another church. One choir member worked with or for this church, so I imagine he simply had a key to the door in his pocket. There was a complete mundanity not only in the setting, or use of the room and institution, but also the use of voice. Hassan's piece was entirely vocal. There were some printouts, and a smartphone on a desk. Beyond that, no modular synths, laptops, or musical instruments; there was no armature, no apparatus—just extremely skilled people opening their mouths, letting out sound. They were just using the room, in an embedded, existing network of buildings, which also happen to be churches. Maybe no one was religious, or maybe they all were. Like anywhere, it was simply a room in a building there for decades, and probably there for many more. You just open your chest and your mouth, and make sound; there doesn't have to be that much more to it. It was wonderful, deeply so. It made me think that there is something extremely important in working with things that already exist, that have been there and will be there later, or that you already carry around inside your body, whether you like it or not.

MH The artwork you describe seems to open up the possibility of that type of connection.

BKW I should add that Hassan's *tainted* is a very deliberate meditation on populism. It can't be coincidental that it opened up a channel to being serenaded by these ancient forms of applied universalism found in the family and the church.

MH Your experience of *tainted* could be seen as analogous to that of someone who, after having eaten at McDonald's for a long time, suddenly discovers the taste of fresh tomatoes from rural Macedonia, or something like that. The brutally simple and emotionally captivating situation of being in a room with singers who use just their voices—no electronic mediation—is like stumbling upon something that, as you say, already existed but feels new every time. It feels like a possibility that was obvious, but forgotten. Indeed, the relationship with the past is what populism is mining—often in the form of a kind of hoax—to minutely construct the idea that some political claim or story would be natural or pre-given. This is one of the pitfalls of the current political moment: we are having real feelings of attachment, real feelings about what is important, and these feelings aren't all that advanced or complicated. They are straightforward, and can be addressed by something as apparently trivial as singers using their voices in a church. Populism mines or aggrandizes these attachments by using a scaling-up model: the nation-state as a family, the political party as a family, an ethnic group as a family, etc., concurrent to making it seem as if the key to all this lies in some B- or A-side past—from which the target group is to simultaneously derive feelings of superiority and being scolded. The political use of love is, simply put, extremely dangerous material in all directions.

Making art today, in this heightened ideological tension, is also about navigating this reality. But what is lost, somehow, is a sense of the future. What we are left with is simply the present, in which we can feel and think, and the past, from which we can post-construct how we got to where we are now. Isn't this too limited?

BKW I have very little appetite for the future at the moment, so it's hard to lament its loss when most of what I seem to want now comes from the past. This also has to do with the Bubble Rubble. Lately, relations between past and future are prone to peculiar reversals, like plays of scale: it's difficult to distinguish between super-structural operations and their symptoms or derivatives. Sometimes you reach for the past, but latch onto the future, or you reach for the future and hit a wall—you can't get there without coming to terms with the past.

1
Brian Kuan Wood, "The Story of Peter Green Peter Chang," *Superhumanity*, February 1, 2017, http://www.e-flux.com/architecture/superhumanity/68641/the-story-of-peter-green-peter-chang/. Last accessed on August 13, 2018.

2
See Metahaven, "Europe Sans: History, Politics, and Protocol in the EU Image," *e-flux journal* 5 (April 2009).

3
Quoted in John Pilger, *Tell Me No Lies: Investigative Journalism and its Triumphs*, New York: Vintage Books, 2005, 423.

4
Marina Tsvetaeva, "Verses About Moscow" [1916], in *Selected Poems*, trans. Elaine Feinstein, New York: Penguin, [1971] 1994, 14.

in April. For me, this is a similar musical sublime as the Ustvolskaya symphony, those ultra-long pieces by Morton Feldman and the dread and acceleration of Source Direct. Don't ever let me out of this fog.

MH_ We won't.

13
Raphael Vanoli—"Lenz" (Shhpuma, 2017)

JZ_ Let's stay in the fog. Can't have a playlist in Amsterdam without the music of one of the city's most extravagantly talented musicians. Plus the man's mind is a labyrinthian library of musical meditation. A beast of a poet. Love Raphael Vanoli.

MH_ A soothing, abstract, tender, magic flute guitar. This speaks to the gravitas of non-conformist electronic music. That is, it's electronic, but also intensely crafted. Thank you, by the way, for introducing his work, and him, to us.

14
Holly Herndon—"Interference" (4AD/RVNG Intl., 2015)

MH_ Your verdict?

JZ_ Love this one. While listening to this track again, and thinking about the title, it occurred to me that the song sounds like many different songs interfering with each other, searching for meaningful synthesis—which they find. This is a favorite.

MH_ We love it too. Working on the music video for this track was relatively insane—the song got into our heads so much, and so intensely, and just wouldn't let go.

15
The Bug feat. The Spaceape—"At War With Time" (Ninja Tune, 2014)

MH_ We don't have it, and can't find it.

JZ_ Ha, didn't see that one coming, which makes this sad song and story even sadder. Stephen Samuel Gordon had one of the finest voices of early twenty-first-century electronic music. His collaboration with Kode9 on *Memories of the Future* (2006) is one of my favorite albums. This song with The Bug, perhaps his final release before his unfortunate early death as a result of cancer, is one of his most poetic and prophetic:

Time seems endless when you've nothing to give
The void seems sexy when you've nothing to live
Place your faith in a final sound
A sound of escape loud and profound

MH_ (shaking, as in, being-moved)

16
Aisha Devi—"Dislocation of the Alpha" (Houndstooth, 2018)

JZ_ Good serendipity, nice follow-up in the blind. Big mood, this one. Devi has been riding such evocative waves in her recent work.

MH_ Yes. Remembering her live show in Vilnius, which was awesome.

17
Bonaventure—"Supremacy" (PTP, 2017)

JZ_ Another big mood. As Bonaventure, musician and graphic designer Soraya Lutangu has released this revolutionary EP with New York comrades PTP (Purple Tape Pedigree) (s/o to Geng). "Supremacy" is the militant opening track of a 6-track EP that also features a collaboration with artist Hannah Black. PTP has been one of my favorite music labels of the past few years, releasing important works by artists such as Violence, YATTA, and Eaves.

MH_ The unrelenting, heavy-industrial, yet spatial timbre of this track is hypnotic and intense and imbued with sociopolitical narrative. It defies consumption, and in a sense, *playlistification*. Electronic music, as the twenty-first century's most liquid medium, navigates its own (il)legibility in a limitless fashion, producing imprints that are pure *sound* and at the same time pure *art* and, simultaneously, politics. Bonaventure embodies this.

18
Kara-Lis Coverdale—"Grafts" (Boomkat Editions, 2017)

MH_ May we resort to citing the *Pitchfork* review? "Coverdale seems to propose a decidedly agnostic vision of what devotional electronics could mean in our contemporary moment, folding a natural awareness of technology's forms into music that feels insistently about being present." Coverdale also worked as a church organist.[4]

JZ_ Another 22-minute track! Patience is maybe my favorite virtue in a composer. Did you get to see her play at Sonic Acts at the Muziekgebouw in 2017? It was as if the room had been built for her music.

MH_ Missed that one, but love her work.

19
Elysia feat. Money Allah—"American Drift" (Blueberry Records, 2015)

JZ_ Sticking with Grand Visions in Music, here's the inimitable Elysia Crampton with Money Allah. Crampton has been developing a singular body of work that explores identity, race, colonialism, ecology, and religion. Her live performances are punk renditions of music theater, equal parts angelic and grunge. It was especially memorable to see her performing at Progress Bar in Amsterdam earlier this year with so many members of the Shadow Channel program present in the room.

MH_ Indeed, her performance at Progress Bar was epic, and in general, huge respect for this artist and their impact and influence. This is someone whose work resonates across many practices and functions as a catalyst to other musicians and composers. Once again this attests to the fluidity of contemporary electronic music when used to its full potential: the fact that the music is concrete in each instance of its performance, but also, a personal, temporal, and spatial fabric of lived experience and performative thought, that can "spread" its own feelings and urgencies. Amazing work.

20
Sofia Gubaidulina—"Silenzio, Five Pieces for Bayan, Violin and Cello, Gidon Kremer, Kremerata Musica" (BIS, 1991)

JZ_ What a mean-sounding setup are the violin, cello, and classical accordion. Like spiders crawling across my spine. Never heard this piece before. Eerie.

21
Oneohtrix Point Never—"We'll Take It" (Warp, 2018)

JZ_ Now we are entering my favorite range of frequencies. DJ, producer, and author of *Sonic Warfare: Sound, Affect, and the Ecology of Fear* (2009) Steve Goodman (better known as Kode9) once spoke of "electrocuting the dancefloor" with music. I have a folder called "electrocution" for when I DJ, and it consists of tracks like "We'll Take It" that do exactly that. Vanoli would call it "*kapotmaken*" (destroy). And after you've destroyed the dancefloor, you can construct a new story with the utopian music of Crampton and Kuedo.

MH_ OMG! And we're saying this independently of the fact that it is also quite hugely trending now, in summer 2018 (and maybe, hopefully still when you—the reader—are reading this in ten years' time).

22
Mika Vainio—"In Silence A Scream Takes A Heart" (Editions Mego, 2011)

MH_ Because most of the music that you play to us is recent and exceptionally good, how can we disagree? Also this! Vault-like cinematic minimalism. And of course, there is his untimely passing.

JZ_ Mika Vainio. One of the most gigantic and generous musicians in the challenging fields of noise, sound art, and improvised electronic music. That title, too. Artists like Vainio, O'Malley, and Haino make me think about Marcel Duchamp's "Sculpture Musicale": an architecture of sound you can dwell in.

23
TCF—"4641b2cae260eb8577230f-730d1e1b3c737e0503fee9f7f-cbb47f59869df9a63" (Unreleased, 2015)

MH_ Amazing, this loops back to "You Suffer" somehow, this time by the track title.

JZ_ As far as I know, this is part of a long-running project by Lars Holdhus using artificial intelligence to compose his music and art. These songs are among the many renderings of the same source material, created and captured by the code he has written. Ineffable and effing beautiful.

24
Fatima Al Qadiri, Hito Steyerl, and Juliana Huxtable—"Nothing Forever" (The Vinyl Factory, 2016)

JZ_ Since we have been talking a bit about opera, classical music, and art, I wanted to end with this special collaboration for the 9th Berlin Biennale in 2016. Perhaps it is a nice song for the end credits of our conversation. The title "Nothing Forever" is also both a subtle warning and a hopeful reminder that sits well with the title of your exhibition, *Earth*. This planet cannot last like this. We can imagine an alternative. Communism will win.

MH_ There are many things to say in response to this, but there isn't the time. The end credits are almost finished. The type is getting smaller, and it is getting centered.

**2018
NO RIGHTS RESERVED**

1
Antwood, *Sponsored Content*, liner notes, https://antwood.bandcamp.com/album/sponsored-content. Last accessed on August, 21 2018.
2
Mykki Blanco, interview by Patrick D. McDermott, *The FADER*, May 17, 2016, https://www.thefader.com/2016/05/17/mykki-blanco-high-school-never-ends-music-video. Last accessed on August 31, 2018.
3
Metahaven, Twitter post, March 25, 2018, 9:21am, https://twitter.com/mthvn/status/977943515987677184. Last accessed on August 31, 2018.
4
Thea Ballard, review of "Grafts," by Kara-Lis Coverdale, *Pitchfork*, May 3, 2017, https://pitchfork.com/reviews/albums/23224-grafts/. Last accessed on August 31, 2018.

Juha van 't Zelfde
Juha van 't Zelfde is a DJ, organizer, and educator based in Amsterdam. He is the founder of Progress Bar, a political party supporting radical club culture. He is a member of the program team of the Sonic Acts Festival. He is also the course director of the MA program Shadow Channel: Film, Design and Propaganda at the Sandberg Institute. From 2014 until 2017 he was the artistic director of Lighthouse in Brighton. Van 't Zelfde has been making radio about internet music since 2006, first at NPS Lijn5 and VPRO 3VOOR12, and later at Resonance FM and Red Light Radio. As an exhibition maker Van 't Zelfde has developed interdisciplinary projects on hope, resistance, and change, including projects for, among others: De Hallen Haarlem (now Frans Hals Museum); LABoral Centro de Arte y Creación Industrial Foundation, Gijón, Spain; and Stedelijk Museum Amsterdam. In 2013, he published *Dread: The Dizziness of Freedom* (2013), which reflects on possible re-articulations of the concept of dread in our times.

Juha van 't Zelfde ● MH

Somewhere in eastern Ukraine, July 18, 2014

The car is in Russia.

Into the house slips the yellow moon.

Peter Pomerantsev
journalist and writer

Art begins when one person, with the object of joining another or others

in one and the same feeling, invokes it once again in himself,

and then expresses it by certain external indications.

a boy, having experienced, let us say, fear on encountering a wolf,

relates that encounter; and, in order to evoke in others the feeling he has experienced,

describes himself, his condition before the encounter,

the surroundings, the woods, his own lightheartedness,

and then the wolf's appearance, its movements,

the distance between himself and the wolf.

All this, if only the boy, when telling the story,

again experiences the feelings he had lived through and infects the listeners

and compels them to feel what the narrator had experienced,

is art.

Расцвели яблони и груши,
Apple and pear trees were blooming,

Apple and pear trees were blooming

Выходила на берег Катюша,
On the steep banks walked Katyusha,

On the steep banks walked Katyusha,

Of her silver eagle of the steppe

Benjamin H. Bratton
philosopher and design theorist

I live in the megastructure.

I'm attached to the heavens, upside down, suspended, indefinitely.

Without beginning or end

136

SOMEWHERE IN EASTERN UKRAINE
July 18, 2014

VOICES ON PHONE (RUSSIAN)
Good morning.
—Good morning. Yesterday was a mess.
I have no words.
What's the matter?
—Where is that motherfucker? Why did
he, your comrade, come back yesterday?
—I don't understand what he did.
—What was going on yesterday? Tell me.
They brought a car up to a crossroads.
Left it there, continued by themselves.
—OK.
The car went in the right direction
and arrived as planned.
Then he started to get strange
incoming calls from ten people.
—What people?
Well, he started to receive
different calls on his phone.
The first, second, third, then the fourth.
Then he started to call other people.
—And then he just turned off
his phone. What a mess.
—And we have no idea where the car is.
The car is in Russia.
—Oh shit, last night I said that I
didn't know where the car was.

ANNA AKHMATOVA, *REQUIEM*
Quietly flows the river Don
Into the house slips the yellow moon
Through the window, its cap askew
It sees a shadow lost in gloom
The moon sees a woman. She's sick, bereft
The moon sees a woman with no one left
Her husband dead, her son in jail
Pray for me.

RONALD REAGAN
I don't know whether you know it or not,
but I have a new hobby.
I am collecting stories that I can actually
prove are told among the Russian people.
They make them up themselves, they
tell them between themselves.
Reveals they got a great sense of humor.
And they've also got a little cynical
attitude about things in their country.

And one of these stories, the
one I'm gonna tell you, I told to
General Secretary Gorbachev.
And he laughed.

The story was an American
and a Russian, arguing about
their two countries.

And the American said, "Look, in my
country, I can walk into the Oval Office,
I can pound the President's desk and
say, 'Mr President, I don't like the way
you're running our country.'"

And the Russian said, "I can do that."
The American said, "You can?"
And he says, "Yes. I can go into the
Kremlin, to the General Secretary's
office, pound his desk and say, 'Mr
General Secretary, I don't like the way
President Reagan's running his country.'"
(audience laughter)

PETER POMERANTSEV
I used to think that propaganda
was about persuading people.
Jacques Ellul, who wrote the classic
study of propaganda, in 1960— French
philosopher—called it mass persuasion.
He didn't say propaganda was good or
bad. He said it was a part of modern
society, a part of technological society,
a part of mass industrialized society.
Whether it's getting people
to wear condoms, or to get
them to become Maoists.

Soviet propaganda used to be, you know,
"Believe in Communism!"
Moscow is the shining beacon
on the socialist hill.
Now it doesn't seem to be about that.
It's just about deconstructing

the other side, disrupting... disrupting
Western narratives... of any sort.

There's a steady stream of disinformation
whose purpose seems to be
to sort of undermine the very
idea that truth is provable.

GIRLS UND PANZER
Let's go!
We'll leave their flag tank hanging
and destroy all the others!
You shall learn what real strength is!
A-URA!

LEO TOLSTOY, *WHAT IS ART?*
Art begins when one person, with the object
of joining another or others to himself in one
and the same feeling, expresses that feeling
by certain external indications. To take the
simplest example: a boy having experienced,
let us say, fear on encountering a wolf,
relates that encounter; and in order to evoke
in others the feeling he has experienced,
describes himself, his condition before the
encounter, the surroundings, the wood, his
own lightheartedness, and then the wolf's
appearance, its movements, the distance
between himself and the wolf, and so forth.
All this, if only the boy when telling the story,
again experiences the feelings he had lived
through, and infects the hearers and compels
them to feel what he had experienced is art.

GIRLS UND PANZER
Apple and pear trees were blooming
Over the river the fog merrily rolled
On the steep banks walked Katyusha,
On the high bank she slowly strode.

As she walked, she sang a sweet song
Of her silver eagle of the steppe
Of the one she loved so dearly,
And the one whose letters she had kept

LEO TOLSTOY, *WHAT IS ART?*
(cont'd)
Even if the boy had not seen a wolf, but
had frequently been afraid of one, and if,
wishing to evoke in others the fear he had
felt, he invented an encounter with a wolf
and recounted it so as to make his hearers
share the feelings he experienced when he
feared the wolf, that also would be art.

BENJAMIN H. BRATTON
1648, Treaty of Westphalia.
This is the moment where the
modern state is codified.
Where all of the sort of structures,
its spatial distribution, is set.
And it's a particular kind of subdivision of
geography by which you sort of imagine
a horizontal map.
And we subdivide the land...
The (Westphalian) land is subdivided.
Not the sea. Not the air.
Not the electromagnetic spectrum,
but the land itself.
And it's a particular kind of topology,
if you think about it. Right?
It's a loop topology.
Inside the loop, there is a certain
regime of sovereignty that comes
with this organizational structure.
There's the right to make the
law, to issue a currency, a flag,
World Cup team, whatever.
And this becomes a kind of standard
format by which the surface of the Earth
is subdivided into these political units.

What I'm interested in is both the ways
in which planetary scale computation,
which I describe as this accidental
megastructure that we've
produced over the last twenty-
five years, has both distorted and
deformed this traditional logic.

The development of planetary scale
computation, this accidental
megastructure that I call the stack,
has both deformed and distorted
this traditional logic.

**ACTRESS IN THE
MEGASTRUCTURE
(RUSSIAN VOICE)**
In the streets, I am no more than a ghost.
I live in the megastructure.

I'm attached to the heavens, upside
down, suspended, indefinitely.
Without beginning or end.

BENJAMIN H. BRATTON
And so the stack is understood as
both an actual massively distributed
technological infrastructure, in which and
on which, and with which we organize
our cultures, economies, and societies,
but also as a kind of abstract model for
how it is that we could conceptualize
subdivisions of political geography
that are not about just horizontal
adjacencies, but actually about vertical
layers, where one site and one person
and one event, one network, may be
claimed, may be part of the jurisdiction
of... multiple... multiple forms of political
sovereignty at the same time,
one on top of another.

BENJAMIN H. BRATTON
(BAHRAIN PROTESTERS)
Exactly what is the relationship and role
between sovereign states and an
apparatus of planetary-scale computation
that has a kind of de facto sovereignty,
a practical sovereignty that has
superseded the sovereignty of the state,
and for which there are no norms?

MARYAM MONALISA GHARAVI
(BAHRAIN PROTESTERS)
Just to first describe some of what I see.
There is... there's a beginning and an end
point, almost like... the interlude to a film
or to a cinematic event that happens to
be a production in which, you know,
the producers are also part of the action.
So there's a conflation of production
and subject matter.
Autographic.

And then...
I see these cinematic tools that are
overlaid and almost as important
as the images themselves.
So I see slow motion and dissolves, and...
of course, a layover of music that is
emotionally very impacting, and perhaps
calling upon a certain kind of viewer.
One who can not only make the images
and what's happening legible, but
can also make legible the emotional
spirit with which this was made.

So, even though people from all over the
world will see this, I think that the video
itself enacts or performs its audience.

But the uprising in Bahrain is almost
completely erased from the narrative,
and I'm thinking not only of, you know,
outlets like the State Department,
or US interests, but also things like Al
Jazeera, which has a very narrow
and concrete narrative about the Syrian
uprising, for example, which is also
ongoing, if one can call it an uprising,
although that's bled into, you know,
the invasion of ISIS and other things.

But a short time ago, the Syrian and
the Bahrain uprisings were almost neck
and neck in terms of ground covered,
or encounter with authorities and so on,
and you saw one of them completely
deleted from the present history.

**ACTRESS IN THE
MEGA-STRUCTURE
(RUSSIAN VOICE)**
A planetary ceiling.
A floating megastructure.
A cloud.
A glittering river.
A mirror.
An untruth.
A lie.
A technology.
A pathology.
A desire.
A platform.
A road.
A map.
A network.
A destination.

(ANNOUNCER VOICE)
The Rolex of chemical weapons.
The Hemingway of Dagestan.
The caviar of unsubscribe.
The Art Basel of the Donetsk
People's Republic.

**INTERCEPTED PHONE CALL
EASTERN UKRAINE
JULY 18, 2014**

**VOICES ON PHONE
(RUSSIAN)**
—Yes?
Come here and bring him with you.
There is no car, no one has seen it.
The one who went to get it came back
without it. You know what I mean.
Where? Who? Where did he end
up bringing it? What a disaster.
—To Bibliotekar.
—This was the group that transported it.
OK.
—On the trailer. I've just phoned them.
—They are already in Russia. They are
bringing another vehicle from Russia.
Aha... and that one... did he
give it to Bibliotekar?
—Without a doubt.
OK, now I got it.

TRUTHLOADER HOST
Two Boeing 777s, two rare aviation
disasters and one airline.
This is the story of the Malaysia
Airlines coincidences.

EURONEWS (RUSSIAN VOICE)
Since fifteen hours a Boeing 777-2000.
en route from Kuala Lumpur to
Beijing, has gone missing.
According to Malaysia Airlines,
the whereabouts of the airliner
have not been determined yet.
The airline states that it hasn't received
any signals from the crew so far.
Contact with the aircraft was
lost two hours after its departure
from Kuala Lumpur.

BENJAMIN H. BRATTON
So you think about something like the
Malaysia MH370, the vanished airplane.
You know, in a way, the fact that
this is so surprising, that this is so
uncanny, is a kind of exception,
in a way, that proves the rule.

TRUTHLOADER HOST
There are still loads of questions
surrounding MH370.
How can a jet of that size, with
world-class technology, go missing,
when a tiny device like an iPhone
can be located with an app?

BENJAMIN H. BRATTON
The idea that something like a commercial airliner could just vanish off
of the surface of the planet that we have
so thoroughly mapped at such a granular
level that it's not just one panoptic
regime, it's multiple panoptic regimes
all one on top of another, that you can
hide something like that, or that something could vanish, is so bizarre in 2015.

But twenty years ago, thirty years ago,
something like that, you know, you could
hide... you could hide an entire country,
and no one would sort of think that
much of it, let alone an airplane.

But, you know, I think the fact that there's
also sort of... apophenia, the political
apophenia, not just "Where does it go?"
but "What caused this?"

TRUTHLOADER HOST
Just over four months later, on July
17th, flight MH17 was traveling from
Amsterdam to Kuala Lumpur, and is

138

shot down by a surface-to-air missile, crashing in a sparsely populated area of Ukraine, killing all 298 passengers and crew. Pro-Russian separatists fighting with Ukrainian forces have been blamed for downing the aircraft.

TANK PASSING, DASHCAM
(RUSSIAN VOICE)
What the hell! He can't do that!
I'll definitely put it on the internet!

MARYAM MONALISA GHARAVI
The citizen journalist, or even just the person on the street who takes a picture, or uploads a YouTube video of something they may or may not be able to describe, and what that shares with, you know, what we think of as a more centralized database is that it's still...
Someone has to make it legible if it's gonna enter a kind of political conversation or a social conversation. And who gets to make it legible, I think becomes the interpreter of those images. It becomes all the more important.

BENJAMIN H. BRATTON
The idea of a completely self-transparent global grid by which every event, every molecule, every everything, could be addressed, could be accounted for, could be calculated, could be governed according to some algorithmic principles, such that nothing could escape, because there is no outside, is itself, at the very least, an incomplete ambition, at the one end, and at the other, you know, a kind of dangerous psychosis.

MARYAM MONALISA GHARAVI
With the... with the, you know...
With the MH17 photographs of the missile launcher, you know, how they're framed becomes just as important as the fact that they were allowed to be entered into a conversation, or, like, uploaded into the conversation. And that framing then becomes as important as the existence of the image, if not more. And so that's why I think the indexical of, like, you know, for example, captioning or circling parts of... highlighting the blurs of the image and giving them... giving them a kind of, like, narrative expression becomes so tricky and makes the work of credibility and verifiability even more important. So you get that sort of, you know, forensic or scientific impetus, like, who can... who can test the image against, you know, these verifiable factors of where it comes from? And I think... I think that, you know... makes people enormously nervous. It makes me enormously nervous on some level.

ACTRESS IN THE
MEGASTRUCTURE
(RUSSIAN VOICE)
JPEGs are hoarded.
The shapes of the trees, the directions of their shadows.
Layers of random facts.
Investigations on the credibility of those facts. Investigations on the credibility of those investigations.

ACTRESS COMMITTING AN ACT
OF AESTHETIC TERRORISM

PETER LAVELLE,
RT CROSSTALK HOST
NATO, the North Atlantic Treaty Organization, has an identity problem of sorts. To have meaning, cohesion, purpose, and reasons to be funded, this alliance needs enemies.
Following the Western-backed regime change in Ukraine, today, Russia gives the alliance a reason to exist.

PETER POMERANTSEV
(US CONGRESSIONAL HEARING)
I mean, conspiracy is... What is conspiracy? Sort of a linguistic sabotage on the infrastructure of reason.

RT HOST (UNKNOWN)
Did CNN edit out criticism of its network during an interview with RT anchor Anissa Naouai?

ANISSA NAOUAI, RT HOST
Certainly at Russia Today, we always try to show both sides of the story. Do we show more of a Russian perspective? Of course we do, because that's the perspective that's being sidelined. But it's an absurd question coming from someone that's propagated the line of the State Department for over fifteen years.

LIZ WAHL, FORMER RT HOST
(US CONGRESSIONAL HEARING)
Essentially, anybody that is an expert is somebody that is willing to... to toe the Russian line and to... to... I mean, they could be from the far left, they could be from the far right, they could have unconventional, deranged theories...

BRIAN BECKER
(ANSWER COALITION),
RT CROSSTALK
NATO has proved very good at bombing Libya.
—Yes.
They've been very good at bombing and destroying Yugoslavia. It's been very good at invading and occupying Afghanistan. But was that the purpose of NATO?

LIZ WAHL
The producers would scour the internet for these... for these experts.

BRIAN BECKER
NATO now is incentivized to come up with new enemies, Russia principally right now, but in other places, to justify its existence, when in fact, NATO should be dissolved.

PETER POMERANTSEV
It's about destroying belief in anything. When you have no belief in truth, you can't believe in anything.

NICOLAY BERDYAEV,
DREAM AND REALITY
Truth as an object which intrudes itself and wields authority over me—an object in the name of which it is demanded that I should renounce freedom—is a figment: truth is not a superfluous thing. [...] Truth is spiritual conquest; it is known in and through freedom.

PETER POMERANTSEV
But also, more insidiously than that... Look, our... I'm going to get very grand now: our global order is based on an idea of a reality-based politics.

LIZ WAHL
And I know that, formerly of Radio Free Europe, Mr. Lack, who has since departed, had gotten a lot of criticism for comparing Russia Today and Russian propaganda to ISIS propaganda.

BENJAMIN H. BRATTON
I think one of the ironies of planetary scale computation and the challenges that it brings to the traditional sovereignties of the modern nation-state is that, on the one hand, global cloud platforms take on the role and provide services that have traditionally been provided by the state. But at the same time, it's not a story of the state somehow virtualizing and going away. At the same time, states themselves become cloud platforms. And one of the ways I think we see this operating is the way in which what we used to call traditional media, television, for example, shift in terms of their relationship to their state sponsors.

PETER POMERANTSEV
Politics in an era of globalization. The breakdown of the sense that... actually, that governments can do anything.
It's that sense of "Who's really in charge?" Your government can do any policy it likes, but a butterfly flaps its wings in China and, you know, a village in Birmingham is unemployed. It's part of the paranoia and part of the sense of globalization, which in Europe... heightened even more by the, you know, the idea of an EU above national governments. So governments used to be like, in the West, "Look how big and strong we are!"
Now they're like, "We can't do anything! We can't do..." It's like, "It's the EU." You know? "It's globalization, sorry." So governments get into this, and get into this game, and actually end up exacerbating the lack of faith in them by saying, "of course, we can't do anything."

NATALIA POKLONSKAYA
(PRESS CONFERENCE)
The right to define and the constitutional order of Ukraine belongs exclusively to the people and can't be usurped by the state or a government official, regardless of the manner by which they came to power, including...

(PHONE ON DESK STARTS
BUZZING, SWITCHES IT OFF)
...bloodshed.

ACTRESS WEARING COLOR
REVOLUTION FACE PAINT

GRIT-TV, HOST
When we say "Twitter revolution," what do we mean?

CLAY SHIRKY
(SOCIAL MEDIA GURU)
The disputed June 12th elections in Iran, when that then erupted into street protests in Tehran, you know, over the course of the next couple of days, there were enough people on the ground in Tehran with cell phones to get messages out, and then those got rebroadcasted all over the world.

VLADIMIR PUTIN
2014 STATE DUMA ADDRESS
There was a whole series of controlled "color" revolutions. Clearly, the people in the countries where these events took place were sick of tyranny and poverty, of their lack of prospects. But these feelings were taken advantage of cynically. Standards were imposed on these nations that did not in any way correspond to their way of life, traditions, cultures. As a result, instead of democracy and reedom, there was chaos, outbreaks of violence, and a series of upheavals. The Arab Spring turned into the Arab Winter.

MARYAM MONALISA GHARAVI
One of the promises of the 2011 Egyptian and Tunisian uprisings was that on the one hand, you have people on the ground, and then you have the data space.
And one of the promises of that was the way in which other parts of the world sort of spilled into the streets as we got news through the data stream of what's happening on the ground there, in zones of conflict. And it was heralded in a way that reinserted them back into this liberal narrative of technological progress and also the importance of exporting democracy.

ABKHAZIAN NEWS NETWORK
AGENCY "ANNA NEWS,"
TWO MEN AT A TABLE: IGOR
"STRELKOV" GIRKIN, MILITARY
COMMANDER, DONETSK
PEOPLE'S REPUBLIC
The unexpected thing, in my opinion, was the sharp change of the motion vector of our president. That is, I have already said that he really started a revolution "from above" by the entry of Crimea.

NATALIA POKLONSKAYA'S
NEW YEAR'S MESSAGE,
DECEMBER 2014
When all Crimeans will be listening with anticipation to the sounds of the Kremlin clock, and proudly will be watching the address of our president, we, as rightful citizens of Russia, will raise our glasses to our motherland, for our great holy Russia. And may God help us: to keep her, take care of her, and strengthen her. In the words of Tsar Nicholas II: "There is no sacrifice that I would not make to save Russia."

ENJOYKIN, "NYASH MYASH"
A coup has occurred
Armed seizure of power
To massive bloodshed the mayhem has led
against the constitution
We don't have a moral right
to abandon our people
It is our task to restore the work of the prosecutor's office in this country
Power
Blood
Nyash Myash
Power
Blood
Crimea is ours

ANNA NEWS, TWO MEN AT
A TABLE (TOLSTOY PORTRAIT):
MARAT MUSIN, ANNA
NEWS FOUNDER
Tell me please, here we witnessed an incredible thing: that seems to be the one nation, the same people—the Ukrainians, Russians. But this stupid machine of brainwashing, it worked. People turned zombie over a short period of time. I understand that they've been "treated" for twenty-three years, but we also have been "under treatment" for twenty-three years. And yet, the military component of it—worked. And when sensible, educated people who are able to understand things for themselves, what is truth and what is falsehood, they are now... they use the slogan "The Big Brother" has betrayed us, when we say: no guys, on the contrary—it's the "younger brother" who betrayed us, went to the policemen, and went to the "Sonderkommando" to kill his fellows, they don't listen. What do you think is the strategy of the United States here? I'm not talking about Slavs killing Slavs—it's their achievement. From the point of view of these technologies and these threats, which obviously will be applied to Russian people and to us here in the nearest (future)...

IGOR "STRELKOV" GIRKIN
Please narrow your question.

VOICE OF VICTORIA NULAND,
US ASSISTANT SECRETARY
OF STATE
So I don't think Klitsch should go into the government.
I don't think it's necessary,
I don't think it's a good idea.
I think Yats is the guy who's got the economic experience, the governing experience.
I just think Klitsch going in, he's gonna be at that level, working for Yatsenyuk, it's just not gonna work.

VOICE OF GEOFFREY PYATT,
US AMBASSADOR TO UKRAINE
I think you reaching out directly to him helps with the personality management among the three, and it gives you also a chance to move fast on all this stuff and put us behind it.

VICTORIA NULAND
I can't remember if I told you this or if I only told Washington this, that when I talked to Jeff Feltman this morning, he had a new name for the UN

guy, Robert Serry... did I write
you that this morning?

GEOFFREY PYATT
Yes. Yeah. I saw that.

VICTORIA NULAND
He's now gotten both Serry and Ban
Ki-moon to agree that Serry could
come in Monday or Tuesday.

GEOFFREY PYATT
OK.

VICTORIA NULAND
So, that would be great, I think, to help
glue this thing, and have the UN help
glue it.
And, you know, fuck the EU.

ACTRESS IN THE
MEGA-STRUCTURE
(RUSSIAN VOICE)
We lost ourselves in a medieval
haze of information.
We were very likely spreading fictitious
information ourselves, but couldn't help it.
To argue is to look in the mirror.
There is no exit, as every new
accusation is a reflection of another.
In upside down reality, there can be
no argument because the response
is always: look at yourself.
Look at your own mess. Who
are you to tell me, after all?

ACTRESS INVOLVED IN A
PSYCHOLOGICAL OPERATION

LIZ WAHL
And the internet, you know, we thought
that it would be this place where...
where, you know, it's wonderful in a
lot of ways, because a lot of different
viewpoints and a lot of different people
have a voice, like never before.
But unfortunately, it's provided a forum
where disinformation, false theories,
people that are just trying to make
a name for themselves, bloggers or
whatever, that have absolutely no
accountability for the truth are able to
rile up a mass amount of people online.

PETER POMERANTSEV
So, up until 2008, the Kremlin left
the internet alone, and it became this
incredible space for social activism,
a very different discourse.
Since then, they've invested a hell of a lot
into astroturfing and alternative internet.
You know, they're trying to find ways
of going into the internet and spinning
it from inside without cutting it off.
So if the whole point of RT and having
all these trolls is not to convince people,
but just to sort of show, "Look how
big we are. We can hire troll farms.
We have TV channels.
We invade other countries and we lie to
you," and that is all... the point of it is the
very brazenness, so the psychological
operation is not about convincing people,
but just to... you know, just to have...
impress, signal just how big and fearless
Russia is, then it's worked really well.

PETER LAVELLE (RT CROSSTALK)
Media wars have entered new territory.
Secretary of State John Kerry, members
of the EU and the military alliance NATO
all have singled out this television station,
RT, as some kind of security threat.
Since when is holding, in broadcasting,
different opinions or narratives a
threat to global media freedom?

ANISSA NAOUI
(RT IN THE NOW)
I've seen lots of your reports, and
in not one report will you find you
questioning the United States

government and their policy.
And we, with our Russian propaganda,
question those arms to the FSA, question
those arms to al-Nusra and other links,
and now, today, we have ISIS.

(LOUD BOOM)

BENJAMIN H. BRATTON
I think, honestly,
I think that RT operates a bit...
operates in this way different
than, say, CNN, in this regard.
I think that the relationship between RT
and the Russian state and the relationship
between CNN and the American
state are... are comparable but
not reducible to one another.

One of the interesting things about
the way RT deals with this is they're
completely open about the fact that
it's a state-sponsored enterprise, and
that there's a specifically Russian
narrative that they are going to define.

And they're going to defend the right to
present this specifically Russian narrative
and to do so as a way of protecting and...
It's protecting the fiction of this particular
organization of political sovereignty.

It's about the staking of the claim to have
the Russian position and the production
of this idea of there being a specifically
Russian position on what happened in
Syria, what's happening in Ukraine, what
happened in Crimea, what happened to
the Malaysia Airlines flight, as if all of
these things that happen on the Earth can
be seen in a very specific way through
a particular narrative... with a particular
lens... from the Russian perspective.

And that would be different than
the Western perspective.

It's not as though something actually
happened in physical space, in
actual... in actual space-time, and
that we can deduce this and measure
it and know it and come to some
kind of understanding of it.

No, there is this perspective and
that perspective and the right to
have this perspective, regardless of
what anything actually is or is not.

(ANNOUNCER VOICE)
The Denmark of international terrorism.
The Midwest of southern California.
The Che Guevara of Uber.
The ISIS of gluten-free donuts.

THE GREAT PROGRAMMER

MARYAM MONALISA GHARAVI
But some of the beginning titles
discuss the prohibitions against, like,
showing women or listening to music
and so that kind of framed a little bit
what images aren't appearing.
You don't really see figures,
like, human figures.
You just see this, like, proliferation
of windows and tabs.

I think that there's a tendency in the
so-called West to think of a lot of these
tools like Adobe, and various design tools,
and hardware and software, as neutral.
And I think this sort of
circumvents that completely.

The logo suggests a weaponization
of software and also, in maybe a
twentieth-century understanding of
the emblem's design, there's a kind
of revolutionary recruitment.
There's a kind of, like,
recruitment of technology.

(ANNOUNCER VOICE)
The Paris of the Holocene.
The Marina Abramović of Neo-
Conservatism.
The Harvard of botnets.
The Dom Pérignon of lab-grown meat.

MARYAM MONALISA GHARAVI
What I find really interesting about
the interest in ISIS consuming M&M's
is the degree to which M&M's are
from the space of the consumer,
the space of the familiar.
And also, M&M's have their
own emotional life.
They're animated, they're cute,
they speak, they flirt.
And that overlay brings to mind the emoji.
They actually look like emoji.

CNN HOST
That... that is a bit of a chilling analogy,
that it's "the ISIS of infectious agents."
Does that mean it is that deadly, that
dangerous, or that it needs to just be
treated with the same kind of strategy?

DR. ALEXANDER GARZA
I think it's a little bit of both, Ashley.
And so, if you think about Ebola as an
agent that spreads throughout and kills
innocent people, it's directly like ISIS.
Right? It infects people and it kills people.

BENJAMIN H. BRATTON
I see this as a kind of... of... a kind
of big data apophenia, call it.
That, when you have... there's just so
much information, in which the actual
cause and effect relationships between
an event, an institutional decision,
people begin to see and deduce
causalities that are not really there.
Right? Where you see one thing
and you see another thing and
you imagine them to have a causal
relationship with one another.

BENJAMIN H. BRATTON
At the level of the interface, though,
I think, longer term, this is where the
capacity for a kind of... a real splintering
in the way in which we perceive
reality at a political level is possible.
You know, if you think of something like
Augmented Reality, right, Google Glass
or Microsoft HoloLens or Facebook's
Rift, something like this, what you have,
in a way, is a kind of an immediate
lamination of, a narration of the real,
that is brought directly into how it is
that we perceive that... that reality.
So it's not just "I see a person across
the room," but "I see their name,
their information about them."
Any interfacial regime, whether that's
Google or Microsoft or anything else, is
a way in which this enormously complex
system of the vast, you know, global
supercomputational network is made
simple enough, is narrated enough,
that people can make use of it.
In the course of doing so, this
incredible reduction takes place.
And in that reduction of all the
possibilities into just a set of buttons
with words on them that you can
click, there is, inevitably, a highly
ideological distortion of all of those
possibilities into a framework.

MARYAM MONALISA GHARAVI
Well, Tolstoy's formulation of art
is interesting in that it's an artifice
that has a truth at its heart.
Whether or not it appears as an actuality
or has a sort of shell of truth, there
is some sort of emotional depth, or
an emotional legibility at its center.
I don't know if there can be any such
thing as a kind of pure art, untouched
or unfettered by the demands and
the power grabs of society. But the
aestheticization of politics allows art
to become politically expedient, or to
empty... empty certain categories and
classifications, and aestheticize them to
the degree that power feels necessary.

BENJAMIN H. BRATTON
When that compression of possibilities

into interfacial regime is one
that is not just providing
things that you can do with
machines, but things that you
might do with reality, that are
subtitling the real —clean and
unclean, ours and theirs, us
and them, halal, haram—the
capacity for a kind of cognitive
fundamentalism is not only a
danger... In some ways, I see
it as almost an inevitability,
such that what you see and
encounter is pre-narrated
for you, by those subtitles.

DIGITAL SCREAMINDENTATION

EUROPEAN COMMISS[...]

Directorate-General for Commun[...]
Media Policy
Media Convergence and So[...]

A

Colloquium on Fake [...]

15:00 – 18:00

14:30 Registration

15:00 Welcome by [...]
Society

15:15 *Fake news f[...]*
- Presentati[...]
- Discussi[...]

15:45 *Rethir[...]*
- Pres[...]
- Dis[...]

16:15 [...]
- [...]

Colloquium on fake news and online disinformation

27/02/2018 - Brussels

Title	Last Name	First Name	Organisation
Ms	ADAM	Montse	EU DisinfoLab
Mr	ALAPHILIPPE	Alexandre	Rai
Mr	ANTONELLI	Diego	Bulgarian National Television
Ms	APOSTOLOVA	Desislava	Freelance
Ms	BAKER	Jennifer	Microsoft
Mr	BELL	Martin	Radio K2, TV Kanal 3
Ms	BENOVSKA	Iliana	Organisation for Security and Cooperation in Europe (OSCE)
Mr	BERMAN	Thijs	Mission of Ukraine to the EU
Mr	BOBYTSKYI	Nazar	Monitor
Ms	BUDAKOVA	Lyubomira	Leiden University Centre for Linguistics (LUCL)
Mr	BURGER	Peter	Dechert LLP
Mr	BURNSIDE	Alec	Mission of Norway to the European Union
Mr	BÅRDSEN	Trond Helge	MCC Ltd
Mr	CAMISANI CALZOLARI	Marco	EAVI
Mr	CELOT	Paolo	Inline Policy
Mr	COUTTS	Rory	State University of Applied Science
Ms	CZUBOWSKA	Karolina	T6 Ecosystems
Mr	DE ROSA	Simona	Mediawijs - imec vzw
Mr	DEMEULENAERE	Andy	Flemish government
Mr	DESMARETZ	Koen	StopFake.org
Mr	DEYNYCHENKO	Ruslan	
Mr	DOTT	Claus	Blue Heaven KG, Modern Unit Management SL.
Ms	DORR	Renate	Zweites Deutsches Fernsehen
Mr	ECHIKSON	William	CEPS
Ms	FLICK	Caterina	Of counsel at Nunziante Magrone Law Firm
Ms	GARCIA VAN HOOGSTRATEN	Catherine	The Hague University of Applied Sciences & [...]
Mr	GONZALEZ	Alejandro	Public sector
Ms	GOUVEIA	Patricia	JM-Madeira
Mr	GRAY	Oliver	Graywise
Ms	GROENEWOLT	Pia	All Digital
Ms	GRUNDMANN	Silvia	Council of Europe
Mr	HEAWOOD	Jonathan	IMPRESS: The Independent Monitor for t[...]
Mr	HEINDERYCKX	Francois	Universite libre de Bruxelles (ULB)
Ms	HULIN	Adeline	UNESCO Brussels Office
Mr	ILIEV	Yanislav	Private Company
Mr	IZDEBSKI	Krzysztof	ePaństwo Foundation
Ms	KABASHI	Festina	EMMA/ENPA
Mr	KAKARNIAS	Theofanis	RTL Group
Ms	KAMARA	Irene	Tilburg University
Mr	KARAGIANNIDIS	George	FightHoax P.C.
Ms	KARAIVANOVA	Gabriela	Council of the European Union
Mr	KASTRITIS	Ilias	Managing Authority of Operationa[...]
Ms	KEILHOLZ	Danielle	Hill+Knowlton Strategies
Ms	KHAN	Mehreen	Financial Times
Mr	KOURTELLIS	Nicolas	Telefonica I+D
Ms	KOZIK	Aleksandra	Edelman
Mr	KRIZAN	Miro	Agency for elecronic media
Mr	KROPLEWSKI	Robert	law office
Ms	KRUK	Vinca	Metahaven

142

previous

Information Skies, Netherlands, South Korea directed by Metahaven (Daniel van der Velden & Vinca Kruk) nominated in the category European Short Film 2017

The Sprawl[1], say Metahaven. Sprawling in a hammock, I would close my eyes and watch the information sprawl. We will be witnessing the same processes again and again, learning painfully to navigate them, mastering a new language that has always been gradually inventing and establishing itself from shreds and scraps. This is the language in which a turquoise tube of mascara looted from the crash site of MH17 is not a fact but a trope. This language is described and studied in The Sprawl: when applied in the interests of particular power relations, it is called «propaganda». It embraces the loss of meaning and fuels fights for multiple shades of evasive truth, while taking good care of preserving the structural status quo, mobilizing «identities» and «values» as a promise of selective wellbeing. Such flow and rhythm of «propaganda» has been made apparent by digital tools and networks, but it's hardly a recent invention or a phenomenon that hasn't been described before. It's just that our attempts to face and grasp the language of «propaganda» are always being slowed down by its persuasive effects — and by the fear to be left alone and misunderstood in one's questioning of the states of affairs that define the subtlest aspects of our everyday life. At one time Socrates was sentenced to death for precisely this.

the interactions between ecosystems, the mechanosphere and the social and individual Universes of reference, we must learn to think «transversally». Just as monstrous and mutant algae invade the lagoon of Venice, so our television screens are populated, saturated, by «degenerate» images and statements [énoncés]. In the field of social ecology men like Donald Trump are permitted to proliferate freely, like another species of algae, taking over entire districts of New York and Atlantic City; he «redevelops» by raising rents, thereby driving out tens of thousands of poor families, most of whom are condemned to homelessness, becoming the equivalent of the dead fish of environmental ecology»[2]. This passage illustrates beautifully the relations between information flows and material phenomena, which has only recently become a trendy yet still questionable issue in the discussions on the nexus between digital platforms and real life affairs — which both are, in the end, real life. Xenofeminism Manifesto has been one of the most prominent and prominently concise recent attempts to work on emancipatory tactics within this phenomenon: «Digital technologies are not separable from the material realities that underwrite them; they are connected so that each can be used to alter the other towards different ends.»[3] Metahaven manage to aestheticize on a large scale — and thus to playfully deconstruct — the proliferative qualities of the language of propaganda in these upgraded conditions. One of the stances of The Sprawl

absurdist poetry, advertising, AI, airport customs control experiences, and the like. At the moment Metahaven are working on a new film, shot in Beirut and Kiev — a sequel to Information Skies (2016)[4], a piece on virtual reality and the texture of truth in the digital world. The chosen settings are eloquent. Ukraine has been the ground for the most explicit, refined, and uncanny narrative collisions, vision distortions, and logical failures. Its war on «propaganda» carried on with «propaganda» instruments — that is, defensive counter-narratives, restrictive value-based choice of allowed marketable discourse, and maladroit sterilization of history — is only a part of «the sprawl», the global proliferation of the phantom language of power, to be taken with food. The Sprawl gets inside this language, and uses design tools as formaldehyde to immerse and store its tropes in for further examination. Moreover, the specimens are immediately supplemented with analytical comments and poetic footnotes wrapped in stylized theatrical generalities — which does not necessarily aim at denunciation of particular cases and asserting any universally applicable optics, but definitely estranges, defamiliarizes (in the sense as coined by Viktor Shklovsky) and illuminates the inventive automatisms of present-day quicksilver propaganda. Its material manifestations come through as systemic aberrations — ultimately, not less real than the status quo that precedes them. That's the reality The Sprawl captures: «Oh, Novorossiya. Imaginary motherland, spiritual Rorschach.» It's fed by the language that appears to be fighting it, because there are no colours within quicksilver. It's rather amusing to expand the metaphor of quicksilver by recalling that it is the colloquial for

Metahaven, The Sprawl (Propaganda about Propaganda), and sprawl.space, 2015-2016.

The mentioned systemic aberrations are there not as the signs that a certain established system has to be fixed and retained. Largely, they are its own products, and the signs of stagnation of particular political languages that are willing to benefit from — but unable to contain — the rearrangements accounted for by information technologies. The Sprawl is about this stagnation. Benjamin H. Bratton, featured in the film, refers particularly to the «relationship between the sovereignty of state and the apparatus of planetary-scale computation». The changes in the notion of space brought, roughly speaking, by the internet, require and inevitably advance the transformation of political infrastructures and the evolution of corresponding languages. The longer and harder these changes get inhibited by reactionary stances — the more disastrous and stupefying are the ways the surface fails and breaks, the more of Guattarian «mutant algae» corrupt the possibilities of balance and new sense. But nonsense is also what sparks poetry — poetry as a transformative twist of language and reality. This is the deterritorialized area Metahaven offer one to enter.

Snippets from Lesia Prokopenko, "Imaginary Motherland. Some Notes on The Sprawl (Propaganda About Propaganda) and a Google Doc Conversation with Metahaven," originally published by *Prostory*, 2018. See https://prostory.net.ua/en/9-publikatsii/krytyka/300-imaginary-motherland-some-notes-on-the-sprawl-propa-ganda-about-propaganda-and-a-google-doc-conversa-tion-with-metahaven. Last accessed on August 31, 2018.

143

Eurasia (Questions on Happiness)—Field Report

next

Eurasia (Questions on Happiness), 2018
fiction documentary, 50 min
Russian, French, Chinese, German, English, with English
subtitles

Eurasia (Questions on Happiness)—Field Report

next

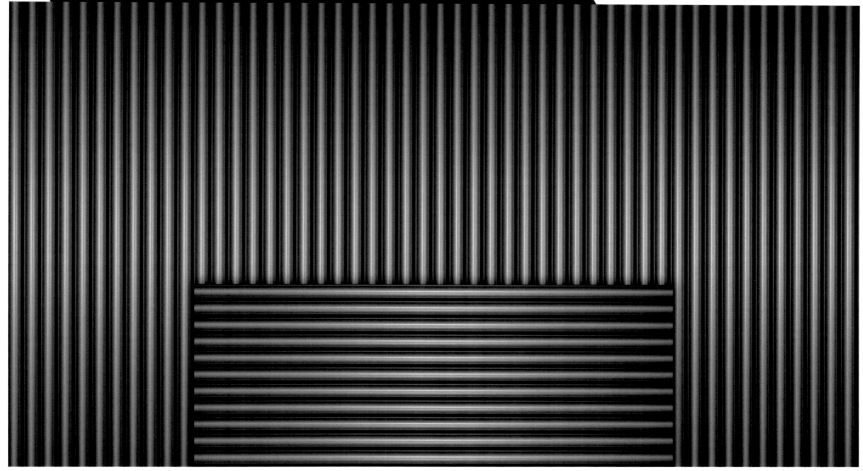

If we're talking about the eschatology
of Lars von Trier, it is a peculiar one.

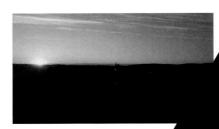

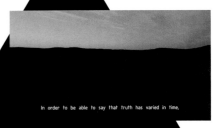

In order to be able to say that truth has varied in time,

one would have to show that a proposition can legitimately be considered true

at a given moment and in particular circumstances,

and that this same proposition at another moment and in other circumstances

cannot be held to be true,

even though it relates to the same object.

Now live-streaming, we speak seriously and I play the role of the political boss,
so I cannot even make jokes.

You will understand this later.

Sociology introduces a relativism

that rests on the relation between the physical environment
on the one hand

and man on the other,

The physical environment presents a relative fixity

The original world survives under successive additions that enrich it.

The laws that ruled the movements of the primitive nebulae

are conserved in the stabilised universe of today.

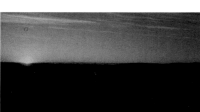

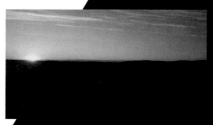

because we are different from one another—that's clear.

One Englishman is a lord, two Englishmen are a team.
Three Englishmen, a club.

One Frenchman is a champion, two Frenchmen, an équipe.
Three French, a couple.

Wait! Not finished.
One Italian, a Latin lover. Two Italians are...

three Italians, four political parties.

The war in Europe is over!

150

She continues in Siberia, Mongolia, Manchuria!

previous

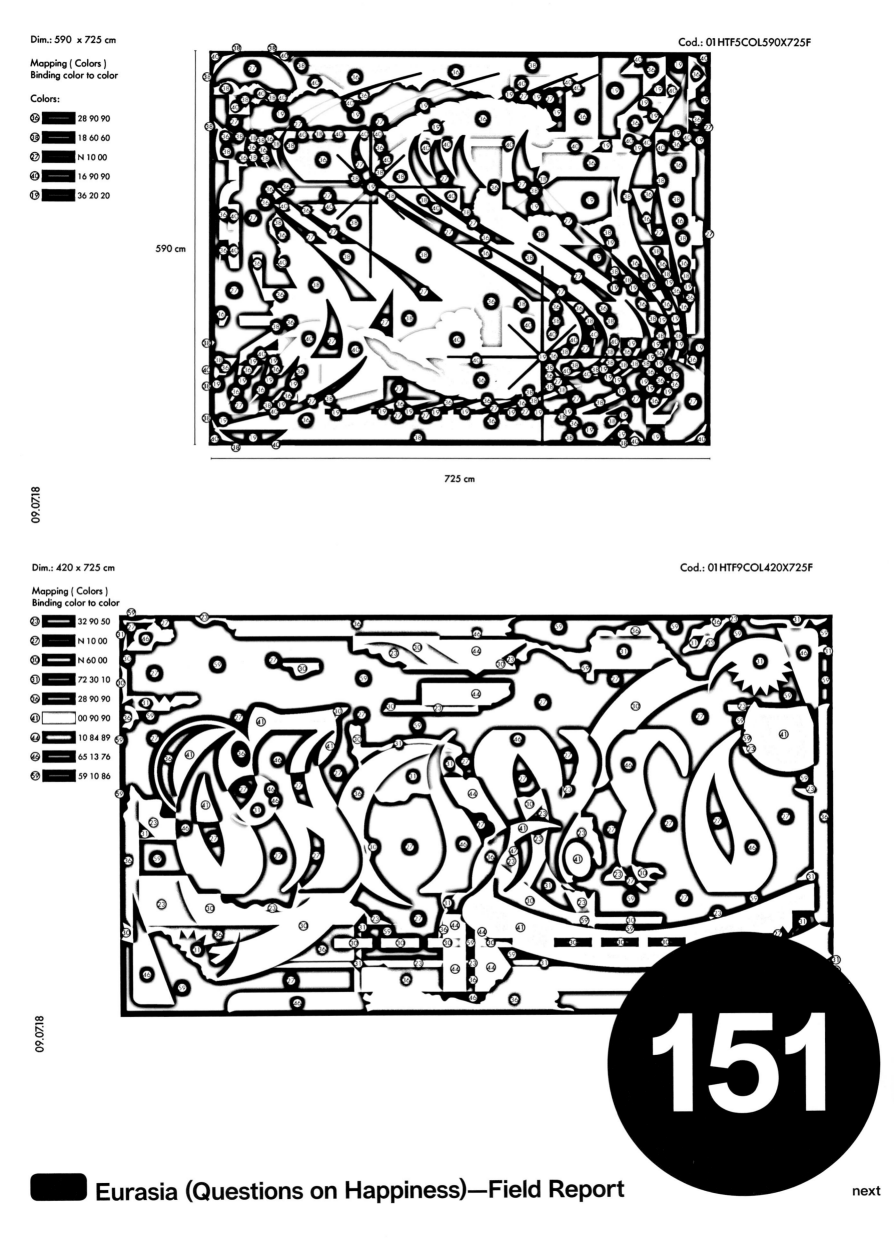

Dim.: 590 x 725 cm

Cod.: 01HTF5COL590X725F

Mapping (Colors)
Binding color to color

Colors:

36 ▬▬▬ 28 90 90
18 ▬▬▬ 18 60 60
27 ▬▬▬ N 10 00
40 ▬▬▬ 16 90 90
13 ▬▬▬ 36 20 20

590 cm

725 cm

09.0718

Dim.: 420 x 725 cm

Cod.: 01HTF9COL420X725F

Mapping (Colors)
Binding color to color

23 ▬▬▬ 32 90 50
27 ▬▬▬ N 10 00
30 ▬▬▬ N 60 00
31 ▬▬▬ 72 30 10
36 ▬▬▬ 28 90 90
41 ▬▬▬ 00 90 90
44 ▬▬▬ 10 84 89
46 ▬▬▬ 65 13 76
59 ▬▬▬ 59 10 86

09.0718

151

■ **Eurasia (Questions on Happiness)—Field Report**

next

Home and Interference 2014–2015

"Home," a collaboration with musician Holly Herndon, is among Metahaven's first forays into moving-image work. It was made shortly after Edward Snowden's revelations about the surveillance program of the United States National Security Agency (NSA) in June 2013. The music video deepens Metahaven's long-standing interest in state and corporate aesthetics, which they investigate here using "data rain" of the NSA's various logos, code words, acronyms, and icons. Herndon and Metahaven reunited a year after making *Home* to collaborate on the video for the musician's track "Interference" that addresses communion in a networked world. Featuring a ripped flag, bodies of water, and Situationist International founder Guy Debord and writer Alice Becker-Ho's *A Game of War* (1987), the video represents Metahaven's move toward more abstract emotive content.

● Home

Music and Lyrics
Holly Herndon

Director and Designer
Metahaven

Videography
Mathew Dryhurst

Photography and Lighting
Robert Couto

Interns
Alyar Aynetchi, Jessica Kao

Icons
National Security Agency (NSA)

Acknowledgments
Thanks to Center for Computer Research in Music and Acoustics, Stanford, CA; Ian Colon; Robert Couto; Suzy Poling; Matt Werth; Juha van 't Zelfde

With support from Lighthouse, Brighton

● Interference

Music and Lyrics
Holly Herndon

Director, Editor, and Graphic Designer
Metahaven

Featuring
A Game of War (1987) by Alice Becker-Ho and Guy Debord

Manifesto
Mathew Dryhurst, Holly Herndon, Metahaven

Line Producer
Lucy Chinen

Videography
Mathew Dryhurst, Metahaven

Camera Assistant
Benedikt "Mad Max" Wöppel

Stylist
Ella Plevin

Clothing
Final Home, UEG, Cottweiler, Christopher Kane, 69, Patagonia, Arielle de Pinto x LVMM shoes, Zucca

Props Assistant
Benedikt Benedikt "Mad Max" Wöppel

Model
Made by Mistake, Rotterdam

Interns
Robbie Blundell, Monika Gruzite, Alexandra Lunn, Eva Nazarova

Acknowledgments
Thanks to Alexander Benenson; Stef Caers; Genevieve Costello; Colin Self; Coralie Vogelaar; WallRiss, Fribourg, CH; Matt Werth; Juha van 't Zelfde

With the kind support of Lighthouse, Brighton; Impakt Festival 2014: Soft Machines, Utrecht; WallRiss, Fribourg, CH

Additional support from Swiss Arts Council Pro Helvetia

The Sprawl (Propaganda about Propaganda) 2015

The Sprawl (Propaganda about Propaganda) opens with images of a dark forest. In the background we hear an audio recording—gathered by security who intercepted the call—in which two men discuss moving a vehicle from Ukraine to Russia two days after Malaysia Airlines Flight 17 was downed by a surface-to-air missile over eastern Ukraine. This event and its aftermath comprise the starting point for Metahaven's expansive exploration of shifting geopolitical structures in the age of digital platforms. The artists' experimental documentary analyzes the rapid spread of disinformation via the internet, while attempting to embody the form and style of online propaganda itself. With one subject rapidly shifting into another, the video installation offers a perceptive take on the contemporary media landscape that has contributed to the rise of a "post-truth" politics. Interviews with contemporary theorists and narrated excerpts of Russian poetry as well as philosophical texts are cut together with viral dance videos and electronic music, producing jarring shifts in tone and genre. By editing analytic commentary, YouTube clips, original footage, and graphic elements into a non-linear, often humorous documentary, the artists show how "fantasy can be designed so as to seem or feel like a truth."

Writer and Director
Metahaven

Soundtrack
Kuedo

Featuring
Benjamin H. Bratton, Maryam Monalisa Gharavi, Peter Pomerantsev

Cast
Georgina Dávid, Gwen Pol, Annabel Reid

Screen Gazers
Georgina Dávid, Xuanhong Huang, Astrit Ismaili, Kees de Klein, Annabel Reid, Sofija Stankovic, Xiaoyao Pippa Xu

Voice
Masha Pruss

Additional Voice
Henrietta Meire

Producer
Sian Habell-Aili

Executive Producer
Juha van 't Zelfde

Director of Photography
Remko Schnorr

Additional Photography
Metahaven

Camera and Lighting Assistant
Elisa Grasso

Music and Sound Design
Kuedo

Sound on Set
Ferry de Pater, Tim van Peppen

Sound Mix
Ranko Pauković

Editing Consultant
Daniel Goddard

Russian Script Consultant
Anastasia Kubrak

Hair and Make-Up
Aga Urbanowicz

Production Managers
Netherlands: Lucy Chinen, Anna Spierings
United Kingdom: Fiona Fletcher

Interns
Anastasia Kubrak, Raf Rennie, Chloe Scheffe, Yee Jin Sha, Solveig Suess, Barron Webster, Joeri Woudstra

Research Assistant
Lucy Chinen

Design Assistant
Kees de Klein

3D Animation
Benedikt "Mad Max" Wöppel

Color-Grading Interviews
Tobias Corba (Fono, Amsterdam)

Camera Equipment
Camera Rentals, Amsterdam

Lighting Equipment
Schram Studios, Amsterdam

Studios
Schram Studios, Amsterdam; NLStudios, Amsterdam

Excerpts from
—Leo Tolstoy, *What Is Art?* (1897), translation by Aylmer Maude
—Anna Akhmatova, *Requiem* (1935–1961), translation by Nancy K. Anderson
—Nikolai Berdyaev, *Dream and Reality: An Essay in Autobiography* (1962), translation by Katherine Lampert
—Qur'ân, Sûrat Taha, 20:132, translation by N. J. Dawood

Translation
Ekaterina Kholyapina and Anastasia Kubrak (RU); Selim Helmi and Remke Kruk (AR)

Music
Kuedo
—"Vertical Stack"
—"Border State Collapse"
—"Case Type Classification"
—"Eyeless Angel Intervention"
—"Event Tracking Across Populated Terrain"
Courtesy of Knives/Just Isn't Music

Enjoykin
—"Nyash Myash"
Courtesy of Enjoykin

Acknowledgments
Abkhazian News Network Agency (ANNA News), Bellingcat, ECO Media TV-Produktion, Enjoykin, Euronews, GRITtv (lauraflanders.com), Internet Party of Ukraine (ipu.com.ua), ITAR-TASS, ITN (Truthloader), My Revolution (Video Diary from Kiev), Neuromir TV (neuromir.tv), Nikolay Ovcharov, RT (TV-Novosti)

Thanks to Suzan Breedveld/NL Studios, Maria Bota, Syb Groeneveld, Ingrid Kopp, Anthony Lilley, Ruth Mackenzie, Charlie McGough, Bas Schram

Metahaven would also like to thank Aernoud Bourdrez, Paul Fuller, Femke Herregraven, Ceci Moss, Joowon Park

Made possible with the support of The Space (Arts Council England and BBC), Creative Industries Fund NL, Media Fund NL, and Dutch Film Fund

sprawl.space 2016

As the online interface for *The Sprawl*, on sprawl.space the viewer can see the "shards" that make up the full version of the film. Nowadays, films live in a thousand and one forms on the internet: as short trailers, fragments, cloud-based copies of copies, endangered data, self-hosted vaults, and so on. As a hybrid, episodic documentary, *The Sprawl*'s story isn't linear. The film lends itself to be seen as a succession of impressions—a trailer, forever unfinished. The duration of each of those video pieces, or "shards," is attuned to an attention span that is less cinema, and more internet. The website has been shaped by the interface design of Metahaven and the viewing algorithms of YouTube.

Design
Metahaven

Design Assistant
Kees de Klein

Programming
Jonas Lund

Senior Producer
Emily Kyriakides

Development Producer
Sian Habell-Aili

Artistic Director
Juha van 't Zelfde

Executive Director
Miriam Randall

Communications Manager
Aleida Strowger

Commissioned by Lighthouse, Brighton and The Space (Arts Council England and BBC)

Produced by Lighthouse, Metahaven

© 2016 Metahaven

Information Skies 2016

Building upon *The Sprawl (Propaganda about Propaganda)* (2015) and featuring one of its actresses, *Information Skies* follows a young couple inhabiting an immersive virtual sphere in which they imagine themselves as heroic characters fighting dragons. As the outside world presses in, they retreat further into their bubble, accepting its universe as authentic. Inspired by the philosophical science-fiction of Russian film director Andrei Tarkovsky, Metahaven creates an ambiguous environment that is at once futuristic, otherworldly, and hyperreal. Contesting the assumption of English as the de facto language of art and culture, *Information Skies* features Hungarian narration subtitled not only in English, but also Korean. The three overlapping visual layers—live action, animation, and graphic computational interface—bring together digital and physical forms to create an augmented reality. Its soundtrack of stirring harpsichord strums and ticking piano notes sets the hypnotic fiction of *Information Skies* apart from the works Metahaven has made within this scope previously. Here, Metahaven further develops their interest in anime as an immediate graphic means of communication. The artists question what counts as reality in an era in which online and offline space have become inextricably bound, and competing versions of the "truth" are increasingly incompatible.

Writer and Director
Metahaven

Soundtrack
M.E.S.H.

Cast
Artur Chruszsc, Georgina Dávid

Voice
Georgina Dávid

Director of Photography
Remko Schnorr

Camera Assistant
Elisa Grasso

Animation
Metahaven, Janna Ullrich

Stylist
Ella Plevin

Clothing
Adidas, Yulia Yefimtchuk

Production Manager
Anna Laederach

Production Assistant
Kees de Klein

Intern
Carmen Dusmet Carrasco

Design Assistants
Kees de Klein, Tereza Ruller

Website Programming
Tereza Ruller, Vit Ruller

Sound Recording and Mix
Split Second Sound, Amsterdam

Translation
Georgina Dávid and David Sarlos (HU); Dongyoung Lee (KO); Nandini Patodia and Alisha Sett (HI)

Acknowledgments
Thanks to Verena Adt; Camera Rentals, Amsterdam; the Laederach family; Maria Lind; Margarida Mendes; Ben van der Velden; Kees van der Velden (1944–2016)

Commissioned by *The Eighth Climate: What Does Art Do?*, 11th Gwangju Biennale, 2016, curated by Maria Lind

Made with the support of Gwangju Biennale Foundation, Mondriaan Fund

© 2016 Metahaven

Hometown 2018

Conceived by Metahaven as a follow-up to their 2016 film *Information Skies*, *Hometown* was filmed in two cities—Kiev and Beirut—reimagined as a single fictional town. Narrated in Arabic and Russian and subtitled in Ukrainian and English, the film is structured around a simple yet contradictory poem. Doubling as a riddle, the script is inspired by absurdist Russian children's poetry. The video features two young women, one Ukrainian and one Lebanese, traversing their respective urban environments, drifting from the bustling city center to overgrown gardens wrapped in barbed wire on the outskirts of town. Set against a surreal electronic soundtrack blending music with ambient sound, shots of tangled wiring and satellite dishes installed throughout the city subtly point out the omnipresence of electronic networks. The live footage is interspersed with psychedelic graphic elements, which, for Metahaven, serve as abstract counterpoints that unite reality and imagination depicting melting glaciers, colored rainfall, planets, and a caterpillar. Throughout the film, the protagonists narrate the murder of the caterpillar and other ethical paradoxes, revealing an attempt to live with, through, and by contradictions.

Writer and Director
Metahaven

Original Soundtrack
LAIR, Mhamad Safa

Cast
Ghina Abboud, Lera Luchenko

Line Producers
Beirut: Jinane Chaaya
Kiev: Tania Monakhova

153

 **Credits**

next

Production Assistants
Sara Ballout, Sasha Kuchirka

Directors of Photography
Karim Ghorayeb (Beirut); Roman Himey, Yarema Malaschuk (Kiev)

Focus Pullers
Nabil Assaf, Roman Himey

Camera Assistants
Eugene Filatov, Aleksandr Lyakhno

Lighting Technician
Oleg Bezbah

Stylist and Costume Designer
Yulia Yefimtchuk

Make-Up
Diala Chaaban, Yulya Zalesskaya

Animation Assistants
Jonathan Castro, Roman Häfliger

Voice Recording
Alligator Friends Studio Kyiv, Vitaliy Lyakin, Walid Sarrouh

Camera Rentals
Media Square, Beirut; Zodiac Rental

Translation
Mohammed Abdallah (AR), Alex Anikina (RU), Oleksandr Vinogradov (UK)

Acknowledgments
Thanks to Mohammed Abdallah; Ashkal Alwan, Beirut; Guus Beumer; Kateryna Filyuk, Izolyatsia, Kiev; Polina Medvedeva; Luba Michailova; Marina Otero; Lesia Prokopenko; Oleksandr Vinogradov

Commissioned and produced by Sharjah Art Foundation for Sharjah Biennial 13, Tamawuj, 2017

Additional production support from Het Nieuwe Instituut, Rotterdam

© 2018 Metahaven

Possessed: Circular Sequence 2018

Possessed: Circular Sequence is an installation made after Metahaven's 2018 feature film *Possessed*. *Possessed* debuted in movie theaters and film festivals as a single-channel documentary feature co-directed with filmmaker Rob Schröder. Presented in a semicircular enclosure of stacked foam bricks and split between three monitors, *Circular Sequence* recalls a castle or tower rendered in pixel-like building blocks. Shot at a former military air base on the border of Bosnia and Croatia, *Circular Sequence* shows a group of veiled figures. Their scarves feature visual references to digital platforms and communist symbolism. For *Possessed*, Metahaven and Schröder worked closely with composer Laurel Halo, who created the original score.

Installation Architecture Assistant
Andreas Nikolopoulos

Possessed 2018

Directors
Metahaven, Rob Schröder

Original score
Laurel Halo

Cast
Olivia Lonsdale, Nick Srnicek, Alex Williams

Voice
Mirna Gaberšnik, Shelby13

Producers
Ernst de Jong, Rogier Kramer

Executive Producers
Wilant Boekelman, Dutch Mountain Film, René Huybrechtse

Line Producer
Constant van Panhuys

Graphic Design and Animation
Metahaven

Design Assistants
Kees de Klein, Christina Wörner

Additional Animation
Benedikt "Mad Max" Wöppel

Cinematography
Remko Schnorr

Additional Cinematography
Metahaven, Rob Schröder

Focus Puller
Ralph van de Weijer

Camera Assistant
Elisa Grasso

Gaffer
Kristijan Vadinjov

Lightning Technician
Croatia: Igor Jurković, Slaven Spinčić

Grip
Croatia: Juraj Stiković
Netherlands: Bjorn Schumacher

Grip Assistant
Luka Haramija

Sound Design and Mix
Ranko Pauković

Sound Recording
Carla van der Meijs

Narrative Writer
Metahaven

Editors
Wouter van Luijn/NCE, Metahaven, Rob Schröder

Assistant Editor
Esgo Groenendijk

Costume Designer
Ella Plevin

Scarves
Metahaven

Make-Up and Styling Assistants
Croatia: Petra Sever, Matea Tunuković

Make-Up
Netherlands: Celine Bernaerts

Line Production and Location Management
Josip Kovačlevantin, Mihovil Pirnat

Production Manager
Croatia: Rogier Kramer

Production Assistants
Jelle Beuger, Ante Lovrić, Chantelle Lue, Vjekoslav Palinić, Maya Perez, Matija Pucak, Valerie van Zuijlen

Third Assistant Director
Josip Kovačlevantin

Data Handler
Valerie van Zuijlen

Dancer and Extras Manager
Croatia: Mario Vrbanec

Group Dancers
Croatia: Stanislav Bajt, Brutala, Iva Čevizović, Mirna Gaberšnik, Andrea Hršak, Petra Mirković, Marijana Pintarić, Petar Rupčlć, Šimun Stankov, Tomislav Žalec

Extras
Croatia: Dražen Čuljat, Saša Savić

Location Scouting and Services
Croatia Infiltration, Airbase catering, Supercatering Slovenia, Political School

Catering
Croatia: Villa Zelenjak Ventek
Netherlands: Sandra Hoffman

Firefighters at the Political School
Croatia: Josip Borovnjak, Slavko Jurič

Post-Production
Rob Maas, Constant van Panhuys

Post-Production Facilities
De Lodge, Amsterdam; Marja Paeper; Remco Smit

Grading
Remi Lindenhovius

Subtitles
Ronald van Biezen

Legal
Jaap Versteeg

Production Accountant
Peter Kersten

Archive Clearances
Genevieve Costello

Citations
—"If I speak in the tongues of men and of angels," 1 Cor. 13:1, c. AD 53–54
—Giovanni Battista Pergolesi (1710–1736), Stabat Mater Dolorosa ("Grave in F minor"), 1736, arranged by Laurel Halo, 2018
—Krist na žalu, "Lord, You Have Come to the Lakeshore," Cesáreo Gabaráin, UM hymnal, no. 344, 1977

Interviews
—Alex Williams, School of Politics, Philosophy and Language, and Communication Studies, University of East Anglia
—Nick Srnicek, Digital Economy, King's College London

Acknowledgments
Thank you to Red Cross volunteers at Grande-Synthe Migrant Camp; Secours catholique, Calais; Vluchtgarage, Amsterdam; Vluchtkerk, Amsterdam; residents around Željava Air Base

The directors would like to thank Karen Archey, Henk Bakker (Nederlandse Spoorwegen), Benjamin H. Bratton, Genevieve Costello, Nicoline van Gog (Nederlandse Spoorwegen), René Huybrechtse, Kees de Klein, Remke Kruk, Anna Laederach, Olivia Lonsdale, Frans Oort, Maria Morata, Gabrielle Provaas, Natasha Savicheva, Nick Srnicek, Queenie Tassel, Vesper van der Velden, Alex Williams, Brian Kuan Wood

The producers would like to thank Yvonne Bruynen; camper Atelier About; fire department of Korenica; fire department and city of Kumrovec, Lianne Hillebrand; Holger Huisman; Ministry of State Property of the Republic of Croatia; Kostas Murkudis; Niels Koopman/Nike; Ottolinger; Plitvice Lakes and its National Park; Ya'ala Szomoru; Theaterkunst Kostümausstattung (costume design), Berlin; Marcha Vermeulen; Samuel Wellington; Willem-jan Wreesmann; Samuel Guì Yang

The Netherlands Film Production Incentive
José van Doorn, Simone Kaagman, Manon van Melick, Ilke Vernooij, Corine Vos

The Netherlands Film Fund
Mirjam Bal, Doreen Boonekamp, Renée van der Grinten, Karlijn Landman, Dorien van de Pas, Sabine Terken, Dick Tuinder

Cinema Delicatessen
Mei-ling Djoa, Katrien Lamers, Daan Vermeulen, Anne Vierhout

Mondriaan Fund
Birgit Donker, Douke IJsselstein, Wouter Koelman

This film is realized within the framework of New Screen NL, a collaboration between Mondriaan Fund and the Netherlands Film Fund, supported by the Netherlands Film Production Incentive.

Distributor Benelux
Cinema Delicatessen

Produced by Dutch Mountain Film

© 2018 Metahaven, Rob Schröder, Dutch Mountain Film,

154

A Blackmagic 4K digital camera mounted on a tripod is filmed standing on a hill, at dusk, overlooking the Eurasian Steppe at the meeting point of Europe and Asia. In voice-over, a passage from Émile Durkheim's 1914 critique of pragmatism cites the philosophical tradition's notion of truth as mutable and multiple. Bookending this eerily sublime vision are two pieces of found television footage: in one, the Russian far-right philosopher Natella Speranskaya expounds on the eschatology of Lars von Trier; in the other, comedian-turned politician and founder of the populist Italian Five Star Movement Beppe Grillo, cracks a joke in the European Parliament.

The sequence establishes an image of an epic landmass, rendered in high-res, and caught within a flux of belief and affect-based notions of truth and resurgent nationalism. The continent of Eurasia, as both geography and geopolitical concept, stands as a locus for both the grand claims of pre-modern projects of unification, and the hyper-fragmentations of a neo-medieval political order. Combining aspects of science fiction, documentary, poetry, and folktale, *Eurasia* weaves a speculative narrative about the eponymous continent under the grasp of data-driven and platform-hosted ideological currents.

In one of the film's sub-plots, a nationalist scheme is prevented the discovery of a small, mysterious sculpture on the outskirts of Yekaterinburg.

In its combination of cinematic footage, archival material, graphic overlay, and animation, *Eurasia* speaks to the politics of the interface, and the manner in which political ideology and thought on the internet are entwined with their encoding as specific forms and iterations of media production. Wrapping facts in fictions, and fictions in facts, *Eurasia* renders an immersion in a material, temporal, and emotional state of "epistemic uncertainty," brought about by an ever more pervasive data-driven cognitive order.

Richard Birkett

Production Assistants
Ifeanyi Awachie, Chris Rawcliffe

● **Russia Shoot**
Akkermanovka, Beloshapka, Dneprovka, Karabash, Kuvandyk, Magnitogorsk, Orsk, Utyagulovo, Yasniy, Yekaterinburg

Cast
Ilya Lim, Timur Saulebaev

Producer
Red Pepper Creative, Yekaterinburg

Line Producer
Kirill Verkhozin

Associate Line Producer
Evgenii Markov

Assistant Line Producer
Mikhail Kremeshkov

Director of Photography
Dima Mishin

Additional Photography
Metahaven

Gaffer
Andrey Khudyakov

Key Grip
Ivan Solovyev

Grip
Valeria Gabysheva

Drone Operator
Anton Smetanin

Stylist
Marina Malinovskaya

Clothing
Nina Donis

Make-Up
Sasha Vanhanen

Props Assistant
Masha Orlova

Model
Made by Mistake, Rotterdam

Driver
Valeriy Leonidovich

Interview Translator
Valeria Tylis

Subtitles Editor
Maxim Yakimov

Studio
Photostudio KISA

Acknowledgments
Thanks to Nina Donis and FAKOSHIMA eyewear

● **Macedonia Shoot**
Skopje, Veles

Line Producers
Vladimir Anastasov, Angela Nestorovska, Sektor Film

Director of Photography
Dimitar Popov

Additional Photography
Metahaven

Focus Puller and Camera Assistant
Kiril Shentevski

Acknowledgments
Thanks to the City of Skopje, Macedonian Railways Transport JSC Skopje, Pepi Manevski

● **Netherlands Shoot**
Amsterdam

Cast
Lucie de Bréchard

Focus Puller and Camera and Lighting Assistant
Ralph van de Weijer

Sound Mix
Wave Studios, Amsterdam

Sound Recording
Soho Radio Studios, London

Props Assistants
Richard Birkett, Lucie de Bréchard, Roman Häflinger

Installation Architecture Assistant
Andreas Nikolopoulos

Interviews
Ivana Dragsic (Freedom Square), Ippolito Pestellini

2D Animation
Benedikt "Mad Max" Wöppel

3D Animation
Theo Cook

Camera Equipment
Camera Rentals, Amsterdam; Bandit, Amsterdam

Studio and Lighting Equipment
Singelfilm, Amsterdam

All Kuedo tracks courtesy of Ninja Tunes

Acknowledgments
Thanks to Dmitrii Bezouglov, Steven Cairns, Zhenya Chaika, Stefan Kalmár, Anna Klec, Estelle Marois, Varvara Melnikova, Olga Polishuk, Daria Sheeborshee, Natalia Sielewicz, Olga Tenisheva

Commissioned by Institute of Contemporary Arts, London; Stedelijk Museum Amsterdam; Sharjah Art Foundation

Produced by Institute of Contemporary Arts, London; Metahaven

With the support of Museum of Modern Art in Warsaw and Creative Industries Fund NL, and with the generous assistance of Strelka Institute for Media, Architecture and Design, Moscow

© 2018 Metahaven

155

next

■ Credits

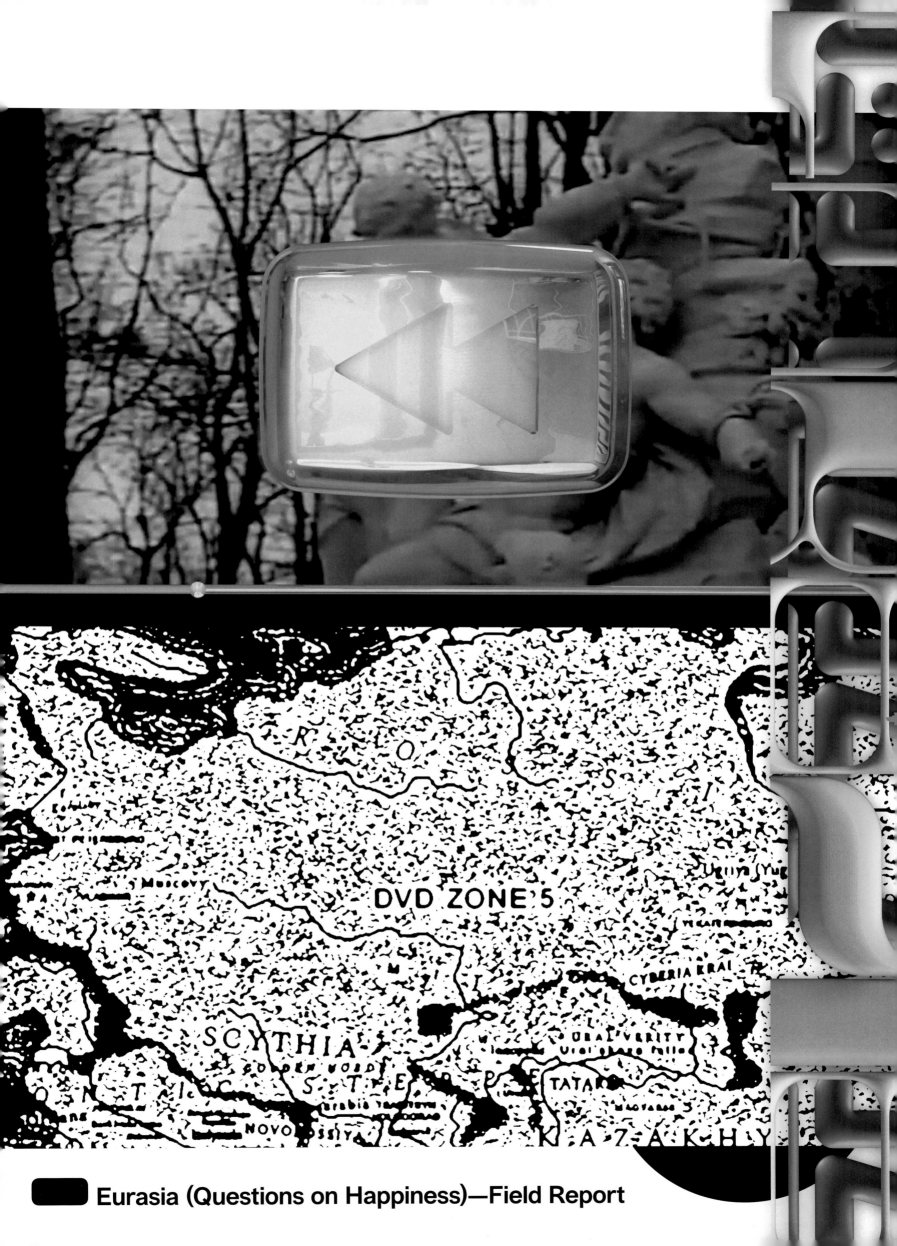

DVD ZONE 5

Eurasia (Questions on Happiness)—Field Report

Appreciation

Our thanks go out to everyone who contributed to this book, by means of essays, exchanges, conversations, or otherwise, and to everyone at the Stedelijk Museum Amsterdam and Koenig Books who helped to make this publication happen.

We thank Karen Archey for her engagement, support, and for recognizing our work in its shapeshifting appearances; Bart van der Heide for his support, which we have felt from close and afar; and Gwen Parry for her editorial prowess, warmth, and wit.

At the ICA, we thank Stefan Kalmár and Richard Birkett for joining us on the life-changing journey of a new film. We thank Richard for his trust, commitment, and for our collaborative insights.

We thank Dongyoung Lee and Kees de Klein for their dedication and precision.

We thank Remke Kruk and Frans Oort for their presence, love, and intellect.

We thank Vesper for her poetry, and for being the light of our lives.

Vinca Kruk and Daniel van der Velden
Amsterdam, August 31, 2018

| suhail | Monday |
| To: Vinca Cc: Daniel | Details |

PSYOP is great! mil-tech of affect meets greek god (which is kind of the same thing anyway). what's not to like?

yes, london def. if you have time, let's hang off-piste.

The Stedelijk Museum Amsterdam is supported by

❌ **Gemeente**
❌ **Amsterdam**

Principal donor

Rabobank

Partner

BankGiro
Loterij

Colophon

Open with